CHARLES I'S PRIVATE LIFE

CHARLES I'S PRIVATE LIFE

Mark Turnbull

PEN & SWORD
HISTORY

AN IMPRINT OF PEN & SWORD BOOKS LTD.
YORKSHIRE – PHILADELPHIA

First published in Great Britain in 2023 by
PEN AND SWORD HISTORY
An imprint of
Pen & Sword Books Ltd
Yorkshire – Philadelphia

Copyright © Mark Turnbull, 2023

ISBN 978 1 39908 290 7

The right of Mark Turnbull to be identified as Author of
this work has been asserted by him in accordance with the Copyright,
Designs and Patents Act 1988.

A CIP catalogue record for this book is available from the British Library.

Typeset in Times New Roman 10.5/13 by
SJmagic DESIGN SERVICES, India.
Printed and bound in the UK by CPI Group (UK) Ltd.

Pen & Sword Books Limited incorporates the imprints of Atlas, Archaeology,
Aviation, Discovery, Family History, Fiction, History, Maritime, Military,
Military Classics, Politics, Select, Transport, True Crime, Air World,
Frontline Publishing, Leo Cooper, Remember When, Seaforth Publishing,
The Praetorian Press, Wharncliffe Local History, Wharncliffe Transport,
Wharncliffe True Crime and White Owl.

For a complete list of Pen & Sword titles please contact
PEN & SWORD BOOKS LIMITED
George House, Units 12 & 13, Beevor Street, Off Pontefract Road,
Barnsley, South Yorkshire, S71 1HN, England
E-mail: enquiries@pen-and-sword.co.uk
Website: www.pen-and-sword.co.uk

or

PEN AND SWORD BOOKS
1950 Lawrence Rd, Havertown, PA 19083, USA
E-mail: uspen-and-sword@casematepublishers.com
Website: www.penandswordbooks.com

Contents

Acknowledgements

Having thoroughly enjoyed the journey of researching and writing this book, I finish it with a much closer understanding of the man who was at the epicentre of this pivotal, and fascinating, period in history.

Along the way, I've been struck by the friendly and helpful manner of archive staff up and down the country, such as Lambeth Palace Library, The National Archives, National Records of Scotland and numerous county archives, together with Longleat House, Worcester Cathedral and The Badminton Estate.

James St Levan kindly gave permission to use a particularly interesting miniature of King Charles I from his collection at St Michael's Mount, and one that I had not seen before. The fabulous Rijksmuseum has also been a great source of images. A unique painting depicting Charles's execution can be found inside All Saints Church, Burstwick, and I am grateful that the PCC permitted me to use a photograph of it. Sadly, the church has closed, leaving the image and its history in a precarious position.

Thanks to Leanda de Lisle for her advice, Keith Crawford and Claire Hobson for reading draft sections, and Stephen Hunt, who visited an archive for me and tackled a particularly long parchment roll. I am fortunate enough to have met talented artist Danelo Yarnold whose artwork graces the cover.

This book would not have been possible were it not for the support and encouragement of my wife, Kate.

Preface

At the age of ten, I first saw a portrait of King Charles I and found out about the War of the Three Kingdoms. Anthony Van Dyck's image of the monarch at the hunt captivated me, and I have read and researched the endlessly fascinating period of history in which he lived ever since.

Considering it encapsulates a devastating civil war, the killing of a king, and political drama that had a profound effect upon families, I'm struck by the way it remains so overshadowed. The Tudor age abounds in books, films, television documentaries and dramas, yet the Stuart age does not. At 118 years, the Tudors' reign is only seven years longer than their poor relations.

One of our most controversial monarchs, Charles cuts a distant figure to this day. His formality is captured in stunning portraits and every horror of civil war was laid at his door by the victors. He is two-dimensional. Condemned as a tyrant, or worshipped as a martyr, his real character is frequently lost, making it difficult to both understand and relate to him. Especially so if we do not put our twenty-first-century standards and bias aside when attempting to do so.

By examining Charles through his relationships, it is possible to peel away the layers of propaganda – his own and his enemies' – and shine a light on the man himself. To approach him on a different level and get that little bit closer. A number of new sources piece together his rarely examined childhood, allowing his character to fully develop within the pages. Fresh approaches to the infamous events of his reign reveal very different aspects of consideration. Overlooked evidence shows that the past is not as different as we might think. My goal has been to create a very intimate biography that appeals to veterans of the period and newcomers alike.

Introduction

Tuesday 30 January 1649, St James's Palace, London.

King Charles wakes and peers at the silver striking clock by his bed. The time is 4.00 am. He draws the curtains around his four-poster and glances down at his servant, who lies on a small pallet bed. Thomas Herbert is awake, but seems troubled. The king by comparison, having read and prayed until midnight, has rested soundly for four hours. Upon getting out of bed, the chill of the winter's morning becomes apparent. Today he will be put to death, therefore the next few hours are crucial preparation for his final moments. An hour of private devotion follows.

Charles Stuart is 48 years old, though he appears greatly aged. He had been 3 years old when his father, King James VI of Scotland, inherited the English throne. After following his parents to England, St James's Palace became his main residence until acceding to the throne, aged 24. In just a few hours he will leave this palace and embark on a final journey, which will take him to an altogether new realm.

When the king emerges from prayers, Herbert brushes his master's hair, which is streaked with white. Charles's beard is longer and much less defined than the Van Dyck portraits of his heyday. Yet, the king remains fastidious in his appearance and checks Herbert over his care: 'This is my second marriage day; I would be as trim to day as may be; for before Night I hope to be espoused to my blessed Jesus.' He decides to wear two shirts to avoid shivering from the chill, which some might misconstrue as fear: 'I would have no such Imputation. I fear not Death'. Such concern is heightened after last night's distressing ordeal, when after taking leave of two of his young children for the last time, the king had collapsed.

He takes an orange studded with cloves in case he might need the assistance of its sharp scent. The blue ribbon and medal of the Order of the Garter, which hangs around his neck, contrasts with his black satin doublet. A familiar part of his appearance, it represents his chivalric beliefs, and his cloak is emblazoned with a silver star of the same order. Finally, Herbert fixes in place one pearl earring, which is surmounted by a small, golden crown.

Soon afterwards the 66-year-old William Juxon arrives. Until Parliament's abolition of episcopacy, he had been Bishop of London, and is also a former

Lord Treasurer. Juxon is a man who the king trusts and respects. Herbert, on the other hand, is a spy, chosen by Parliament to replace the royal servants they had dismissed. He reports on everything that occurs around the prisoner – not that the king blames him. Indeed, he has only just given the man a written testimonial, to help protect him against potential Royalist reprisals. At this point it all becomes too much for Herbert, who breaks down, falls to his knees and craves forgiveness. It is readily granted.

Now to dispose of all earthly belongings. There are little left. As if appreciating the troubled kingdoms his eldest son is to inherit, the king bequeaths his annotated Bible, 'which in all the time of his Affliction had been his best Instructor and Delight'. Young Charles should frequently read and meditate upon it, and exceed in mercy over rigour. For his second son, the Duke of York, a 'jewel' of a mathematical instrument is assigned. Religious books are selected for his daughter Elizabeth, which will 'ground her against Popery' and youngest son Henry is to receive works written by his grandfather, King James. Lastly, the king's gold watch, which had belonged to his father, is to be conveyed to the Duchess of Richmond. Charles has been a father-figure to her for over twenty years.

With these bequests committed to Mr Herbert's care, the king and Bishop Juxon engage in prayer and readings for some time. Matthew: 27 – the passion of Christ – moves the king, referring to Jesus being 'shut up in the hands of his enemies'. He thanks Juxon for such a poignant choice, but the bishop explains it is the actual lesson of the day. The king judges this a 'seasonable' preparation for his end. As time wears on, a knock comes at the door. Herbert does not stir. A second rap ensues, and the king instructs him to answer. Colonel Hacker, who is to lead the king to the scaffold, explains in a 'trembling manner' that it is time to depart. The silver striking clock approaches 10.00 am. The king tells Herbert to keep it in memory of him; he had, after all, obtained it to assist the man, who had recently slept late. After kneeling in brief prayer, the king rises and takes the bishop's hand. 'Come, let us go.'

Colonel Hacker escorts the party into St James's Park, where soldiers stand with pennants held aloft. A drumbeat becomes steadily louder. As if the cold and noise are not enough to contend with, the king's spaniel races after him, but is caught and taken back inside. Juxon stands on the monarch's right, while Colonel Tomlinson is bareheaded on the left with Herbert behind them. They begin to walk, led by files of halberdiers, with more bringing up the rear. Troops line either side of the route to Whitehall. Naturally fast-paced, the king asks if the going must be so slow.

Along the way, he speaks of funeral arrangements with Colonel Tomlinson, a man he has taken a liking to. A stranger then approaches and walks alongside, staring hard at the king, and is only removed after Juxon intervenes. Whitehall Palace looms and the party climb the wooden staircase that leads inside.

They proceed through the gallery and Holbein Gate, below which is a main thoroughfare. Windows offer a glimpse of the scaffold, which is hung with black. Entering the privy gallery, studded with over 100 paintings, the faces of the king's European counterparts look back at him: the Duke of Savoy, King of Hungary and Emperor Charles V. From here, he is escorted into his private lodgings along with Juxon and Herbert. A four-hour wait ensues.

Charles's death is an infamous piece of history, but his life, specifically his personal life and character, is far less prominent. History has left him a two-dimensional tyrant or martyr. By focusing on his relationships, I hope to offer fresh insight into the man behind the crown.

Chapter 1

Precious Jewell

5 August 1600, Scotland.

Falkland Palace was just one residence of King James VI, the 34-year-old King of the Scots. The park was well stocked with deer, many of which had been gifts from the ageing Queen Elizabeth I of England – perhaps a ploy to keep him suitably occupied with hunting, his favourite pastime. Though she refused to name her successor, James was the strongest claimant to the spinster's throne. While he patiently waited upon destiny, it was better to shoot at deer rather than English troops. Hopes were pinned on a peaceful inheritance.

Already thirty-three years into his reign, James's position might have seemed agreeable. Aged 25, he had married Anna, sister of Christian IV of Denmark. By 1600, the Stuart line had been secured in the person of 6-year-old Henry Frederick. There was a daughter, too, tactfully christened Elizabeth after her Tudor godmother. Although the third child, Margaret, had just died, Anna was pregnant once again. James, however, knew first-hand how unstable his kingdom could be. The throne had been thrust upon him when, not long after his first birthday, his Catholic mother had been forced to abdicate. She had fled to England for refuge and was later executed on the orders of Queen Elizabeth. But nothing could prepare the 'cradle-king' for 5 August 1600, a day that would shake him to the core. One that neither he, nor Scotland, would forget in a hurry.

Alexander Ruthven, brother of the Earl of Gowrie, arrived at Falkland Palace that day with some startling news. A man had been discovered who knew the whereabouts of a 'huge amount of gold' and James was urged to go to Gowrie House to find out more. Alexander wouldn't declare the full details, but eagerly requested a share of the fabulous proceeds. James hesitated. Alexander insisted that the royal household be left at Falkland to allow for a discreet journey. He employed 'incredible cunning and confidence, with his very sweet address, expression and words'. Sufficiently tempted, James followed with very few attendants, all of whom were unarmed.

On arrival at Perth, the Earl of Gowrie met the small entourage and escorted them to his home. James was led inside by the two brothers and then left alone in a secluded bedroom. When the Gowries returned, they brought a third man who wore armour and a helmet. If the situation wasn't already suspicious enough, James realised he had been led into a trap.

Next, the brothers spread a rumour James had 'suddenly departed at the postern gate'. Believing this news, the royal retainers called for their horses and made ready to follow. Deep within Gowrie House, however, James was set upon in a 'hideous clamour'. The armour-clad man rushed at him and held a knife to his throat. James tried to persuade him to 'desist from the foul, detestable and treasonable crime'. He begged him to listen to reason. A pardon was offered. Being told that he must die, James fought his assailant with only the 'spirit of almighty God' and somehow opened a window to cry for help. Realising that the game was up, the Earl of Gowrie rushed to the bedroom to deal a killer blow, but after being intercepted by some of the royal party, he was killed before James's very eyes. As the 'monstrous breath of his body abandoned its home', Gowrie's brother, Alexander, was also felled.[1] The king had been saved.

The above account is James's version and the full circumstances of this incident remain a mystery. Fifty years later, when Arthur Wilson penned his *History of the Life of James I* he was frank. 'Whether the Gowries attempted upon the Kings person, or the King on theirs, is variously reported.'[2] If James did have a motive, the exact nature is open to debate. Certainly, he owed the Gowries a huge sum of money, and perhaps sought to kill off the debt along with the family. Another reason might have stemmed from rumours that Queen Anna had also visited the Gowrie bedroom, although in very different circumstances. There was also a third party who might have benefitted from the plot: England. In October 1600, Queen Elizabeth's Secretary of State, Sir Robert Cecil, admitted to a 'purpose in Gowry to have made a welter in that kingdom [Scotland]'.[3] Whatever the truth, James ordained that 'in all times and ages to come' the anniversary should be kept for 'public preachings, prayers and solemn thanksgiving to God'.[4] Annual fireworks would remind everyone of this conspiracy and James's miraculous preservation – until 5 August came to be overshadowed by 5 November.

On 19 November 1600, after proceeding against the two dead brothers, James had their corpses hanged, drawn and quartered in Edinburgh. On that same day, at 11.00 pm, his second son was born at Dunfermline Palace. James did not fail to notice the significance of the date – he had been born on 19 June, his eldest son Henry on 19 February, and daughter Elizabeth on 19 August. A jubilant James handed £16 to the bearer of this good news. The very next morning, as the ordnance of Edinburgh Castle exploded with joy, James raced to Dunfermline to see his wife and son. But as the rotting Gowries dangled from their nooses, so the life of the sickly baby hung in the balance. He had been born 'in so much weakness' that baptism was hastened without the usual ceremonies.[5]

As the days wore on, the royal baby clung to life. Leanda de Lisle suggests he was born 'with a lingual deformity, possibly ankyloglossia, or "tongue tie"', thus making feeding difficult.[6] A second christening more than made up for prior lack of pomp. At that moment the French Duc de Rohan and his brother were engaged on a grand tour, and despite English discouragement, they crossed the border to Scotland. As if anticipating the future, Rohan observed that James was witty, knowledgeable, and eloquent enough 'to govern his own kingdom and others besides'.[7] James, for his part, welcomed these influential Huguenots and invited them to become 'gossips' (or godfathers) to his new son. The godmothers were the Countesses of Mar and Huntley.

Dressed in a gown of lawn, wrapped with cloth of gold, Charles was carried by Rohan into the royal chapel at Holyrood House. The Lord President, Alexander Seton, bore the ducal crown before them. Beneath a silk canopy, which had been worked in gold and silver by the child's grandmother, Mary, Queen of Scots, the Bishop of Ross performed the ceremony. Baby Charles was given the same name as his father (the king was, in fact, Charles James), and invested as Duke of Albany, Marquis of Ormonde, Earl of Ross and Lord of Ardmonoche. The festivities culminated in a great banquet and £100 was scattered to the crowds outside. James dished out ennoblements and knighthoods, as well as ordering the firing of the castle's artillery not once, but twice, for his double-christened boy.

Duke Charles continued at Dunfermline surrounded by a close group of personal attendants. An old woman called Marian Hepburne was his 'rokker' while Jane Drummond – a friend of Queen Anna's – also cared for him. Margaret, Lady Ochiltree, later recounted how she cared for Charles 'night and day' and nearly twenty years later was still making 'dayelie petitions' (or prayers) for his welfare.[8] Though of a fragile constitution, the boy was made to look every inch a prince. His wardrobe included a suit of scarlet serge, another of yellow satin and a velvet belt with dagger. On 18 January 1602, the 1-year-old Charles was joined at Dunfermline by a new baby brother. Prince Robert's christening saw the court bedecked in purple velvet, but living less than six months, black mourning rapidly swept it all away. Death was also stalking Queen Elizabeth I. Her long life had created suspicion that England would never acknowledge her death if 'any old Woman of that Nation' might be employed to 'personate the Majesty of a Queen.'[9] In November 1602, Elizabeth gave 'Jesuits, priests, and their adherents' thirty days to leave England.[10] Four months later, she also departed.

On 24 March 1603, after languishing in a deep melancholy and refusing to eat or take to her bed, Elizabeth finally died. One visitor in those final days had been her cousin, Sir Robert Carey, who 'did catch at Her last breath, to carry it to the rising Sun then in Scotland'.[11] As the Tudor age ended, and Richmond Palace was sealed off, Carey slipped through the gate and escaped with this momentous news. It would not be the last time that he blindsided people by his speed and foresight, and he went on to form a unique bond with the new king's second son.

Bolting north like the wind, Carey reached Edinburgh at midnight after only two days. In his memoirs, he recalled 'the king was newly gone to bed'.[12] Exhausted and dirty, he knelt before James and confirmed that England had uniformly consented to his accession. Though carrying nothing official from the English Privy Council, he produced a sapphire ring. It had been given to one of Elizabeth's ladies-in-waiting some time ago, with instructions that upon her mistress's death, it should be delivered to James as proof of her end and his beginning.

This remarkable journey secured Robert Carey's place in history and forever associates him with the start of the Stuart age. It also resulted in his appointment as a Gentleman of the king's Bedchamber. But contemporaries, such as the Lord Mayor of London and members of the Privy Council, scathingly condemned Carey's behaviour as being contrary to decency, good manners and respect. The matter overshadowed their protestations of loyalty to the king and led to the reversal of Carey's appointment, but he would not remain in the cold for very long. To smooth matters over, King James wrote a placatory letter to the English Secretary of State, Sir Robert Cecil. Expressing gratitude for 'so wise a counsellor', he expressed a wish to say as much from his own mouth. Within a week, he was preparing to leave his homeland to do just that.[13] His family were instructed to follow later – all bar Charles, who was not deemed well enough for such a journey.

The 2-year-old was assigned to the Catholic Alexander Seton, Lord Fyvie, who had carried the ducal crown at the boy's christening. Fyvie had four daughters, the eldest being seven years older than the prince. The first three and a half years of Charles's life were a constant battle against ill health within the confines of Dunfermline Palace. Unable to walk or talk, and trapped within his fragile shell, perhaps he was indulged by the Fyvie girls, as well as frustrated by their abilities. When Fyvie's long-awaited son was born in 1602, he was named after the under-developed royal, but died soon after. The Bishop of Dunkeld, a staunch Royalist, would later write that Charles looked on the Setons 'with more than ordinary affection'.[14] Fyvie later became Earl of Dunfermline in honour of his charge.

Though King James did not see his offspring before he galloped into England, he did pen some words of advice to Prince Henry:

> Let not [my accession] make you proud ... be therefore merry but
> not insolent ... choose none to be your play fellows but them that
> are well born.[15]

By comparison, James passed merrily through the North of England, 'Banquetting and Feasting by the way'. The English turned out in droves to see him – a fact that made the king uncomfortable. He had never been the object of such wonderment and as much as he considered himself appointed by God, he wasn't particularly divine-looking. Seeking to escape the gawping multitudes by way of hunting expeditions, he ordered his new subjects to restrain themselves from chasing him. But many, like Robert Carey, saw this accession as 'the way to Advancement ... The Court being a kind of Lottery'.[16] James passionately believed in the union of his kingdoms and was eager to please every section of his new populace to achieve it. This was his destiny. But too many olive branches would inevitably alienate in the long run – James, after all, sat on a throne and not on a fence.

April passed in a blur. The new queen was asked not to cross the border until the old one was laid to rest. Meanwhile, despite being delayed by his 'fat horses failing him', Sir Robert Cecil met his new monarch at York.[17] Not everyone was as welcoming of James and the army of Scotsmen accompanying him, and this momentary state of flux provided opportunities for the discontented. Outrages occurred in the West Marches and riots broke out across the English-Scottish border. Inside the Tower of London, a man was questioned about treasonable threats, having vowed to make the new king pay the price if he initiated toleration for Catholics.

Back in Scotland the mood was sombre. People were said to have wept at James's departure, as much as some in England did at the prospect of his accession. Duke Charles's presence at Dunfermline was no consolation to the Scots. In fact, in his vulnerable state, he was easily overlooked. Even the king passed over his second son when writing to the queen and anticipating seeing a 'couple' of his bairns – there being only three royal children.[18] With no immediate plans to move Charles, Lord Fyvie kept the king informed about the boy, and a report dated 29 April 1603 offers an insight into the prince's younger years:

> that precious jewell ... is (praisit be God) for the present at bettir
> health far then he was, and, to mak your majestie mair particular
> accoumpt, eats, drinks, and uses all naturall functions as we wald
> [wish] in onye child off his graces age.

Fyvie certainly put a spin on the positive aspects. Charles's sleep was not as sound as could be hoped, but God willing it would be fine in no time. The 'greate weaknesse' of his body was more than made up for by the 'strenth off his spirit and minde'. He looked 'stately' and bore a majesty in his countenance that could be required of any prince, even one four times his age.[19] Behind Charles's pale face, the battles with his health had already started to shape his character. Fyvie's words begin to form a recognisable portrait of the king that Charles would become. But for the moment, to Fyvie and many other courtiers, he was simply a 'jewell'.

As the months rolled by, plague kept James from London, but it could not prevent his reunion with Anna and his two eldest children. The following month the quartet departed on a royal progress, feted by many of England's most influential families. Outside this bubble, authorities were rounding up more suspects, accused of plotting to seize both the king's person and the Tower of London. Labourers in Sussex, Essex and Hertfordshire were indicted for treasonable speeches. In Scotland, too, Lord Fyvie wrote about disorders arising from the monarch's absence.

Events came to a head towards the end of 1603. Resentment over the number of Scotsmen around James left Englishmen referring to his accession as a peaceful invasion. The Scots were no less happy with the imperious English, whose kingdom fell by 'inheritance' to the king and was therefore a mere accessory to Scotland. Some disaffected Scotsmen returned home and drew up a petition, informing James that unless he granted their demands, it would be 'impossible to effect' the union of the two kingdoms and peace would be compromised.[20] The fracture stemmed from religion. The petitioners were Catholic noblemen, and the Venetian ambassador whispered that many more of the king's confidantes harboured the same faith in their hearts. Suspicion of Queen Anna was long-standing.

Religion was the biggest threat to James and his kingdoms. It divided swathes of his people, but at the same time united extremists. By December 1603, after his hand was forced, he ordered the resumption of laws against Catholic recusants, as well as the suppression of superstition and popery. James and his Catholic subjects were on a collision course. The paths of Prince Charles and Robert Carey would also cross before 1603 was out, when Carey made a second prophetic journey north.

'When I was at Norham,' Carey wrote in his memoirs, with the benefit of hindsight, 'God put it into my mind to go to Dunfermline, to see the King's second son.' Although he found Duke Charles a 'very weak child' Carey stayed two days with his noble friend Lord Fyvie, whom he 'had long known'.[21] Carey would next meet Charles around a year later, by which time the boy had embarked upon an epic journey of his own – one which would impress even the intrepid Carey.

Chapter 2

Sweet Duke

On 6 March 1604, the shipbuilder Phineas Pett launched a vessel like no other. It was 25 feet long, with a 12-foot breadth, 'garnished' with paintings and carvings. One week later, it sailed to the Tower of London, where King James, Prince Henry and many nobles 'took great pleasure in beholding [it]'. A special gift for Henry, the excited prince took possession of the vessel on 22 March and travelled as far as Paul's Wharf, where he used a great 'bowl' of wine to name it *Disdain*.[1]

Further up the Thames at Westminster, James's first Parliament was under way. The king had opened it with such a long speech, exhorting everyone to work together, that its printing was delayed. The Catholics were said to entertain hopes that the king might steer a middle course in religion. They petitioned for liberty of conscience and even promised to abstain from plots against his life. For his part, despite royal proclamations, very few priests were banished and 'no great diligence' was said to be used towards their expulsion.[2]

In April, Prince Henry declined a gift from France that was nowhere near as exciting as the *Disdain*. It was customary for the King of France to hold a Scottish company of 100 men-at-arms. By tradition, command lay with the King of Scotland's eldest son, but it was now deemed beneath Henry. To avoid offending the French, the post was bestowed upon the 3-year-old Charles. It was a prophetic appointment because he would go on to express a desire for soldiering.

A better gift arrived in the form of a surprise visitor in May. Doctor Henry Atkins came to Scotland with an apothecary in tow, having been allocated £100 for the prince's medication and 'safe passage' to England.[3] Upon arrival, Atkins found Charles attempting to walk, led by the hand of an 'ancient gentlewoman' who was his nurse. The boy did 'carryeth him self chearfully & merily'. Charles was set to emerge from his chrysalis and escape Dunfermline – not that he realised it at the time, rebuffing the doctor's attempts to examine him by calling for music. He happily imitated the tunes of the musical instruments with his 'tender voyce' and considering he could not stand without support, marvelled at those who danced galliards around him.[4]

Admitting the scale of the challenge to Robert Cecil, Atkins wrote 'at my cominge the duke was far out of order'. He concluded that the joints of Charles's knees, hips and ankles were 'great and loose' and not knitted together. This was later speculated upon as rickets.[5] To make matters worse, the boy was suffering from diarrhoea and great thirst, attributed to teething, though he would not 'permitt any to feele his gums'.[6] By June, Atkins was thanking God that with 'easy remedyes he is soe well recovered that … his stomack & mouthe & other partes' were well.[7] Following this news, instructions to convey Charles into England duly arrived at Dunfermline on 15 June.

Two days later, the doctor sat down to dinner after preparing another update. The Almighty had blessed Charles – and in turn Atkins – with a bout of well-timed 'happy health' that proved 'concurrent' with the king's orders. Adding a postscript of concern about 'slow proceedings' that might jeopardise this opportunity, he called for a curtained litter with spare horses and a second coach to avoid any unforeseen delays. Lord Fyvie added that he would 'not mislike' the opportunity of accompanying the duke to England, but only if he was to be the senior rank in attendance.[8] Atkins and Fyvie were ready to cash in their services while stock was high.

Queen Anna was kept closely informed of the 3-and-a-half-year-old's progress. She had the Earl of Shrewsbury read one of the doctor's letters aloud and found 'nothynge displeasynge' about the state of her son's 'boddy'.[9] On 3 July, she was told that Charles, though not as bold as Ajax, could now walk the length of Dunfermline's great chamber like a 'gallant soldier all alone' and without a staff.[10] Whether accurate or not, the statement conveys the teetering hopes of all parties, Charles included, who was excited at the prospect of seeing both his mother and London. To Atkins, 'wit and beauty' strove for superiority in the boy, who was a 'vive image' of his father.[11]

As the prince persevered with walking, the humiliation of every stumble and fall was hard to bear, and in later life he would hide his vulnerability behind a regal mask. But it instilled in him a determination to overcome adversity and a tenacity to succeed against all odds. The king must have followed his son's progress with newfound understanding, temporarily bedridden by mobility issues of his own; while en route to Rochester to review the fleet, the queen's horse had kicked his leg.

Charles's journey, set for 17 July, coincided with the resignation of the Lord Lieutenant of the Marches, leaving a void in border authority. While Scotland's precious jewel slowly made his way south, thefts of horses and oxen spiralled. Overseen by Lord Fyvie, an army of attendants surrounded the duke; from couchmen, littermen and those who repaired saddles and harnesses, to men who bathed the horses' legs. Charles's bed was carried within the cavalcade, while George Knevett, a groom, rode ahead to give notice of the royal's impending arrival to his various hosts. William Meredith, yeoman of the king's wardrobe, would apply hangings to the rooms assigned as the duke's bedchamber.[12]

Berwick was the first stopover. Doctor Atkins was relieved to have left Scotland. So too, for different reasons, was Charles, who 'very well brooks and likes his journey'.[13] He would have been excited to see the countryside and coast, as well as to receive local dignitaries who hastened to him. The unfolding adventure was the most momentous event in his life so far, emphasising his importance after so long in the sickly shadows. Just rewards for his personal struggles and perseverance.

From Berwick, the next stop was Bamburgh Castle, built on a stunning outcrop overlooking the sea. The following day they made for Alnwick Abbey, and then, Bottle, Newcastle and Durham, arriving at Auckland on 28 July as a guest of the bishop. It was here, resting for three nights, that Charles met Sir Robert Carey once more. The king had ordered Carey to see his son 'furnished with all things necessary', but he also considered the opportunities the boy's presence would provide.[14]

Travel continued via Selby, Aike, Cowling and Fountains Abbey, to Gawthorpe Hall, near York, which they reached on 4 August. The duke was 'honourably entertained' for three nights by Sir William Wentworth, a father of twelve, whose eldest boy was 11-year-old Thomas. There is a high probability that Charles and the future Earl of Strafford met here for the first time – Charles would end his days believing his fate to be divine punishment for the death of Thomas. Sunday 5 August 1604, the fourth anniversary of the Gowrie Conspiracy, provided a timely reminder to Charles of the dangers his family faced. Doctor Atkins sycophantically recounted how they spent 'ye Lords Day consecrated to his divine service' while also celebrating the happy and joyful memory of the king's 'blessed deliverance'.[15] Quoting his favoured Roman poet, he revealed how he had prayed for the king as Horace did for Augustus. Around the time of Charles's visit, Sir William Wentworth also regaled his son Thomas with family legends of future greatness.

Though the 'sweete Prynce' was said to be in better health 'then ever he hadd before', all down to Atkins, a pause was planned. A few days were to be passed at Worksop Manor, which stood in 'good and holesome ayre and ther [Charles] may rest & be quiett'.[16] Apart from the rigour of the travel, his health was threatened by 'the sickness in those parts'.[17] By 10 August, James was complaining about a lack of updates and demanded the 'gysts' of his son's journey.[18] For four days Charles had been pleasing himself with music. At Worksop his love of the hunt was born after seeing the bucks coursed and killed and taking pleasure 'in viewing the quarries of deer'.[19]

Written notice was then sent to Mansfield, Nottingham and Leicester to host the royal party. The Mayor of Leicester was required to provide suitable accommodation with twelve beds, and seven hogsheads of beer, along with all necessities for a kitchen. He swiftly turned over a mansion for the purpose, decorated with welcoming boughs, and a banquet was given in Charles's honour. The brief visit left a bad taste in the mouths of officials when they found many Flanders fruit dishes had been broken and other items stolen.

Anyone still alive forty-one years later, when the town was sacked by Royalist troops in the Civil War, might have cast their minds back and wondered at the calibre of those that orbited royalty.

As summer continued, temperatures and plague deaths soared. There was also a warming of relations with Spain as peace negotiations got under way in the capital. King James was struggling to instil unity between his own kingdoms, without continuing an unofficial war with Spain. Meanwhile, from Althorp, Charles proceeded via Pauls Perry and Wing until finally, on 21 August 1604, after travelling for over two months, he reached Windsor.

Days earlier, the Treaty of London had been agreed. King James had promised to withdraw financial and military support from the Protestant Dutch, in exchange for Spain's agreement to cease military intervention in Ireland and recognise his Protestant monarchy. For Lord Cecil, the Crown's lack of money was the driving force – 'necessity knows no law'.[20] Peace gave the new dynasty breathing space, but it would prove fleeting. The Spanish still expected James to lessen the persecution of Catholics, while English Protestants believed their greatest enemy had just been appeased. It was a see-saw that the king attempted to ride for the rest of his life, using his children as checks and balances, only to alienate both parties in the process. It would overshadow Charles's first twenty-four years, but for now, he happily settled back into the heart of his family.

After the Spanish peace, *Rex Pacificus*, as James came to be known, set his sights on a different title – King of Great Britain. Anxiety over the union of his crowns reached such a level that the Venetian ambassador thought James 'cares for nothing else'.[21] The Earl of Worcester complained that the king would never be satisfied 'until this work begun be thoroughly effected'.[22] It was a topic that monopolised the Privy Council's time. Scottish and English commissioners failed to reach agreement, but James was, at least, proclaimed King of Great Britain in October. At that point, Shakespeare was writing *King Lear*, which centred around a split kingdom, with half of Lear's realm being given to the Duke of Albany. For the real-life duke, aged 4, the idea was not altogether unimaginable.

Chapter 3

Charles of Scotland

As the end of 1604 beckoned, King James received a personal warning of the simmering discontent in England. At Royston, his latest bout of hunting was interrupted when a note was discovered tied to the neck of a hound. It called upon the royal to leave, claiming the locals can no longer 'afford to support the Court'.[1] The Earl of Worcester was as equally tired of the unending sport, lasting from 8.00 am until 4.00 pm. A need for stability made James consider the little Duke of Albany's role.

Charles was quickly absorbed into Stuart politics. His title was reviewed and archives were consulted over the Dukedom of York, the last holder being Henry Tudor, later King Henry VIII. But a grander position looked to be on the table: that of King of Scotland. In November 1604, a report circulated that King Henry IV of France, intrigued at the prospective union of Scotland and England, wondered whether the Scots would 'desire' the king's second son as their monarch.[2] Such a prospect would prevent Scotland losing the status of a kingdom, as well as the presence of a ruler. This statement, from Charles's future father-in-law, demonstrates a dramatic change in the boy's prospects.

On 3 January 1605, the Attorney General declared that the term 'Charles of Scotland' might even be considered offensive. James was eager, for the sake of unity, to replace the labels 'Scottish' and 'English' with that of 'Briton'. Twelfth Night revelry provided a mix of excitement and joy, as well as serious reflection for the 4-year-old, when he was made a Knight of the Bath and Duke of York.

Alongside a posse of new knights, he made his way to the Holbein Gate with its chequered stone and flint frontage and octagonal towers. In a room on the upper floor, the group had supper. With their coats of arms behind them, they flanked Charles, who was borne by the 70-year-old Earl of Nottingham, Lord High Admiral of Armada fame. Ceremonial spurs were issued, and then the knights were shaved and bathed. Donning special habits with long sleeves and a hood, they processed to chapel for prayers, and the next day went 'downe into the Parke in their Hermits weedes'.[3] The rituals and religious devotions must have left a deep impression on Charles. One spectator, however, was less than inspired – Sir Dudley Carleton wrote 'we have a Duke of York in title but not in substance'.[4]

As part of the ceremony, each knight swore to maintain the rights of the church during his lifetime. Charles would later become passionately attached to the Order of the Garter, and the chivalric honour and symbolism it embodied. His installation of the Bath was the first taste of such principles. Being at the centre of pomp and feted by so many – all much older – must have enchanted the boy. Two of the new knights at his side, Robert Bertie and William Compton, were ennobled by him after his accession twenty years later – Bertie as Earl of Lindsay, and Compton as Earl of Northampton – but their bonds were rooted in the ceremony of the Bath. Both men would go on to become Royalist commanders in the Civil War and died in Charles's cause. Of the eleven other knights that day, Charles would one day invest Bertie, Compton, Sir William Cecil and Sir Thomas Howard with the Garter.

The entertainment was augmented by a court masque. The Elizabethan banqueting house, made of bricks, timber and canvas, was originally intended to be temporary. As he watched his wife take centre stage beneath its ceiling of painted vines and fruits, King James dreamed of a replacement that would assert the permanence of the Stuart dynasty. Queen Anna, now six months pregnant, sat encapsuled in a vast scallop shell with her ladies, 'their faces and arms up to their elbows painted black'.[5]

After entering London, Charles had been installed at Whitehall Palace with his parents, while his older siblings had their own households elsewhere. This gave him a unique perspective of government, keeping him close to his parents and at the centre of events. Now Duke of York, it was time to consider his staff. On 8 February 1605, the king declared his gratitude to Lord Fyvie for delivering the duke in such 'good and sound estate'.[6] Old Marian Hepburne, a one-time 'rokker', was also dispensed with, resulting in the loss of some of Charles's original companions, but also heralding a new start. The post of tutor was filled by Thomas Murray, a diligent and honest Scotsman. With Queen Anna's essential blessing, Sir Robert Carey and his wife, Lady Elizabeth, were given charge of the duke's household and care of his person. It was a fortuitous appointment.

If Sir Robert is to be believed, many great ladies became 'suitors for the keeping of the Duke' but quickly abandoned all aspiration when they noted his weakness. Charles still could not walk 'nor scant stand alone' and was 'so weake in his jointes, and especially his ankles, insomuch as many feared they were out of joint.' This is at odds with Doctor Atkins' glowing reports, but both men had their own agendas. Charles grew 'better and better every day' due to Lady Elizabeth's diligent care. She had a transformative effect, winning 'many a battaile' with the king against measures such as cutting the string under Charles's tongue to better aid speech, or putting him in 'iron bootes' to strengthen his sinews and joints. The Careys would have charge of Charles until he was 11 years old. He never forgot their devotion.[7]

While these household changes were under way, the Privy Council's advice was sought about a petition that the duke should have the 'regency of Ireland', with an Irishman of undoubted loyalty as deputy.[8] For all his weakened state, talk of the boy becoming a cypher King of Scotland, or Vice-Regent of Ireland, are stark reminders of his status.

By early March 1605, a heavily pregnant Queen Anna was escorted to Greenwich Palace in preparation for her confinement. She went with the Prince of Wales and Duke of York, who were later joined by Princess Elizabeth. It was a family affair in the full sense when the queen's brother, the Duke of Holstein, arrived for a tournament to celebrate James's Accession Day. Against this backdrop, the king searched for a solution to the problem of religion. Puritans were proving ever more 'troublesome and annoying', even publishing a book entitled *The Errors of the King of Great Britain*, which criticised their ill-treatment. James was resolved to deprive them of their benefices and expel them from the kingdom. Yet, he remained equally prepared to enforce the law's 'severity and bitterness' against Catholics.[9] This double persecution was an attempt to steer his kingdoms between the two extremes and it was replicated in foreign policy.

On 8 April, the overdue Queen Anna finally gave birth at 2.00 am. The baby girl – christened Mary after the king's mother – meant that Charles was no longer the youngest child. Parliament was similarly overdue, plague having forced a prorogation in 1604. In May 1605, Sir William Heyricke supplied gold and pearls for Prince Henry, along with diamonds and rubies for Charles, perhaps adornments for the anticipated state opening. The Earl of Dunfermline wrote from Scotland that in 29 years it was 'never so calm and quiet'.[10] It was an ominous silence. As devastating as plague was, for the Stuarts, it proved to be their saviour by delaying Parliament yet again. The sixteen months between sessions gave the Gunpowder Plot time to unravel.

At this time, Viscount Cranborne wrote of the perfect health of that 'precious jewel the D. of York'. Displaying great determination to surmount his physical setbacks, Charles also devoted the same focus to his studies. In June, Thomas Murray informed the king that his second son was capable of all things 'which his art or industry may afford'.[11] One of the duke's earliest letters is from this period:

> Sweet, sweet Father, i learn to decline substantives and adjectives. Give me your blessing. i thank you for my best man. Your loving son, York.[12]

As indication of the boy's desire for learning and adventure, Murray went on to beg for reasonable entertainment on his behalf. This is not elaborated upon, but six months later, Norman Lisle was appointed as the duke's musician. Plague also led to the brothers being packed off to the country for safety, which resulted in a few months' quality time together. At the end of June, they travelled to Surrey as guests of Lord Lumley, the 70-year-old collector and connoisseur of art and literature. They stayed at Nonsuch Palace, so named because there was supposedly no other palace of equal magnificence.

Built by Henry VIII, it consisted of two courts, one of stone and the other of timber. Adorned with plaster statues, slate had been 'fastened onto the timber … like a coat of armour'.[13] Lord Lumley's father-in-law had purchased Nonsuch from the Crown but upon inheriting it, Lumley sold it back to the royals and continued to reside there as custodian. The Lumley inventories evidence a vast art collection that was spread amongst his three properties. They included works by Holbein and Dürer, while Nonsuch's library was the second largest in private ownership, having been formed from Archbishop Cranmer's. This was later acquired for Prince Henry, along with pictures and medals, which then went on to form Charles's own collection.

The duke must have relished watching his athletic elder brother hunting or exercising with his pike, and might even have admired the artworks or library, benefitting from Lumley's expertise. The old man had no heirs, three children having died in infancy, so he doted somewhat on the boys who became regular visitors. 'We have this summer been greatly refreshed with the presence of two fine princes,' Lumley wrote to the Earl of Shrewsbury on 11 September, before thanking him for the gift of a 'fat and sweet red deere'.[14]

Spending summer with Henry imbued Charles with a strong bond to his brother, demonstrated by one of his undated letters from this period.

> Sweet, sweet Brother, I thank you for your Letter, I will keep it better than all my graith; and I will send my pistolles by Maister Newton. I will give anie thing I have to yow, both horss and my bookes, and my pieces and my cross bowes, or anie thing that you would haive. Good Brother, loove me, and I shall ever loove and serve yow.[15]

The parliamentary session was set for 5 November 1605. As peers and MPs made ready to converge upon London, Lord Cecil wrote of the king and queen's 'pleasant and healthful' country progress. He noted that all was as 'quiet' in the city of London.[16] On the evening of 27 September, a stranger called on the Archbishop of Canterbury. The Norfolk man introduced himself as one who had informed on a 1603 plot to replace the king with his cousin, Lady Arabella Stuart [also known as Arbella]. He now wished to acquaint the prelate with a matter tending to the 'same purpose'. Archbishop Bancroft delicately probed further. The man was a Catholic recusant and wished for protection of conscience. As the night drew on, he took his leave, promising to return in the morning. When he failed to show, the primate was left much troubled that he had let the man go but vowed that it shall be 'a warning unto me'.[17]

If the Archbishop of Canterbury was unnerved, the king was positively merry. He was at Royston in October, sending thanks to Lord Cecil for a gift of fruit. The peaches looked 'very fair' but were 'not so good in taste'. A further letter to his overworked 'beagle' expressed faith in good servants that will 'sweat and labour' for his relief and quite prophetically declared 'swan like' he would live and die in purity and innocence. On 28 October, the king rose at 5.00 am to get his fill of hunting before heading back to London.[18]

Thomas Percy, a gentleman pensioner, called by Charles's lodgings on 1 November. Speaking to one of the household, a lady called Agnes Fortune, he made enquiries about the little boy's movements. Where did he ride, how could his chamber be reached, and who attended him? Whether Agnes alerted the authorities or not, in four days she would realise the implications.

Chapter 4

This Poor Boy's Innocence

'a roaring, nay, a thundering Sin of Fire and Brimstone, from the
which God hath so miraculously delivered us all'.
King James VI & I's speech to Parliament,
9 November 1605

Nearing midnight, on 4 November 1605, a solitary figure arranged thirty-two barrels and two hogsheads of gunpowder in a vault beneath the House of Lords. Alongside coal and wood, this stash had been hidden by a great store of billets and faggots. Guy Fawkes, a Catholic and a soldier, was used to handling munitions of war. But while preparing a train of fine powder, which would give 30 minutes' respite, he was discovered by guards.

Replete with a 'fals lantern, match and a tinder box', he had been booted and spurred for a quick getaway. Instead, he was thrown into the Tower for his part in the most detestable plot ever 'conceaved by the hart of man'. Fawkes' intention was to have 'blowen up all, at a clapp' when the king was at Parliament the next day.[1] Princess Elizabeth would have been crowned and married off to a good Catholic to establish a new dynasty.

When Parliament did assemble in the shocking aftermath, James took the opportunity to assert his belief in divine right, noting that kings are Gods 'being His Lieutenants' and Viceregents on Earth. He reminded everyone that he had now been exposed to 'Two more special and greater Dangers than all [other kings]'. It had been his interpretation of a strange letter, warning of a 'dangerous blow', which caused a last-minute search, therefore he was the saviour of nobility, bishops, knights, gentry and judges.[2] As for Thomas Percy, a cousin of the Earl of Northumberland, as early as 1603 it was said that the man could not look the King in the face by 'owl-light'.[3] He had been assigned to do away with the 5-year-old Duke of York had the boy not been present at Westminster.

Living in Whitehall Palace, Charles must have been acutely aware of the plot and that he was an intended victim. Six days later, when a shell-shocked James met the Venetian ambassador and talked about his 'special protection', the Duke of York entered the room. Heartened by his son's presence, the king declared 'This poor boy's innocence' had more power with God than the 'perfidious malignity' of men.[4] Like any young child in the middle of a momentous event,

Charles would have experienced the many emotions, overheard whispers and looked in upon it all as he came and went. At Whitehall, he was in the hub of Stuart government, watching the business of monarchy at first hand. Perhaps this proximity to power, with few young friends, helped form his serious-minded approach to life and kingship.

The seismic fallout of the plot very nearly split the royal family. There followed calls for the Prince of Wales to reside in Scotland. A suggestion of settling Charles in the North of England was also raised. On 3 April 1606, Thomas Fairfax, a Yorkshire soldier-diplomat, wrote to the Earl of Shrewsbury in favour of the idea. 'We flatter our selves that his majesty will send downe the duke of york,' Fairfax admitted, in the hope that the Bishop of Durham might take on the role of tutor. After all, the late treason had proved 'to[o] great an adventure'.[5] The idea was never adopted, but Fairfax's son and grandson would both take a more direct hand in Charles's life during the Civil Wars.

As King James battled to suppress Puritans and Catholics alike, Parliament granted financial subsidies, but questioned his expenditure. Inventories of the Duke of York's household were headed by Sir Robert and Lady Elizabeth Carey, whose wages equalled those of all six royal surgeons. Thomas Murray, his tutor, was of Puritan persuasion. An honourable man with much integrity, he kept his distance from court politics and proved a significant role model for Charles – something of a father-figure. In time, Murray would connect his pupil with various artistic and military leaders of the day and encourage awareness of foreign affairs. He was married to Jean Drummond, a cousin of the queen's lady-in-waiting, and their daughter was wedded to the son of Prince Henry's tutor. In this way Murray linked all three royal households and such a network kept Charles very much informed. It also maintained a tight ring of Scottish influence. There were precious few friends of the same age, but the tutor's nephew, William Murray, became a companion. Another was Thomas Carey, son of Sir Robert, who Charles 'much beloved'.[6] He would form a lifelong bond with Thomas and William, despite William's fickle nature.

In April 1606, with the kingdom still reeling from the Gunpowder Treason, a village constable's pursuit of a felon was enough to spark panic, occurring just after the king had passed by. It was quickly alleged that James had been stabbed to death and believed by the Court, this news led to an extraordinary council meeting before the queen who was pregnant again. London descended into panic as everyone 'flew to arms'. Shops were closed and cries were made against 'Papists, foreigners and Spaniards'. Hurrying back to the city, James was welcomed as one 'risen from the dead'.[7] Within Whitehall Palace, Charles must have felt there was a blade perpetually poised above his family. Death claimed a Stuart scalp two months later when the queen gave birth to a daughter, named Sophia, who died the following day.

The sombre atmosphere was alleviated in July when the queen's brother, the King of Denmark, made a state visit. It was a magnificent affair. Christian arrived with a small fleet of eight ships, his own sporting three tiers of brass ordnance, with blue and white pennants fluttering from every mast. King James and Prince Henry met Christian amidst the music of bands and thunder of cannon, and took him by barge to Greenwich. There the 5-year-old Duke of York and his sisters, 9-year-old Elizabeth and 1-year-old Mary, welcomed their uncle. Charles's presence at such an event casts doubt on a 1651 biography, which claimed that he crawled 'upon all foure, in a most unseemly manner' until the age of 7.[8] His debilitating health concerns were being conquered.

This was the biggest royal event that Charles had taken part in and it was also his sister's first visit to court.[9] When the Kings of England and Denmark progressed through London, the capital was hung with azure cloth, 'set with scutcheons, streamers and pendants'.[10] A route of gravel was made so that the royal horses would not slip. Buildings were hung with cloth of arras, silks and tapestries, and conduits ran with claret. Grand pageants touted the beneficial alliance of Britain and Denmark, personified by James and Anna's union, and Somerset House was renamed Denmark House.

Around this time, Charles wrote to Henry that he did 'keep your haires in breath, (and I have very good sport)'.[11] He ended with a wish that the king and prince could see his feats. The king, however, was in no fit state during the Danish visit. James and Christian rolled around in drunken stupors. One servant was so inebriated that she fell into Christian's lap and covered him in 'wine, cream, jelly, beverages, cakes, spices and other good matters'.[12] Christian also managed to upset the ageing Lord High Admiral, using two fingers in a dispute over the time being 2 o'clock. Though Charles was not present at Theobalds, there is no doubt that James's commonplace debauchery played a part in forming his son's notoriously abstemious manner.

Just months after his sixth birthday, in February 1607, Charles's future became interlinked with that of Venice. An ongoing wrangle between the Republic and the Papacy was exacerbated by the interference of European powers. France supported Venice, while Spain pushed the Vatican's cause. It revolved around a power struggle between the maritime state and its Catholic clergy, with the King of Great Britain hovering on the periphery. As Zorzi Giustinian, the Venetian ambassador, waited for an audience with King James, he was met with an extraordinary sight when the Duke of York emerged 'with an harquebus on his shoulder'. Charles was portrayed by the artist Robert Peake at this time with a pale complexion, long face and large forehead. But his eyes stood out even at that age, just as they did in later life – there is a sparkling determination in them. With such resolution, he went 'right up' to the ambassador and declared he was 'thus armed for the service of the Republic'.

The envoy answered that Venice would be proud of so 'big and brave' a captain, and under his leadership she was sure to win a great victory.[13]

The king did not show the same clarity of purpose. He had a natural affinity with the Venetians, but would only consider alliances if the French king did the same. In May, Prince Henry pledged his own support in a letter to the Doge, for once following in Charles's wake. This use of the two boys made a great impression on all concerned, not least Charles. He relished playing his role, strong enough to bear a harquebus and speaking with what appeared to be a confident bearing. A Venetian future is an under-explored aspect of his life, and offers an interesting 'what if' had he never come to the throne. A more whimsical suggestion was raised in August 1607, this time as a result of heightened tension between the Dutch and Spanish. Ambassadors hinted that the Spanish Netherlands might come under the dominion of King James by matching his second son with a Hapsburg. Had this option played out, Charles would have finished up in direct conflict with his sister Elizabeth and her Protestant husband.

When the outgoing Venetian ambassador took his leave that year, he made a detailed observation of the royal family for his successor. This handover document gives personal insights of one who was close enough to the Stuarts to judge them – a man who had, for example, indulged Queen Anna in the Italian language. Though King James was labelled 'a bitter enemy' of our religion, he was termed placid, averse to cruelty and a lover of quiet. Of the royal offspring, the Prince of Wales was of noble wit, but took little delight in study and was only persuaded by his father's strict entreaties. An occasion was recounted when an exasperated James threatened to leave the crown to Charles, who was 'far quicker at learning' and studied 'more earnestly'. Suitably chided, Henry had returned to his chamber and in a fit of rage declared if his brother was so learned, he would make him Archbishop of Canterbury.

When the king heard of this, he did not see the funny side and took Henry's outburst 'in no good part'.[14] As Prince of Wales, Henry was naturally treated as a superior being, receiving more attention and having key involvement in affairs of state. There is no evidence to suggest that Charles took this ill; he understood it was the way of things and always respected hierarchy and order. Rather, he hero-worshipped his 'loving brother'. By 1609, Charles's writing gives a sense of his growing self-confidence and maturity:

> Nothing can be more agreeable to me, dearest brother, than your
> return to us; for to enjoy your company, to ride with you, to hunt
> with you, will yield to me supreme pleasure.[15]

In a bid to keep up with his sibling and impress him, Charles revealed that he was reading *Conversations of Erasmus*, from which he hoped to learn the 'purity of the Latin tongue and elegance of behaviour'.[16] He also owned a very special set of books, containing history, poetry and drama, by authors such as Ovid and Cicero. They varied in language between Latin, Italian, Greek and French, all of which he studied. What's more, they were small enough to be used while travelling. A 1658 biography rings hollow when it claims that in Charles, 'no Overtures of merit' were observed, compared to Henry's brilliance.[17]

It was often Henry who appeared to harbour jealousy. He teased and doled out mockery as much as any elder sibling, as alluded to in a book by Sir Charles Cornwallis in 1626. This mentions Henry's 'rough play and dalliance' with Charles and how he also tried the patience of his sister. Interestingly, it refers to a shared flaw in the two brothers, claiming that Henry's speech was 'slow and somewhat impedimented' stemming from 'custome and a long imitation of some that did first instruct him, then by any defect in nature'.[18]

Little Princess Mary, the youngest Stuart, fell ill in September 1607. Her sickness particularly troubled the king who was devotedly attached to her, and a doctor was summoned with haste. When the Earl of Worcester sought out the queen at Hampton Court on 16 September, she anticipated the meaning and sent him on to the king. Following 'violent paroxysms', Charles's sister had succumbed aged only 2.[19] Once again, he became the youngest surviving child and his persistent nickname 'Baby Charles' was indicative of the tragic ends of his siblings. Maybe it scared him that he might be plucked next. Or perhaps it served to imbue a sense of God's favour, sparing him despite his most fragile of beginnings.

Lady Elizabeth Carey was as much the reason for his increasingly robust health as divine providence. Considering the death of Princess Mary and Henry's brief illness that October, she fired off a letter to the king, as she was wont to do when it came to Charles's welfare. Complaining that the household was increasingly starved of finances, she added a warning that Charles 'oftentimes is not so well fed' because of it.[20] It was probably owing to her kind and wise management that the prince survived. Sir Philip Warwick, writing much later, also confirmed that Charles was 'born sickly' but temperance and exercise gave him 'as firm and strong a body as most persons I ever knew'.[21]

A cold spell heralded the year 1608, which was more intense than any 'within the memory of man'. The Thames froze and the city was almost in a state of 'siege'. But nothing could stop Queen Anna's annual masque from going ahead. The Venetian ambassador marvelled at the apparatus and cunning stage machinery, but what captivated him most of all were the queen's jewels. Bedecked in gemstones, she received universal applause. This array of jewellery also played an integral part in her day-to-day role as queen consort and enhanced the image of Stuart monarchy.

Such lustre and magnificence dazzled subjects and foreign observers alike. A diamond ring fashioned like a tortoise, or a jewelled 'C4' monogram (referencing her brother, Christian IV) could mask a drained treasury and garner added respect. To the goldsmiths and jewellers that supplied them, her defaulted payments were notorious. In lieu of hard cash, she would often pawn an old ring or brooch to pay for the creation of a new one, in a never-ending cycle that kept spectators gasping. Many were gifted to foreign heads of state, or ambassadors, and others helped secured loans. James shared this love of jewellery, and Charles most definitely inherited it. Stones of another kind helped set that year's masque apart from any that had gone before it. The occasion christened James's new banqueting house, or great hall. Replacing that of his predecessors, which had been built 'merely in wood', the king proudly showed off the new stone edifice.[22]

Often referred to as a precious jewel, Charles was used once again to enrich the relationship between Britain and Venice. When the Venetian ambassador retired that year, Charles interrupted the audience. It was evident that he was 'the joy of the King, the Queen and all the Court' and notwithstanding official business, James began to laugh and play with his son, betraying a relaxed and genuine affection. He held him aloft and called for the Venetian to make him a Patrician of Venice, a remark that the ambassador felt was not made by 'mere chance'.[23] The king had never felt threatened by his second son in the same way as he did the Prince of Wales. Whereas Charles was obedient, Henry was imperiously independent. Though playing second fiddle in terms of status, Charles seems to have been his parents' favourite, and was emotionally closer to them than either of his older siblings.

For all the politics of it, a Venetian venture was no flash in the pan. Just short of his ninth birthday, the ambassador found Charles in excellent health and of a manner 'far in advance' of his age. The studious boy, savouring the attention, declared that he hoped to visit the man in Venice, intending someday to present himself to the Doge. On a later occasion, when the envoy doled out praise on Prince Henry, King James was quick to point out that the Duke of York 'your soldier' is no less promising.[24] Indeed, so serious were the Venetians about Charles, that when their diplomat, Marc Antonio Correr, was knighted, the man assumed it had been conferred so that he might follow the Duke of York who was to enter 'the service of the Republic' and who hoped one day 'to be seen walking' in the Piazza of St Mark.[25]

Of the other royal children, it was Queen Anna's reported intention to find Princess Elizabeth a German or Italian husband. The long-standing view for Prince Henry was marriage to the Spanish Infanta, but healths were now being drunk to a daughter of France. Instead of being saddled by matrimonial diplomacy, at this stage the Duke of York remained free to pursue his love of horses and hunting. Aged 8, he enjoyed 'the benefit of yor Maties gratious favour' to hunt in Waltham Forest, but was careful to promise that afterwards, 'I will employ my tyme at my booke the best I can'.[26] James took a close hand in his children's education and was so satisfied with Thomas Murray's tutorship that he gave him a signet for 'penning and framing [the duke's] missive letters in divers languages, directed either to ourself or foreign princes'.[27]

Charles was becoming more independent. A grant of £50 per annum was provided, allowing him to confer small gifts and rewards, and take a more active part in the culture of politics and influence. In the summer of 1608, Holdenby House, in Northamptonshire, was purchased as a seat for him. Thomas Murray had travelled to Durham to scout out the castles of Raby, Brancepeth and Barnard, but found them 'very far out of order' and decayed. Instructions were given for their repair, particularly for 'using [Raby] Castle hereafter' but once again, a northern venture did not get off the ground.[28]

That summer's regular progress to Nonsuch coincided with a visit by Princess Elizabeth. Henry and his sister were devoted to one another. Of similar ages, and having lived together for a short time, they corresponded avidly. By comparison, Charles rarely saw her, and up until this point there is no evidence that they were particularly close. But he was spending more time with his brother, and this coincided with an increased involvement in political affairs.

Chapter 5

Little Servant

When Henry was created Prince of Wales in 1610, Charles basked in his brother's glory. June was turned over to ceremonies, pomp and celebrations. First Henry was made a Knight of the Bath and an obligatory masque followed. *Tethy's Festival* was amongst the most 'picturesque' of its kind.[1] Charles danced the part of Zephyrs wearing silver wings and 'a short robe of green satin embroidered with golden flowers'.[2] He was flanked by two 'sea slaves', while twelve girls of his age twirled around him, each one a nobleman's daughter. A sword worth 20,000 crowns was then presented by Charles to his brother. In the second half, Anna took centre stage as Queen of the Ocean, supported by thirteen of her ladies, each representing a river. Princess Elizabeth was the Thames. Charles's debut inducted him into the art of the masque and allegorical acting, which would appeal to his sense of honour but also blur the lines between myth and reality.

Charles also began taking a greater part in King James's audiences with foreign ambassadors, such as those of Saxony, Holland and Venice. The latter met with the entire royal family and observed that Charles was his parent's 'joy'. The Venetian also conveyed his regret that the Duke of York stood without a sword, considering his frequent representations as a 'champion of the Republic'. When the king revealed his son's new intention 'to go into the Church', Charles intervened and reasserted that he was still 'to carry arms' for the Doge.[3] Perhaps James was teasing Charles about a church role in the same way that Henry had over his studious learning? The few references to a religious career all seem given in jest, and none were endorsed by Charles. Even 1609's Twelfth Night masque contained a prophesy that he would 'shake a sword And lance against the foes of God and [his father]'.[4]

With Charles approaching 10 years old, the royals began attending more events as a group. He thrived on this inclusion. Having once lamented the family's long absence, he had found it only bearable through his memory of them, coupled with the hunting of deer. It's surprising that no portrait ever captured the dynasty together, despite their patronage of many artists. One key engagement was the launch of the *Prince Royal,* a new vessel named after Henry, though the warship got stuck between the dock gates. By comparison, there was no holding Charles back when he took delivery of his own state barge. Painted and gilded inside and out, with a carved lion and crown set upon a pedestal, he was proudly rowed up and down river, attended by his footmen in their gold-spangled uniforms. Three teachers were also assigned – two of them French – to instruct him in singing, dancing and tennis, along with his own company of actors.

But the marked increase in marriage negotiations during 1611 was sign enough that the siblings would soon be broken up. A frenzy of outmanoeuvring took place between wooing ambassadors as the two eldest Stuarts were hunted down. Prince Henry was linked not just to Princesses of Savoy, France and Spain, but also the second sister of the Grand Duke of Tuscany. If Protestants were preferred, then Saxony, Brandenburg or the Palatine would surely oblige. Princess Elizabeth had no less an array of suitors, ranging from the Elector Palatine, King Philip of Spain, the Landgrave of Hesse, or Prince of Piedmont. At one point, when the King of Spain's second daughter was put forward for Prince Henry, Lord Cecil snapped with 'heat and scorn' that second for second would mean she was suitable only for the Duke of York. Spain replied that their daughters 'wed Crowns only' and not second-born sons.[5] Little did they know what the future would hold.

St George's Day of 1611 proved to be one of the most memorable days of Charles's life. His investment with the Order of the Garter was marked by artist Robert Peake, who captured the new knight in a supremely confident pose. Flowing velvet robes and white satin linings are sumptuously enhanced by a golden chain, suspending a figure of St George. The Garter band at his leg comprised of 412 sparkling diamonds. Twenty-seven years later, Charles reflected that the Order did 'provoke and encourage' pursuit of glory and heroic actions, while increasing a man's prowess, wisdom, justice and 'princely endowments'.[6]

To his dying day, Charles would daily display the blue ribbon around his neck, and his passionate interest in the Order was encouraged by his mother, who presented him with thirty-six books on the subject. Covered in crimson or purple velvet with silver gilding, after Charles became king, he proudly displayed them in his cabinet room at Whitehall Palace, where they accounted for two-thirds of the books on the shelves. He also inherited Anna's passion for art – a courtier once remarked that the queen loved 'nobody but dead pictures'.[7]

Both of these passions would eventually come together in *Landscape with Saint George and the Dragon*. Painted by Peter Paul Rubens around 1630, Charles was portrayed as St George, demonstrating his desire to be the saint incarnate. Such symbolism hammers home his belief in all that the Garter stood for. When Anna spoke to ambassadors about her family in 1611, it was the Duke of York whom she 'especially praised'.[8] She nicknamed him her 'little servant', perhaps in view of his sweet temperament and eagerness to please, while he addressed her as 'most worthy mistress'. Charles doted on his mother, made clear in a tender letter decorated with many neat flourishes:

give me leave to declare by these lines the duty and love I owe to
you, which makes me long to see you. I wish from my heart that
I might help to find a remedy to your disease; the which I must
bear the more patiently, because it is a sign of a long life.

Gout had, Charles commiserated, deprived him of his mother's company as
well as 'many good dinners', but he vowed to make up for it with some good
recipe that would either 'heal you or make you laugh'.[9] Such warmth was
not present in letters to his father, who Charles both loved and feared. His
headstrong brother, by comparison, often appeared to go up against the king.
In May 1611, during a hunting expedition, James threatened Henry with his
cane. Matters were made a whole lot worse because a large part of the company
went with the prince when he peremptorily spurred his horse and left. When he
inevitably came to beg his father's pardon, James couldn't resist having the last
word, asserting that Henry was 'no sportsman'.[10]

The more time Charles spent with Henry, the more familiar he became with
his brother's influential friends. On 1 May, the pair went a-maying to Highgate,
home of Lord and Lady Arundel, where a banquet of candied fruits and biscuit
bread was provided. Arundel was a leading Catholic peer and collected art on
an industrial scale. On another occasion he was present when Henry rode at
the tilt with a host of teenage companions, the Landgrave of Hesse included.
Between their contests, they listened to music, spoke endlessly about horses,
and on account of it all, went late to dinner. Charles, by comparison, 'dined
alone at his usual hour'.[11] The difference in the brothers could not have been
more apparent – one an extrovert, the other an introvert – with early signs of
Charles's appreciation of routine and order. There is a particular confidence
and ease in the way he set his own course, comfortable with his own company.

That summer, Charles went on his own royal progress, taking the 75-year-old
Lord High Admiral to 'make war' on the king's deer.[12] The Earl of Nottingham
was a white-bearded elder statesman. He had defeated the Armada in 1588,
and then twenty years later – aged 70 – travelled to Spain to seal a peace treaty.
Hunting alongside this national hero was well-timed because, at the turn of the
year, Charles had been designated the earl's successor as Lord High Admiral.
It was a much-coveted title, which in time of war was 'undoubtedly the greatest
post' in the kingdom and worth £150,000 per year.[13] One rival had been none
other than Prince Henry.

With his eleventh birthday looming, Charles prepared to face another
shake-up of his household. Lady Elizabeth Carey was to bow out with 'greate
greife', but Sir Robert Carey was unwilling to melt into the shadows.[14]
Instead, he applied for two posts: Master of the Robes and chief Gentleman
of the Bedchamber. Prince Henry intervened. He was not in favour of the man
having any position, let alone two. But Carey played his cards wisely and

appealed to the queen, who ruled in his favour. Rank and influence were vital to Robert Carey, and though he could often be stubborn and somewhat of a needy character, there were many worse candidates for his place. Thankfully for Charles, Thomas Murray's position as tutor was safe.

Another loss in 1612 occurred when the Earl of Salisbury, the king's dutiful 'beagle', breathed his last. James was greatly disturbed. A plethora of young men stepped forward to catch the king's roving eye and hook themselves one of the vacant government posts. But for the first time, James placed his obsession for hunting second to national interest and superintended all business, applying himself 'courageously and indefatigably'.[15] One of his most touching acts occurred in September when he laid one of the ghosts of his past to rest.

The corpse of King James's mother was brought from Peterborough Cathedral and reinterred in Westminster Abbey, twenty-five years after her death. Mary, Queen of Scots, was conveyed to London in a torchlit procession, dubbed a 'translucent passage in the night'.[16] James described it as 'the duty we owe to our dearest mother'.[17] On the evening of 11 October 1612, the body was interred in the south aisle of the Lady Chapel, opposite that of her nemesis, Elizabeth I. Mary's tomb was crowned with a white marble effigy and a Scottish lion stood proudly at her feet. The inscription referenced her 'most ancient stock' and paid homage to her beauty of form, innocent mind and honour, declaring her murder to be an 'unheard-of precedent, outrageous to royalty'.[18] The matriarch of the dynasty had barely been interred than the sacred building was made ready to receive another of her clan.

Chapter 6

Weep Forth Your Teares

When the Protestant Elector Palatine sailed up the Thames, he was accompanied by a flotilla of eleven boats and landed at Gravesend. Frederick had come to marry his betrothed. After two days' rest, he was conveyed by barge to Whitehall Palace. The guns of the Tower of London gave thundering notice of his arrival, and amidst trumpets, drums and heartfelt cheers, Prince Charles escorted his future brother-in-law into the great chamber. The royals stood on a dais ten steps high, flanked with guards dressed in scarlet and gold. Princess Elizabeth turned a healthy shade of pink when Frederick boldly kissed her.

The visit should have launched a plethora of court events, but proceedings were overshadowed by Henry's health. With few equals in the handling of arms, the prince's rigid regime of exercise included tennis, swimming, tilting and hunting. Very soon it was a fever that had him sweating. He even struggled to hold a game of cards with Charles. Racked with headaches and suffering from 'rushes of moisture and blood to the head', a double-tertian ague took hold.[1] Amongst other remedies, the doctors bled Henry from the arm and shoulder, shaved his head and applied a dead pigeon to it. Sir Walter Raleigh, from the Tower of London, sent a potion that gave temporary respite. Ignorance then turned to fear, and concerned that he might be contagious, his family were prevented from visiting. Henry called out for his sister, who resorted to disguise in a failed attempt to get to his bedside.

The very last time Charles saw his brother, he gave him a miniature bronze sculpture of a horse. It was one of a set of eighteen, coincidentally matching Henry's age. Struggling to speak, Henry could barely offer any thanks. Doctors asked the prince to commend himself to the Almighty, the true physician who treats by 'remedies immortal'. It seemed as if their hopes had already expired, leading Henry to insist they 'make still an effort'. Two hours after midnight, on 6 November 1612, the delirious Prince of Wales died at the very 'flower' of his high hopes.[2] He had intended to escort his sister to Germany following her marriage, but in the wake of his death, that union was postponed.

The loss was a catastrophe for Charles. As a taste of things to come, King James 'apprehending the worst' had already left London for his country retreat at Theobalds, and rumours soon abounded of poisoning with suspicion landing squarely upon the Spanish.[3] When Henry was carved up in a post-mortem, his stomach was declared to be 'without any manner of fault or imperfection', but this did not lay rumours to rest.[4]

In Scotland, it was said that everything ceased at court. The king took to his bed, declaring himself the saddest father in the world. The queen's life was thought to be in the 'greatest danger' and she cried incessantly, refusing to admit anyone to her chamber.[5] Princess Elizabeth went days without eating and shed so many tears that Frederick did not know what to do. A streaker even broke into St James's Palace, now Charles's home, declaring himself the ghost of the dead prince and drawing thousands of curious spectators. The situation called for leadership and displaying a grief beyond his years, 11-year-old Charles was thrust into the breach. The king, however, was well enough to decide that his surviving son would not inherit the income from the Dukedom of Cornwall, nor would he be declared Prince of Wales. In a bid to keep Charles from popery, two sober divines would be instructed never to leave him.

Overnight, Charles was condemned. His Venetian aspirations were reduced to ashes and flourishing development arrested. Now he had to become Henry – he had to take on his late brother's mantle and shoulder the unrealistic expectations of all and sundry. Henry's tragic loss proved difficult for people to comprehend, resulting in a tsunami of grief, and upwards of thirty lamentations and eulogies were published about the prince who was 'Heav'n and Earth's Delight'.[6] John Ward composed mournful music entitled *Weep forth your Teares and doe Lament*.

> Oh had he liv'd our hopes had still encreased,
> But he is dead and all our joyes decreased.[7]

Poet Joshua Sylvester blamed everything on the nation's sins, and those asses, hags and hermaphrodites who had provoked God's vengeance. Francis Bacon said Henry had 'excited high expectations among great numbers of all ranks'.[8] The Earl of Dorset opined 'our rising sun is set'.[9] The pressure to live up to all of this must have been immense, and from that moment Charles lost his own identity. Though acclaimed as 'popular and amiable with everybody', he now had to contend with many disparaging comparisons. Though his health was excellent, his slim build was condemned as 'so slight and so gentle' that many would 'fain see him stronger'.[10]

After Henry had lain in state for one month, Charles was called upon to lead the nation in mourning. There was much similarity between Henry's funeral in December 1612, and that of Diana, Princess of Wales, in September 1997 when 12-year-old Prince Harry walked behind her coffin. Having just turned the same age, Charles did likewise for Henry, though with no family in support. Elton John sang 'Candle in the Wind' for Diana. 'A funeral Elegie for Prince Henry' mentioned a 'candle in the sunne'.[11] Sir Simonds D'Ewes recorded that it was 'the first public grief that ever I was sensible of ... so general as even women and children partook of it'.[12]

At 10.00 am that winter's day, 2,000 mourners marched in the funeral procession to the sound of fife and drum. Two hundred poor people led it, followed by an array of all ranks, from servants to earls, and household officials. Henry's coronet was borne by a knight, followed by heralds, banners, ensigns and the black-clad mourning charger. The coffin was laid on a 'great open carriage' drawn by six roans, topped by Henry's effigy, which was dressed in his robes and complete with a lifelike plaster face.[13]

Prince Charles, on foot, represented the royal family, flanked by the Duke of Lennox and Earl of Northampton, and followed by the Elector Palatine. Trumpeters played the funeral march and 'drew tears' from the eyes of all who heard.[14] So long was the process that when the front reached the abbey, the rear was only just departing St James's Palace. The resulting service lasted two hours. As his brother was laid to rest and Charles stifled both sorrow and nerves, the archbishop's sermon offered no comfort, declaring that princes shall fall like others.

Grief was not confined to Britain. It was reckoned that French Huguenots had 'built their hopes' on the dead prince.[15] Henry's demise also put paid to the king's ideas for financial relief, which could have been expected from his marriage. Charles inherited much; there was his brother's collection of artwork, statues and books, along with coins and medals worth £3,000. Many of Henry's household were transferred, including Abraham van der Doort, who would later inventory the royal art collection, and Edmund Verney, who would die bearing the royal standard at Edgehill. His brother's potential brides were also offloaded, making Charles the focus of endless suffocating negotiations.

An English translation of a book about civil and military aphorisms made use of Charles's portrait. The dedication ominously stated that 'all eyes are upon you ... men looke upon your worthy Brother in your princely selfe; holding you the true inheritor of his virtues'.[16] Another publication prophesised that Charles would be a second Charlemaine 'or rather the perfections of all the Edwards & Henries'.[17] He did not just have to live up to Prince Henry, but centuries of monarchs too.

Not to be outdone, the king rededicated his book *Basilikon Doron* to his surviving son, extolling many opinions about government. This would undoubtedly influence the 12-year-old, who was in especial need of guidance. Part of its treatises covered Scotland, and James's view that sedition and instability were down to a fracture between Kirk and monarchy. In England, by comparison, both were harmoniously united. The union of the three kingdoms and their churches was unfinished business that Charles would one day have to deal with, and he wholeheartedly embraced the notion of divine right of kings, which formed the bedrock of Stuart authority.

The most pressing task at hand, however, was Princess Elizabeth's marriage. Her brother was required to take the lead role in a second public ceremony some months later. It occurred amidst rumours of unrest, and 500 musketeers were raised to guard against 'intended treacherie'.[18] Apothecaries provided the princess with 'unycornes horne', most likely walrus, rhinoceros, or narwhal, which was an ingredient of poison antidotes.[19] Such were the rumours over her brother's fate. The Elector Palatine was made a Knight of the Garter and fireworks preceded the big day. A set piece that would have appealed to Charles portrayed St George on horseback before a dragon.

On St Valentine's Day 1613, Charles escorted Elizabeth to the Banqueting House at Whitehall Palace, with her golden hair flowing loose and her train borne by thirteen ladies. Bride and groom were resplendent in cloth of silver. A tilting extravaganza took place the next day with James, Charles and Frederick running at the ring. In *Basilikon Doron*, James described this sport as vital learning in how to handle arms. The aim was to thunder down the tiltyard and hook small, suspended rings on the end of a lance. Charles won the day by carrying off four.

The cost of the wedding ran to over £50,000, with a dowry of £40,000. Elizabeth lavished rings and chains upon all and sundry at her arrival in the Palatinate after obtaining them on credit from Abraham Hardret. Charles's newfound position saw him besieged by petitioners, not least his sister, who almost immediately called upon her 'onlie deare brother' for assistance to pay this debt:

> beseeching you to keepe me still in your favour and not to forgett
> me it being one of my great comforts to be assured of your love
> and favour … I beseech you still to remember to further Hardrets
> business.[20]

The nuptials left many exhausted. Charles fell ill after his sister's departure, but considering the stresses and strains he had been subjected to, this is unsurprising. He played his part impeccably, which is testament to his inner strength and wellbeing. Though he did not share Henry's athletic build, Charles would go on to improve his physique through mastery of both pike and crossbow. There was also his love of the hunt. James was impressed enough to call him his 'true and worthy son', eager to suggest that this talent was inherited, but four years would elapse before he was formally installed as Prince of Wales.[21] During this time the king kept 'Baby Charles' firmly in his place financially, socially and emotionally.

Barely two months elapsed between Charles becoming a teenager and an uncle. On New Year's Day 1614, Elizabeth gave birth to her first child, a son named Frederick Henry. Gold plate was shipped to Heidelberg for the christening and the king granted his daughter a pension of 12,000 crowns, while Henry Peacham wrote verses about her 'pure and peerelesse excellence'.[22] The baby provided much-needed relief over the succession, but simultaneously saw a certain side-stepping of Charles. After being compared to his elder brother for twelve years, he was now overshadowed by his sister.

To balance the diplomatic scales, Charles's future seemed chained to a Catholic bride. When a princess of Savoy was proposed, their ambassador presented him with some Milanese armour, which was apt – the next ten years would see Charles caught in a furious crossfire over his marriage. It provided another area of disagreement between England and Scotland, the latter favouring their old allies, the French, while English Puritans recoiled at the thought of any Catholic bride. The Spanish, judging the prince on his sweet disposition, felt certain he could be turned back to the 'religion his predecessors lived in'.[23] They severely underestimated both his future adherence to the Church of England and his determination.

The year 1614 provided the prince with his first experience of a very different relationship: that of monarch and Parliament. Royal finances were in a parlous state and the king was raising money through a dubious levy on imports called 'impositions'. Parliament assembled under an atmosphere of mistrust and concern. Both king and prince rode to the opening where foul weather 'marred much of the show'.[24] Hoping that it might be known as the 'Parliament of love' out of a willingness to satisfy his needs, James promised to maintain religion, peace and prosperity.

After fifteen days, the Archbishop of Canterbury observed that nothing had been done except declare the Lady Elizabeth and her offspring next in succession after the prince. Attention turned to the king and the monopolies he doled out to favourites, such as the Lord Admiral's lucrative wine licences. James warned that if MPs did not stump up cash, they 'must not look for more Parliament's in haste'.[25] Parliament, unsurprisingly, dug in its heels and resolved that money would only be forthcoming if the king abandoned impositions. One speech declared royal courtiers to be spaniels to the king and wolves to the people, whereas another writer deemed Parliament more of a cockpit than a council.

The 21-year-old Thomas Wentworth was one of the members. His father had played host to Charles when, ten years earlier, the prince had journeyed to England. Wentworth's marriage, in the same year as Princess Elizabeth's, had also been delayed due to bereavement – in his case, the loss of his mother. His bride was a daughter of the Earl of Cumberland and he was soon after knighted. Newly returned from a year's tour of Europe on account of his father's declining health, Wentworth was full of drive and he rounded on impositions. Going one step further, he declared that in France such taxes had led to the king's murder. This was too near the knuckle for James, who had the Yorkshireman arrested.

In the House of Lords, the Bishop of Lincoln caused a near riot when he branded the Commons a factious and seditious assembly. It marked the bishops' cards. At the start of June, James followed through on his threat and

31

dissolved what became known as the 'Addled Parliament'. Sir Ralph Winwood wrote that he had never seen so much faction and passion, coupled with so little reverence to the king. James turned his attentions to the City of London and after applying for a loan of £100,000, he was gifted £10,000 to soften the refusal. Taking up his plight, the bishops and nobles clubbed together and came to his rescue with a modest sum.

The desire to marry his sons to Popish princesses was blamed for this political turmoil because it 'dis-heartneth the Protestant, and encourageth the Recusant'.[26] Seven years would pass before another Parliament was called, but the topics that caused so much dissention would rumble on across the decades. Samuel Rawson Gardiner, the nineteenth-century historian, stated that in the wake of the Addled Parliament, many came to desire a change 'in the relations between the authority of the Crown and the representatives of the people'.[27]

Thus ended Prince Charles and Thomas Wentworth's first direct experiences of Parliament. Before 1614 was out, Wentworth's father died, leaving him head of a household worth £6,000 per annum and responsible for nine siblings. One day, both men would come to the fore in Parliament and palace.

Chapter 7

Steenie

Kronborg Castle dominated the island of Zealand and a strip of water that provided access to the Baltic Sea. As ship after ship sailed past Denmark's royal fortress, each paid dues to the king. But Christian IV was no longer within the sandstone-clad walls that July of 1614, and only a handful of people knew it. Riding out in utmost secrecy, he had gone to Copenhagen and boarded a ship for England. Routing some pirates on the way, he no sooner landed at Yarmouth than post horses were commandeered to convey him to London.

The energetic King of Denmark was a force of nature who loved dancing, drinking and developing his nation. His long face had a softness to it, with a trademark lovelock on the left side. As he dined at an inn near Aldgate, most of his own subjects still assumed he was ensconced in Kronborg. Once fed, he took a Hackney carriage to Denmark House to surprise his sister. The queen's mood had been low, but this impromptu visit was a perfect tonic, and she welcomed her brother with 'warmest demonstrations of affection'.[1] Prince Charles joined them, while King James, 60 miles away, begrudgingly cut short his hunting. It was said that Christian sought James's support over foreign affairs, and matters were duly discussed between bouts of hunting, bearbaiting and fencing.

On 1 August, James, Christian and Charles travelled to Woolwich and inspected the *Merhonor*, a 40-gun warship that was being rebuilt. Soon afterwards, James took his leave, but Charles and his uncle moved to Gravesend and boarded the *Prince Royal*. The weather was foul, but Christian and Charles shared a love of the navy, and Charles gave a tour of the vessel. Christian then presented his nephew with one of the three ships he had brought to England. The visit made a significant impression upon Charles, who formed a 'very great' affection for his uncle.[2] The novelty and audacity of Christian's shock arrival may even have influenced Charles to make a similarly secret foray to Spain in 1623.

The visit coincided with gossip over James and Anna's marriage; the king had eyes for another, his great favourite Robert Carr. Invested as a Knight of the Garter on the same day as Charles, and created Earl of Somerset, Carr went on to be appointed Lord Chamberlain. The young Scot had come to the king's attention after breaking a leg during a tilting match, and since then they had been inseparable. A desperate plan was needed to drive a wedge between them.

Just weeks later the handsome George Villiers, half James's age, was brought to the queen's apartments. Anna took Charles's sword and handed it to her husband, who then knighted Villiers. Though staged, mother and son had taken a direct hand in manipulating the king, and the results were dubious to say the least. Charles was not, by nature, suited to politics. His chaplain, Dr George Carleton, made complaint about 'shameless' people vying for preferment and singled out the prince as being above this den of vice. He praised his 'sober, grave, swete' temperament and declared him to be without evil inclinations.[3] The king's interest in Somerset duly waned, but a monster was created in his stead. James was utterly spellbound by Villiers. Little did Charles realise it, but his own relationship with the new man would define the first half of his life.

The 'suddane newes' of his father's fall while hunting marred Charles's fourteenth birthday. He wrote from London that day with 'humble and hartie prayers to God' for the king's safety.[4] Less than one year later, there was another health scare. At Royston Palace, on 23 October 1615, the king was 'sorrowful trubled' for two nights by a pain in the 'granelle' (or testicle). The prince's tutor, Thomas Murray, drafted a letter to notify the queen. Key amendments were made by Charles in his own hand, which provide a personal insight into his thoughts. Murray had opened the letter with 'My only deere Maistresse', but Charles, striking it out, replaced that with 'Madame'. There was no change in his affection – he assured his mother that one of his 'greatest worldly comforts' was her health and preservation.[5] This was merely Charles maturing. On the topic of the king, he amended the wording to confirm that all was now well. The letter had perhaps been held back so that confirmed positive news could be shared. The prince's place at the centre of court and family would soon be threatened by Villiers.

As the tenth anniversary of the Gunpowder Treason came and went, James was increasingly unnerved by flourishing relations between France and Spain. Should the two Catholic powers unite against Great Britain, his life and throne might be endangered once again. Wooing ambassadors were deployed against both countries, and negotiations began for the hand of 9-year-old Princess Christine of France. What Charles thought of the prospect is not known, but he had no say anyway. In Paris, Christine 'much more desired' Charles than any other suitor. Her eldest sister, Elizabeth, had been promised to the King of Spain, but had come down with 'blonddie flue'.[6] If she died, the intention was that Christine would replace her, but the latter declared she would be cut to pieces first.

Throughout April 1616, the king and eight of his senior officials – four English and four Scottish – pored over the terms. Eight points were drawn up, with three deemed non-negotiable. These ranged from the age at which the parties should marry, who would pay for Christine's return to France if Charles predeceased her, and the 'joyntur royall' due if either of them should die.[7] The prince's passion for foreign affairs gave him a good grasp of European politics and how he might influence them. But many felt that he was being cast in the wrong part. His late brother, for example, had plumped for a Protestant crusade over a Catholic marriage.

When the robes adorning Prince Henry's funeral effigy in Westminster Abbey were stolen around the same time, his very values and memory seemed violated. But times had changed – the heir had changed. Many wished that Charles was more like his famed brother. Men like General Edward Cecil had found Henry an enthusiastic militarist and hoped Charles might inherit 'the virtue which his brother did possess'.[8] To try and mould the prince, Dudley Carleton, English ambassador to the Netherlands, secured some 'models of artillerie and other necessaries for war'. These wargaming pieces carried a price tag of £1,000, but to Cecil and Carlton, the benefits were clear. The prince might use them to 'make himself perfect in his chamber' as much as if he was in the field. They could also convey 'the verie practice of everie thinge, either defensive or offensive'.[9] But nothing could assist the prince with the war he waged against George Villiers.

At the start of 1616, Charles had taken a ring from the hand of his father's new favourite. He admired it, kept it and then lost it. It smacked of an attempt to assert himself against the interloper, who was burrowing his way into James's affections. Villiers complained to the king. As a stark sign of the man's ascent and Charles's relegation, the prince was severely taken to task, left in floods of tears, and banned from his father's presence. The meteoric rise of George Villiers stunned everyone. Becoming the man by whom 'all things must pass', he was made Baron Whaddon and Viscount Villiers.[10] Towards the end of May the trio were strolling in the gardens at Greenwich when the jealous prince turned the fountain on his rival. The spray soaked the viscount's fine clothes and coiffed hair, but it was Charles who was humiliated when his father boxed his ears.

Held back at home by a jealous father and all-powerful favourite, Charles found an outlet through foreign affairs. He sought out news from England's ambassadors and formed diplomatic relationships with foreign courts and heads of state. Isaac Wake, ambassador in Turin, was honoured to have the prince 'lend an eye' to his despatches.[11] Charles extended a letter of friendship to the Prince de Vandemont, and corresponded with the Dutch House of Orange. In return, he was feted by foreign princes; when Count Maurice of Nassau enquired after Charles's health, the English ambassador revealed he had last seen him 'uppon a high bounding horse'.[12] In October 1616, the prince expressed a great desire for Venice's 'felicity' and admitted to being 'brought up' with a particular affection for the state.[13] He enquired about the support they were offering the Duke of Savoy, posed questions about Mantua and discussed disturbances in

France. Charles regularly summarised his discussions and presented them to his father. Such audiences exposed him to politics, but one ambassador felt there was a certain indiscretion in the prince, who cannot 'keep his sentiments to himself'.[14] It is a flaw that many would go on to echo and demonstrated a lack of political aptitude, as well as a desire to appear more influential than he really was.

Towards the end of 1616, the fate of Savoy became of great concern to both France and England. The small dukedom controlled the Val Telling passes. If the Spanish took possession of Piedmont, they would hold keys to the 'gates of Italy' and could open or close them at will.[15] The Duke of Savoy desperately sought assistance. As Queen Anna went on to admit, her husband was unable to show his goodwill to Savoy, or keep his promises, because of a 'lack of means'.[16] When James finally announced his son's investiture as Prince of Wales, he did so in a bid to help secure the best possible dowry.

The occasion was set for 4 November 1616. James expected the greatest part of the nobility to attend the event, but at the same time kept the purse strings tight. His debts to the royal jeweller amounted to £10,000, and that year he extracted a promise from Anna not to exceed an annual expenditure of £15,000. On Thursday 31 October, the prince came by river from Richmond with the Lord Mayor and city companies in their barges. It made for a goodly show despite the frugality and the fact that Charles was ill. Queen Anna, too saddened over memories of her eldest son, did not attend.

The following day, twenty-six men were singled out to become Knights of the Bath, and the court was described as 'full of joy and festivity'.[17] The knights processed from Durham House, but to avoid 'needless expense' all other ceremonies were to be conducted in private. One contemporary suggested the lack of solemnity was because Charles was 'loth' to take part and declared he was of a 'weake and crasie' disposition.[18] The prince must have been anxious, and probably anticipated the opinionated judgements that would surely follow. Two weeks later, on his sixteenth birthday, he would be stricken with the green sickness. Perhaps indisposition saved him from embarrassment for the knights had feasted and fornicated in the city. Two fought a duel, others stole away the wives of leading citizens and put them to 'the squeake', while raucous behaviour spilled into The Mitre, a tavern in Fleet Street.[19]

Kneeling alongside the Secretary of State, who read out the patent, Charles received the crown and title of Prince of Wales. That evening, in his robes and coronet, he attended a banquet. From a gallery above, King James looked down upon proceedings and totted up the cost. Considering their early hostility, it was observed that Villiers and the prince exchanged 'many mutual smiles'.[20] Charles had come to understand the need to get along with the man, even if many others found it ever more impossible. Lord Ellesmere, the Lord Chancellor, was refused an earldom because Viscount Villiers 'will hardly suffer any to leap over his head'.[21] Other long-standing ministers were 'bought off' so that Villiers could take their posts, such as the Lord High Admiral and Master of the Horse.[22]

The Bishop of Ely put his foot in it during the ceremonies by praying for Prince Henry and not Charles. Later that month, the new Prince of Wales took possession of a specially-made jewel: a crowned heart set with 200 diamonds, which contained a portrait of him alongside his parents and sister. Charles was not living in the past. He was willing to embrace his future – God's will – with a duty to his loved ones and the dynasty. Unfortunately for the Stuarts, their reputation was sinking abroad on account of James's lack of money and resulting hollow promises. At around this time, a cartoon from the Low Countries portrayed the king with his pockets drawn out.

Chapter 8

The Scotch Journey

I am no Harry the Eighth 'who made up mignons to undoe them
for his own ends'.

King James VI/I

After thirteen years' absence, James decided the time was right to visit
Scotland. The year 1617 would be his Golden Jubilee, marking fifty years as
King of Scotland – a fact that might incline the Scottish Parliament to grant
a celebratory payout. 'The Scotch journey' was an investment, but funds
were needed to pay for it before the fruits could be considered.[1] Forced loans
were demanded from wealthy individuals, and the king considered holding
the East India Company to ransom over their patent. Even George Villiers,
now Earl of Buckingham, was condemned for suggesting the trip be delayed.
Charles shared his father's enthusiasm for the venture, harbouring a desire to
see Scotland again.

In March, the impatient king was on the road. His cavalcade included sixty-
one carts for all the goods carried along with him, but a brooding Charles had
been left behind in London. He wrote to his father in May, admitting that he
would have been glad 'to see the Cuntrie whair I was borne and the customes of
it'.[2] James's purpose was to further a perfect union between his kingdoms, and
make reforms to the Scottish Kirk. The Earl of Dunfermline – Lord Chancellor
of Scotland and Charles's old Governor – counselled caution over the many
projects which the king was 'turning over' in his mind. Far better, he tactfully
suggested, to test the water.

The Venetian ambassador in England wrote that a rumoured 'change in
religion' was causing Scottish nobles to leave the country to avoid a conflict of
interest.[3] In 1607, the king had failed in a bid to align the country with England
by becoming a Scottish 'Defender of the Faith' and head of the Kirk. Now, upon
reaching Edinburgh with two English bishops in tow, James began debating
with their Scottish equivalents. Promisingly, the Scots granted 80,000 crowns
by way of welcome and the burghers of Edinburgh, in their scarlet gowns, gave
£10,000. There was a pageant at Linlithgow and the University of Edinburgh
penned verses in the king's honour, but as Parliament got under way, nothing
could disguise the undercurrent of opposition. James unashamedly urged them
to 'imitate England'.[4] The English prelates were, however, looked upon with

increasing suspicion when William Laud donned a surplice at a funeral – it too much resembled Catholicism.

Another death, this one of the French king's chief minister, also generated a stir. Charles, who, with his mother, was one of the counsellors left governing England, expressed great joy. While walking in the palace gallery, the Venetian ambassador came across the prince who laughingly asked if the envoy's 'melancholy' was because of the murder. The dead favourite had been pro-Spanish, and with his demise the European see-saw tipped, leaving France set to distance itself from Spain. After his flippant greeting, Charles spoke with 'prudence and intelligence'.[5] His outburst may have stemmed from hope that a Spanish bride was now less likely.

There was indeed a significant anti-Spanish faction around the prince. His tutor and close confidante, Thomas Murray, was certainly against such a match. He had received reports that negotiations would 'prove fruitlesse' because the Infanta was 'allready contracted to the sonne of the Kinge of [Bohemia]' and the King of Poland's son was also pursuing her. England's ambassadors echoed the warnings; Thomas Edmondes, in France, was suspicious that Spain would not 'proceade syncerely with us'.[6] Sir John Digby, in Spain, advised Charles only to marry a Spanish princess if a Protestant could not be found. Then the hard-pressed Duke of Savoy gazumped Charles in the marriage market and made successful overtures for the marriage of Christine of France to his son, Victor Amadeus. Two years later, Charles felt no loss of face when he wrote to congratulate Victor, who replied with assurances of his 'perfect and sincere devotion'.[7] He and Victor would become brothers-in-law when Charles eventually married Henrietta Maria, youngest sister of Christine. It was a lifelong brotherly friendship that would end with Victor's death in 1637.

Meanwhile, in Scotland, James's wooing met with limited success. Having hoped to 'see the Kirk settled, the Kingdom reduced to good order, Lawes needing reformation reformed', the disappointed monarch returned to England.[8] Travelling through Lancashire, he shot across the bows of all Puritans by declaring in favour of lawful sports upon Sundays and Holy Days, so that 'the meaner Sort, who labour hard all the Week' should have recreation to refresh their spirits.[9] However, it seemed that the royal family were the ones needing a lift. Christmas 1617 proved sombre, owing to the king's melancholy and the queen's languishing condition. Prince Charles's Twelfth Night masque 'proved dull', notwithstanding the use of goats and Welsh speeches. Its creator, Ben Jonson, was called upon to return to bricklaying, but there was praise for the prince, who 'danced very well'.[10] Bonfires and fireworks then marked the birth of the king's second grandson, named Charles Louis, and the jubilant James celebrated by taking his favourite minister up another notch. In 1653, Arthur Wilson wrote that the Marquis of Buckingham had reigned as 'sole Monarch' in the king's affection. 'No man dances better, no man runs, or jumps better;

and indeed he jumptd higher than ever Englishman did in so short a time'.[11] Buckingham was even permitted to choose the next Secretary of State.

The Venetian ambassador described how when the king walked, he liked to be 'supported under the arms' by his chief favourites.[12] James's face was now ruddy and his hair white, perhaps making Buckingham cast an eye to the future. Gone were the days of Charles's petulant resistance, having subordinated himself to the strange relationship that existed between his father and Buckingham. Thomas Murray warned against neglecting the favourite, but he must have watched the impressionable prince with some concern.

James likened Buckingham to St Stephen – nicknaming him 'Steenie' – on account of the favourite's sweet features. Charles, too, used the soubriquet, but could still occasionally run up against him. In July 1618, 'a lytel few words' passed between them and made for court gossip. The Earl of Kellie urged the Lord Treasurer of Scotland to 'suppress them what you can' as this minor issue had been stirred up by their 'followers'.[13] The factional build-up around prince and favourite demonstrated a weakening of James's position. Only one man truly reigned supreme, and it was neither king nor prince.

Soon afterwards, Charles discovered he had apparently incurred the king's wrath over proposals that he be made sole benefactor of his mother's jewels. Buckingham was the informant. The nonplussed prince countered that his father had pushed for this to happen, and was puzzled that the king had not declared 'himself openly so angry'. That Buckingham was such a powerful intermediary between father and son is stupefying. More so that Charles accepted what he was told. Instead, feeling 'grief' over having upset his father, he craved a penance so that he might be forgiven. Calling on Steenie to intervene and 'mend any thing that is amiss', Charles pretty much prostrated himself at the favourite's feet.[14]

The summer progress of 1618 was one with a difference. As he embarked upon it, Charles was described as 'very grave and polite', of a good constitution and very well turned out; recognisable qualities that defined him.[15] He was now also a 'free brother' of the East India Company, an organisation that received its charter in the year he was born. July saw him set off for the south coast with a busy schedule, staying at Chertsey Abbey in August. Here, Daniel Mytens, an artist brought to England by the Earl of Arundel, was frustrated in his attempts to 'fynde occasion to drawe' the prince. Out hunting most of the time, Charles was then 'suddainly to departe' prompting Mytens to give up and return to London.[16] The prince and his party went on to visit the Isle of Wight and dined at Carisbrooke Castle, where celebratory shots were fired from the ordnance.

On returning to the mainland, Charles was met by the mayor and corporation of Portsmouth. In a speech of precisely 43 minutes, the Recorder, Immortal Whatman, compared their guest to King Edward VI. Charles was his 'heire and image' – a welcome change to constant comparisons with Prince Henry.

The poetic Whatman went on to reference the '*mirabilis annus*' of 1588 and declared that Neptune was no recusant, judging by the support he gave against the Spanish. He ended with a call for Charles to be 'a prudent and a valiant lion' in defending the kingdom, and to govern it wisely when the sceptre should 'distend to be wielded by your hand'.[17]

The anti-Catholic rhetoric and comparison between the prince and his Protestant predecessor, who had furthered a religious reformation, betrayed popular depth of feeling. Anger, fear and concern over a Catholic marriage threatened to dominate and define Charles. Resentment was so high that when one of the Spanish ambassador's gentlemen accidentally hurt a child in the road, a London mob chased him back to the embassy. The baying crowd hurled a 'shower of stones', smashed windows, cursed, yelled and forced the door.[18] Despite the incident, a Spanish marriage made 'continual progress' in the king's heart, regardless of the queen's apprehension.[19] Reputed to have little authority at court, she deferred to her husband, but felt that any marriage could wait another four or five years.

The prince prepared to rejoin the king and queen at Windsor in September 1618. James was said 'never to be weary' of hunting.[20] By comparison, Anna was in poor health and soon confined to Hampton Court, with the king visiting twice every week. Her absence dulled Christmas for a second year running. In the New Year of 1619, Anna spoke to Sir Edward Coke about her debts, as well as anxiety that her son should 'grow up in virtue and honour'.[21] Her last wish already seemed realised, and according to Charles's childhood nurse, Lady Ochiltree, who wrote two years later, he was of such 'comelie cariage' and 'good vertewes' that his 'fame spreeds in all nations'.[22] The prince's eighteenth birthday portrait was decorated with his motto 'if you want to subjugate everything, submit yourself to reason'.[23] The queen would no doubt have been pleased to see Charles doling out 'princely bounty' when planning a house of correction in Berkhampstead, where 'poor and idle people' could be put to work.[24] There was also something akin to the present-day Prince's Trust when James delegated to Charles the idea of an educational institute for 'bettering the teaching of youth' and encouraging 'men of art'.[25]

When the prince's 'lustrous eyes' which betokened a 'prudent vivacity' began alighting on ladies of the court, it became clear that he was a romantic at heart.[26] At the end of January, the king, prince and Buckingham made a short visit to the home of Sir Nicholas Bacon. Gossip centred on a beautiful young lady called Anne Gawdy, granddaughter of Sir Bassingbourne Gawdy of Harling. The prince was said to be 'so far in liking' of her that he was named the 'father' of some lines penned in her honour:

> Heaven's wonder late, but now earth's glorious ray,
> With wonder shines; that's gone, this new and gay,

> Still gazed on: in this is more than heaven's light –
> Day obscured that; this makes the day more bright.[27]

Charles had spent some time incorporating the words 'new and gay' as an anagram of Anne's name. Weeks later, heaven's light did burn brightly in London. Like a portent, the Banqueting House at Whitehall Palace was engulfed in flames, caused it was said, by a candle being carried under scaffolding or 'oiled paper and dried fur' of the Twelfth Night Masque scenery.[28] The Lord Chancellor, Earl of Arundel, and Duke of Lennox were all quick on the scene, but within two hours the hall was lost, along with many official documents stored there. Having housed Queen Anna's famous masques, its demise heralded a scene change, and the exit of a leading player from the Stuart stage.

Chapter 9

Crown of Thorns

On 2 March 1619, a fearful comet rose in the constellation of Virgo. The Earl of Northampton wondered at the meaning of this 'Blasing Starre'.[1] Beneath it, Charles raced to his mother's sickbed at Hampton Court and embraced her one last time before she died. Having shunned remedies that might have lengthened her days, she was described as 'more comely' in death then ever in life.[2] Anna had avoided making a will, ordering the royal doctor, Theodore Mayerne, to warn her when the end was near. In the event, she managed only a verbal intimation that Charles, the child she 'ever lov'd best' was to inherit everything.[3] Her property and goods were reportedly worth between £200,000 and £400,000; therefore, it was no surprise that King James staked his claim. Predictably, Charles was willing to yield.

The body of the much-lamented queen, who had 'benefitted many and injured none' was brought to Denmark House, where her ladies took turns watching over it.[4] The cost of the funeral was forecast at £24,000 and was set for the end of April. The date was so far off due to a want of ready money and credit could not even be secured for black mourning fabric.

Having been at his mother's bedside, Charles was no sooner called to his father's. At first it was nothing but a pain in the foot, but this soon changed to a violent fit of the stone. Three attacks followed in succession, enough to convince James that he was about to die. The monarch ate little, was 'trobled wth the vapors' and 'inwardly somewhat hotte'.[5] He then made a last speech to gathered Privy Councillors and Prince Charles. Described as 'religious' and 'wise', he spoke of continuity and welded both heir and officials together for a transition of power.[6] To Charles, he particularly commended the Marquises of Buckingham and Hamilton, the Lord Chancellor, and Sir John Digby, who had led marriage negotiations with Spain. He exhorted his son to respect religion and bishops. It must have been bewildering for Charles to face losing both parents in rapid succession and then inheriting three expectant kingdoms, all at the same time.

Unopened despatches mounted up around the royal sickbed, but despite the bleak forecasts, James pulled through. In mid-April, he was able to sit up a short time and some weeks later, journeyed to Theobalds in stages, including being carried in a Neapolitan chair by the Yeomen of the Guard. Dressed in red livery with embroidered roses on back and breast, the Venetian ambassador had once likened them to 'teriffic giants'.[7] James slowly took back the reins of government and itched for a dose of hunting; when he killed a buck, he proceeded to bathe his 'bare feet and legs' in the blood to cure his gout. All the while, his dead queen continued to lie in state.[8]

Embarrassingly, the funeral was put back not once, but twice. Queen Anna's plate was coined and some of her jewels and chains gifted to ambassadors to mask the financial crisis. Ten weeks after her death, on 13 May 1619, her body was escorted from Denmark House to Westminster Abbey. Charles, the only member of the royal family present, rode before the coffin, which was pulled by six horses. The streets were crowded with spectators, one of whom was killed by falling masonry from Northampton House, near Charing Cross.

John Chamberlain described the funeral as dull. Sir Edward Harwood thought it not as splendid as expected. Once Anna had been entombed in the Henry VII chapel, near her son and two daughters, another procession begun and four cartloads of her trunks were escorted to Greenwich Palace. Notwithstanding the queen's last wishes, her jewels were picked over by the king, who immediately disposed of a portion to his beloved Buckingham. The squandering of these valuables was clearly a tiring job – James entirely forgot about the French ambassador's audience and went to bed. Though Charles was overlooked when it came to his mother's belongings, his relevance and position had become clearer than ever in the face of the king's mortality. One ambassador even considered Buckingham 'as great a favourite' with the prince as with his father.[9]

If Charles looked doomed to inherit the favourite, then August 1619 provided a good counterbalance when he was given a council to administer his Scottish affairs. These leading Scotsmen, all experienced figures, gave Charles vital exposure to the business of government. Council members were the Earl of Dunfermline (Lord Chancellor), Earl of Mar (Lord High Treasurer), Earl of Melrose (Secretary of State), as well as the Duke of Roxborough, Sir George Hay, Sir William Oliphant and Sir Gideon Murray. Part of their scope was keeping up-to-date records of the prince's Scottish holdings, scrutinising proposed grants, and the disposing of places, gifts and wards on his behalf. Charles's business was 'soe moderated' to avoid any 'just occasion of grevance' being made. The prince sent them a copy of his English signet, requesting that a similar one be prepared for Scottish use. There should only be one difference in design – precedence of the arms of England and Scotland, and his specification was that the latter 'must have the first [place]'.[10]

This council was swiftly deployed. When Charles issued instructions regarding his lands and finances in readiness for the next Scottish Parliament, he found himself reverently rebuffed. They warned his approach might lead to the 'alienationn of the subjects mynds', which would be extremely damaging considering this was the first parliament he was involved with.[11] It was prudent advice, but compared to Buckingham's autocratic handling of the English council, Charles must have felt somewhat inferior. Yet, he held a healthy respect for these Scotsmen and, on his accession, he confirmed three in their government posts for life. All but one was dead by the time Charles became embroiled in his wars with

Scotland in 1639 – perhaps their absence was telling? Whenever he worked with a council, rather than a single favourite, Charles's cause invariably fared better.

Another symbolic death in 1619 was that of Robert Peake, the artist responsible for many images of the prince's childhood. But there was also a significant birth. On 17 December, Elizabeth grew her Palatine brood. Her fourth child, and third son, was named Rupert, after a fifteenth-century Holy Roman Emperor. When news reached King James, who was 'at table supping', he drank a health to the new-born, gave a purse of gold to the messenger, and told him to throw open the doors of his son's chamber. Charles 'always rejoiced sincerely' in his sister's prosperity, but his love would soon be put to the test.[12] When the Holy Roman Emperor died in March 1619, Ferdinand, King of Bohemia, looked set to be elected his successor. Bohemia, however, deposed Ferdinand and offered their crown to the Elector Palatine, James's son-in-law.

The whiff of danger had James practically wash his hands of Frederick and Elizabeth. Charles, however, offered to assist 'with my countenance but also with my person if the King my Father will give me leave'.[13] The fine sentiment perfectly fitted with the prince's chivalric ideals, but there was no hope in reality. Frederick was torn over the decision before him. Eventually accepting the Bohemian throne in September 1619, he was crowned two months later. Few offered their support, leaving his family almost alone against the might of the Catholic Hapsburgs.

At the turn of 1619, King James had written a meditation about the Lord's Prayer and dedicated it to Buckingham, describing himself as the favourite's 'politike' and 'eeconomike' father.[14] Before the year was out, another royal publication was dedicated to Charles, describing the difficulties faced by monarchs – that crowns may as well be composed of thorns rather than jewels. Buckingham's natural obligation to the prince was 'redoubled by the many favours that you daily heap upon him'. James stated that by following his lead, Charles showed 'what reverent love you carry towards me in your heart'.[15] The words are tinged with an emotional blackmail. When it came to the thorny issue of Bohemia, the obedient Charles did not step out of line. He resorted to offering Frederick advice: give King James an account of the justice of the cause, and the 'laws and freedom' used as a basis for Ferdinand's deposition.[16]

The Twelfth Night masque of 1620, *News from the New World Discovered in the Moon,* was a titanic three-hour performance led by Charles (cast as 'Truth') and Buckingham. The pair 'contended against each other' in a good-humoured dance-off, vying for the king's adulation.[17] Both men behaved more like brothers and the old king their doting dad. Elizabeth, meanwhile, also struggled for her father's attention. As Catholic forces massed to sweep them from Bohemia, she urged James to 'have a care for your son-in-law and me'.[18] Predictions were already being made that Frederick would be a 'winter king' – gone by the summer. Ever the penniless pragmatist, James wished to avoid a religious war and was therefore branded as 'wary'. The melancholic Elizabeth felt certain that those surrounding her father were against her, declaring 'though they have English bodies they have Spanish hearts'.[19] Despite Charles being termed the 'rising sun' by the Venetian ambassador, he remained careful not to outshine his father.[20]

When Sir Robert Kerr, one of the prince's most trusted companions, was embroiled in scandal, the king's favour was required to save him. As with most of Charles's closest servants and friends, Kerr was much older – by twenty-two years. He had been Groom of the Bedchamber to Prince Henry, but had transferred to Charles's household in 1613, the year prior to Buckingham's debut. Some six years on, a quarrel arose over the French king's favourite minister. Kerr supposedly asserted that the Frenchman had 'small merit' and was meanly born. Another of the prince's household, Charles Maxwell, took these similarities to Buckingham as an insult to the latter, with whom he wished to ingratiate himself. Months later, in February 1620, Maxwell gossiped to Buckingham about the episode, challenged Kerr to a duel, and was then killed. There were rumours of friction between Kerr and Buckingham – Buckingham perhaps hoped to weaken Kerr's influence with the Prince of Wales, and in turn cement his own.

Kerr was arrested and charged with murder. Charles intervened with an earnest entreaty to his father, supported by the Duke of Lennox and Marquis of Hamilton. A Scottish faction was mobilised to save their man, and although remitted to manslaughter, a branding of the hand remained. The prince stepped in again and this was exchanged for exile, leaving Kerr to spend many months in Europe collecting works of art, which he would eventually present to the prince. That same year, Kerr's wife died. Charles's affection for his faithful servant remained as strong as ever, which Kerr repaid with lifelong fidelity. In 1621, Charles wrote to the Countess of Derby successfully suggesting Kerr as a match for her daughter, Lady Anne Stanley, assuring 'what hee wants in meanes hee hath in neernes about my person'. The countess's subsequent approval of the suit was a 'great faver to mee'.[21]

The spring of 1620 was filled with celebrations. In March, Charles gave a ball and banquet at Denmark House with many 'mistresses and valentines'.[22] After losing a tennis wager with Buckingham, he covered the entire bill. It was also the seventeenth anniversary of the king's accession to the English throne. The prince readied himself for the state tilting at Whitehall, despite pleas from the Lords of the Council, who fretted over the 'preservation of his life'.[23] Undeterred, Charles performed sundry feats of arms alongside the Marquises of Buckingham and Hamilton. Considered as eminently military as his brother, in one pass he wounded Lord Montgomery in the arm. Such skill elicited the 'great joy' of the people.[24] But for all this bravado, still no action was taken over Bohemia. Elizabeth petitioned Buckingham, asking him to tell her father that 'the enemie will more regard his blowes then his wordes'. Prince Charles was warned that this 'slakness' discouraged potential allies. Frederick then received the emperor's ultimatum to leave Bohemia by June.[25]

Eight weeks before that deadline, the king and a bareheaded Charles rode to St Paul's for a Sunday service of thanksgiving. Though the Bishop of London mentioned Bohemia, he spoke primarily about fundraising to restore the edifice of the cathedral. Many, such as the City of London, were willing to pledge financial support to Frederick and Elizabeth, but waited for a royal lead. Instead, the king granted £2,000 to St Paul's and ordered churchmen to refer to Frederick only by his electoral title. The Dutch commiserated that James was 'practically neutral'.[26]

Disappointed by the postponement of April's tilting, Charles had wished to 'make show' of a feather received from his Spanish mistress.[27] The marriage negotiations had brought little else but a feather, and at heart, he was not particularly desirous of the match. The Earl of Kellie wrote that 'the prince himself' had ordered him 'not to speike of it'.[28] Charles was conscious of the unpopularity, but the Infanta's blood links to Emperor Ferdinand made it doubly controversial. Around this period, it was an altogether more mysterious, even undesirable, lady that was occupying Charles's attention.

The furtive prince urged Buckingham to read and then commit an undated letter to the 'safe custodie of Mister Vulcan' – in other words, burn it. After receiving a chiding from his father, Charles revealed that 'well relished comfites ye sent' took the sting out of it.[29] He mentions having met the person 'that must not be named' once already and that he would meet again with her on Saturday. Tantalisingly, she has not been identified. In 1621, gossipmongers were kept busy when the prince placed a gold chain worth £3,000 around the neck of Frances Howard, Duchess of Lennox. Described as an unusual honour, it linked Charles with 'the hansomest woman that ever was in her time'.[30]

Pauline Gregg, in her 1981 biography of Charles, comments on claims that he had an illegitimate daughter called Joanna (or Joan) Brydges. Dr Jeremy Taylor, later one of Charles's chaplains, went on to marry Joanna several years after his master's death, but Gregg describes how, during the Civil Wars, Charles had given Taylor a ring with two diamonds and a ruby. She assumes there was 'no reason' why he would have received these other than to pass them on to Joanna.[31] At the turn of the nineteenth century, Reginald Heber alleged he saw a letter written by Lady Wray, a granddaughter of Jeremy and Joanna, who made the claims about Joanna's royal heritage. Heber describes a portrait of Joanna as having a 'plasing oval countenance' and standing in an arbour, suspending a branch of laurel over a bust of King Charles.[32] Unfortunately, both Lady Wray's letter and the painting, if they existed, have been lost.

It took six months from the April sermon at St Paul's for James to follow public opinion. Catholic troops were not just intent on removing Frederick from Bohemia – his ancestral lands were now fair game. Three towns had fallen in the Lower Palatinate, and the situation looked hopeless, leading Elizabeth to enquire whether her father might now assist. Had James committed troops from the start, it would likely have galvanised a Protestant alliance, but at what cost? Whether they could have won out against the emperor is uncertain – but James's inertia certainly damned Frederick. Even Elizabeth's pet monkey, Jack, who attacked her staff, showed more teeth.

Summoning the council in October 1620, James called upon the Spanish to retreat from the Palatinate, though remained silent over Bohemia. Yet, Frederick's small band of allies did not give up hope, more so when the prince and Buckingham began displaying a unified zeal towards the cause. That month, the Margrave of Brandenburg-Ansbach, Duke of Württemberg and Margrave of Baden wrote a joint letter to Charles commending his courage and resolution. They begged him to hold fast, warning that their 'violent enemy' was redoubling efforts.[33] A matter of weeks later, Württemberg reassured Charles that his nieces and nephews were safe in his home. The desperation was palpable. A steady campaign began to build with Charles at its head. Described as being in better financial shape than his father, due to his 'prudent frugality and order', he generously donated £10,000 to his brother-in-law. The Bohemian ambassador, after being 'practically abandoned', was brought to court in Charles's own carriage as a symbolic gesture. Within council, the prince spoke strongly in support and played a 'large share' in coaxing his father.[34]

The king's change of heart occurred in 'a moment' and he drank toast after toast to the 'prosperity of his children'. One casualty of this U-turn was Sir John Digby, the English ambassador to Spain. When the king had been at death's door a year earlier, he had recommended Digby as one who had 'suffered' for the Spanish match. In October 1620, he was made a scapegoat for it – the king invited him to a 'hunt of hares' and then publicly stood him up. The ambassador became persona-non-grata to all and sundry. The prince was 'angry and bitter' and told Digby that his sister's welfare was paramount over his marriage.[35] Twelve thousand troops were to be raised from Scotland and the king assumed this war footing would also stir MPs into clearing his personal debts. France, quick to make the most of this change of heart, offered Charles the hand of Princess Henrietta Maria. This, despite her not yet being 11 years old, stemmed from a desperation to make the King of Great Britain become 'either French or Spanish'.[36] But it all came too late. Frederick was defeated at the Battle of White Mountain, near Prague, in November 1620 and was forced to flee to Breslau.

James wrestled with a conflict of his own when Parliament assembled on 30 January 1621. Charles went with his father in state, wearing a rich coronet, flanked by Sergeants at Arms carrying maces and Gentlemen Pensioners their halberds. The king reaffirmed that he was of the same religion as his subjects and would defend it with 'pen and person'. Cap in hand, he told MPs no monarch had reigned so long and received so little, yet spent so much for the public good. Finally, he mentioned his daughter and son-in-law along with the miserable state of Christendom, in which he would spend 'his own and his son's blood'. Having dealt with his own desires, he anticipated theirs; grievances would be addressed if their complaints did not become witch hunts.[37]

At that year's state tilting, Charles, riding in his colours of tawny velvet with silver embroidery, had been pitted against the Earl of Dorset. Though they 'brake their staves very successfully', Buckingham fared worse against Lord Herbert. The introverted prince avoided the after-party, but Sir Simonds D'Ewes was there, and a decade later recalled the 'effeminate and curious' Buckingham and his 'delicacy'.[38] True, the favourite was a sickly individual – both king and prince regularly visited his sickbed or tended him with letters. For Charles, it was a transformation. As a young child, he had been as weak as his brother had been glorious. Now he was the one with the tiltyard prowess, boundless energy and robust health, outshining his surrogate sibling. There was also another role reversal. Charles was becoming more of a chief minister, while Buckingham behaved like a prince of the blood.

Despite the wrangles with MPs, a sanguine Charles 'very regularly' took his seat in the House of Lords and closely followed the debates. He was 'most anxious' to learn and become conversant with proceedings.[39] His courtesy won Charles much favour and his attendance was deemed the 'best of schools'.[40] But the prince was far from a mere spectator. When Sir Henry Yelverton compared Buckingham to the tyrannical Hugh Despenser, a close favourite of King Edward II, Charles interrupted the man's scandalising speech. Yelverton was sent to the Tower, but the prince and Buckingham secured clemency.

At one juncture, Charles wrote rather ministerially to Buckingham to give counsel that the king should not 'wholly discontent' MPs and advised 'I should have [the king] command them not to speak any more of Spain, whether it be of that war, or my marriage'. The letter assures Buckingham that the royal council are all of the same opinion. Charles also reveals that General Edward Cecil, advocating war in defence of the Palatinate, had requested senior command. On that matter, the prince tactfully declared 'in earnest, I wish the gentleman well' but counselled that Sir Horace Vere should retain superiority and not be 'discouraged or disgraced'.[41]

Charles's advice was not only directed to his father, but also to Parliament itself, intervening to explain or clarify the king's words. He urged them to show their teeth, and their bite too, warning that failure to live up to expectations would bring dishonour. They should oblige him, he ventured, considering he was now 'entering into the world'.[42] The confidence in these letters is noteworthy, as is the way he manages MPs with some astuteness.

Despite calling for Parliament to be gagged over his marriage, Charles got out his pen in March 1621 and wrote directly to Philip IV of Spain. He expressed hopes that a fresh embassy from Lord Bristol would bring the match 'unto an happy issue' and signs off as his 'most loving Kinsman'.[43] The new Spanish monarch was of the same generation, and not wishing to burn his bridges, there was another possibility motivating Charles. The Venetians reported that Bristol had orders to bolt the restitution of the Palatinate onto the marriage terms. Treading two very different paths – war and marriage – was simply the means to an end, but such contradiction risked all-round disillusionment and accusations of double-dealing. It was his father's practice, and Charles, a chip off the old block, would often pursue opposing courses to his detriment.

The situation in Britain fooled nobody, especially Elizabeth and Frederick. The couple, now homeless, sought refuge in Holland that April, and were aghast over talk of any marriage with Spain, whose armies swarmed across the Palatinate. Nor did the 12,000 Scottish troops materialise. King James's finances were so parlous that when secret jewels were discovered in Denmark House, he used thirty-seven diamonds to stud a picture of himself and sent it to his daughter. The gold chains from which they had been plucked were sent to the Tower to be coined. Elizabeth wished there were 'a thousand soldiers for every diamond' or that her father had simply sent hard cash. This she said 'with all her heart'.[44]

As 1621 wore on, James, most likely feeling managed by Charles and Buckingham and manipulated by MPs, declared there were 'many kings' in his realm.[45] In November, the House of Commons documented their privileges in the official journal, opposing the king's assertion that these stemmed from his bounty alone. James summoned the clerk and tore out the offending page. A lecturer of St Paul's preached against intermarriages between Protestants and Catholics at all levels of society. It was a line picked up by Charles's own chaplain, Doctor Hakewill, who wrote a book against a match with Spain and then dared present it to the prince. This controversy blew Charles's household apart. His faithful tutor and secretary, Thomas Murray, knew about Hakewill's intentions and was placed under house arrest. By 1622, Murray was a 'stranger at Court' after over fifteen devoted years of service.[46] Thus two moderate and sober men were removed from the prince's side.

That same year, Charles was swimming with Buckingham every evening at Eton, but this relationship would drag him into ever deeper water. Buckingham's allies, who favoured Spain, were parachuted into the gaps in the prince's household, such as Catholic Endymion Porter, who became a 'gateway to all favours'. He had once duelled a man in defence of the Spanish ambassador's honour. If Porter was a gatekeeper to the prince, Buckingham was said to be the sole access to James's entire court, powerful enough to reverse favours granted by the king. The monarch did not 'eat, sup or remain an hour' without the man.[47]

By the end of the year, when Charles's wave of popularism crashed, he found his actions at Westminster the subject of criticism. He had acted contrary to the authority of Parliament and followed his father 'like his shadow'. A lead had been taken from ministers 'most hated'.[48] Hopes that the heir might offer a fresh alternative were increasingly dashed, and when Charles was appointed a Privy Councillor in 1622, it affixed him to his father's unpopular government. But at this moment, the prince was blissfully unaware of these seeds of discontent and believed he could single-handedly rescue the Palatinate and bring home a Spanish bride. As matters came to a head, he was to make a remarkable decision.

Chapter 10

Jack and Tom Smith

In April 1622, King James hosted the Imperial ambassador to a feast, which contained an array of confectionery 'sugar soldiers'.[1] The sight of James devouring them no doubt set tongues wagging, considering his reticence to support his son-in-law with real troops. In September, the fall of Heidelberg, capital of the Electoral Palatinate, confirmed the utter defeat of Frederick and Elizabeth. At the beginning of 1623, the Holy Roman Emperor handed the territory to the Catholic Duke of Bavaria, giving Prince Charles added impetus to act. After years of fruitless negotiations with Spain, he decided not to let his phantom marriage hold him or his sister's cause back any longer.

In February, Charles and Buckingham came up with a novel way of breaking the impasse that had rendered Britain impotent. They would go directly to Madrid. Not only that, but incognito, personally putting Spanish intentions to the test. When they revealed this secret plan to the king, he began to cry and shriek. This pathetic outburst showed the depths to which James had plummeted, both mentally and physically, but it did not move his boys one bit. He declared that he would be undone if 'Baby Charles' was killed or imprisoned by the Spanish. Now 22 years of age and eager to break free of his chains, the 'baby' argued the benefits of the expedition. He would boldly strike at Spain, carry off the Infanta and restore his sister and brother-in-law to their lands, resuscitating their family honour. Buckingham was curt and rude with the ageing monarch, who backed down after being browbeaten.

Following a restless night the king had a hysterical relapse, leading Charles and Buckingham to resume their remorseless double act. The prince would take Endymion Porter, his Groom of the Bedchamber, and Francis Cottington, his new secretary. Both men had experience of Spain; Porter had lived there for a time, while Cottington was a former diplomat. The king called for Cottington and asked his opinion. Completely unaware of the plan, the stammering courtier 'protested exceedingly' but to no avail.[2] Charles swore James to secrecy before sending Porter off to secure shipping. This all took place at Theobalds, a mansion that had come into royal possession as a result of a house swap. From one of its many galleries, which the tortured James must have paced, the Tower of London could supposedly be seen on a good day. On 17 February, the court prepared to move to Newmarket as if everything was in perfect order.

Charles wrote a letter to his sister, to which the king added some lines, and sent his household to Newmarket ahead of him. Amidst this cover, he and Buckingham rode post-haste to Tilbury, and then on to Gravesend, Rochester, Canterbury and Dover. They used the aliases of Jack and Tom Smith and wore 'fair-riding coats' with false beards.[3] Though escaping the Mayor of Canterbury's scrutiny, at Dover the game was up. The mayor exuded a 'Supercilious Officiousness' and Buckingham was forced to 'vail' his beard and claim that he was on his way to inspect the fleet.[4] It did the trick, and the pair went on to meet Cottington and Porter. At 5.00 am on 19 February, the four men sailed for Boulogne, while behind them the English ports were closed to prevent compromising news leaking out. Before long, rumours were rife about the journey that 'perplexes everybody'.[5]

The council, on their knees, begged James for the truth. When the king caved in, he admitted that his son passionately desired to test Spanish intentions, and gave a brisk exoneration of Buckingham. Secretary of State Calvert hoped the prince would outride the news to maintain his cover. But the royal jester, Archie Armstrong, was cutting and offered to change caps with the king. Whoever had let the prince go, he asserted, was the real fool. When James countered that his boys would return home safely, Archie retorted if that happened, the cap would go to the King of Spain for having let them escape his clutches. The king continued his blustering excuses – he, too, along with his father and grandfather, had left Scotland to bring back their brides.

Prayers were offered to prosper the prince's journey, but the Archbishop of Canterbury was asked to employ 'moderation' in the wording and avoid unnecessary 'dangers or doubts'.[6] The intrepid Sir Robert Carey, who had ridden from London to Scotland following the death of Elizabeth I, recalled that the Madrid trip 'made a great hub-bub in our court, and in all England besides'.[7] Sir Simonds D'Ewes called it 'so strange an accident as after ages will scarce believe it'.[8] As the three kingdoms came to terms with this revelation, Charles, in Paris, donned a bushy periwig and watched the Queen Mother at dinner and Princess Henrietta Maria preparing for a masque.

Leaving the city at 4.00 am on 23 February, the small party headed for Madrid, travelling over stony roads and mountain passes. One noteworthy village was so bad they judged the 'devil himself doth inhabit'.[9] The travellers competed over the number of falls from their horses; Cottington twelve, Buckingham seven, while Charles remained in the saddle throughout, though he had the best mount. During the first week in March, they approached the residence of the English ambassador in Madrid. While the Spanish king had intimation of Charles's arrival, he tactfully kept the secret until approached by Buckingham and Bristol. King James had written to Philip to 'dispose' of his son as he pleased, referring to him as the 'King of Scotland' in a bid to make the match more attractive to the Infanta.[10] Philip duly drove to the fields outside

Madrid, spoke to Charles privately in his coach, and then allocated his guest a suite of rooms in the Alcázar Palace.

Back in England, James delighted in stories of his son's journey and a fleet was readied to transport the prince's household, headed by the *Prince Royal*. Charles had listed eighty-six people that should join him, but his father added fifty-nine more, including Archie Armstrong, the court fool. Robert Kerr, Groom of the Bedchamber, was one of the first to sail, along with Viscount Andover and Lord Compton, both of whom had become Knights of the Bath alongside Charles in 1605. There was also the long-serving and pompous Robert Carey, his Chamberlain, who was given power of martial law over the household while at sea. Attempting in vain to have a kinsman added to the passenger list, he then protested over who should look after the chapel plate. Two chaplains were given the job and briefed by King James not to engage in 'polemical preaching or controversy'.[11] In the event, unable to gain access to Charles within the Alcázar, the chaplains would soon return home. Worryingly, Sir Robert Aytoun reported that unless Charles sneaked out to the ambassador's residence, he could not attend Protestant services.

The Tower of London's jewel house was scoured and precious items such as a large square diamond called 'The Mirror of France' was sent on loan to the prince. Others were selected as presents to be doled out. A gift was also earmarked for Buckingham, who was to be made a duke. Decisions were taken about which London mansions were to house the bride's entourage on her arrival in Britain, such was the hope for a successful conclusion. But by mid-March, matters went awry. The Earl of Bristol was calling the Spaniards the 'most perfidious' of people and claiming they would rather throw the Infanta 'into the sea' than marry her to the prince.[12] Frederick and Elizabeth felt abandoned and were counselled by many to withdraw from James's protection, especially when he advocated a truce with Spanish forces. For Elizabeth, a cessation would be to 'bind one's own hands'. James, however, preferred peace over what he saw as Frederick's devotion to 'fire and sword'.[13]

By April 1623, King James was reading and burning all letters from Charles. Fake news was rife. He objected to building work on the Infanta's chapel, on account of nesting birds, and then remarked that it was a 'temple for the devil'.[14] In Madrid, Charles and Buckingham were side-lining their envoy and going it alone to try and clinch terms. Rumours spoke of the Infanta's preference to take the veil than marry a heretic. Coupled with Charles's mixed messages, matters nosedived. He urged the fleet to come and take him home, but at the same time requested his tilting armour, horses and field tent. When more of his household arrived in the Bay of Biscay, they found an order to return to England, which was then countermanded.

Though there seemed no chance of restoring the Palatinate, Charles did find a match in the King of Spain. They struck up a good friendship. The pious and studious Philip was outwardly sombre, accentuated by rather large lips, drooping eyes and plain dress, but the two delighted in a shared appreciation of the arts. Philip gave Charles gifts and took him to enjoy the pleasures of the country, such as holy day processions of flagellants and bare-footed friars whose heads bled from crowns of thorns. Spanish hopes for Charles's conversion were quickly dashed when he argued with a Jesuit who branded his entourage 'fanatical heretics'.[15]

Steadfast refusals to see the Infanta came as a serious blow to Charles. He had seen her only fleetingly when their coaches had passed one another. It had been orchestrated; Charles, peering out of the curtains, glimpsed enough to take the bait. The days were so busy that Endymion Porter scarcely had 'time to dress'.[16] At Easter, the prince's patience paid off when he was permitted to speak to Donna Maria, but the words were drafted for him by the Spanish. Humiliatingly, she then 'made no reply' to him.[17] Nevertheless, the prince's affection for the Infanta seemed to double. If Charles's own heart was racing, back in England the Lord Treasurer's was described as 'sick' over the extraordinary charges being racked up. Then, on 9 April, Charles's former tutor, Thomas Murray, died: 'His spirits being so farre spent what by age what by greef and paine of his desease'.

It was a sad end, distanced from his former pupil in both person and politics. Sir Robert Aytoun said of Murray that 'no man that hath lived in suche a qualitie as he did ever died so poor'. It was a sign of his honesty. Mrs Murray and the children were left with £200 per annum. 'Times ar hard and the Prince is not heer'.[18] In the face of Spanish procrastination, Charles might well have wondered whether Murray and others had been justified in their opposition to the match. He soon decided to reassure family and friends, telling his sister that on no account would he proceed unless terms included a deal to restore the Palatinate. To the Marquis of Hamilton, he admitted the jaunt to Spain must have seemed 'strange to many', but it would not lead to any outcome that would cause honest men 'to blush for him'.[19]

June approached. Charles had laid a wager that he would be back in Britain by the tenth of that month. Despite being tired of his stay, he pushed the date back and paid out forty pieces. Buckingham, having received the patent for his dukedom, shed tears over his absence from the king. But most of the prince's household were sent home. They were led by Sir Robert Carey, whose three-score years made Charles concerned that 'the heate of the yeare coming fast on' might distemper him.[20] The cavalcade arrived in England where they were confined to talk of 'generalities' and mentioned only what 'the king wishes'. The official line was that marriage was imminent. In reality, Charles desperately flirted with the Spanish over the oppression of English Catholics. A white dove took to following him, which the Spaniards dubbed as the 'Holy Spirit' desirous of his conversion. One persistent priest was punched by Edmund Verney.

Finally, the Spanish suggested that the prince should return home and address the burdens of English Catholics as evidence of his intentions. His good behaviour would lead to the Infanta's despatch. When informed, Charles flew into a 'violent rage' and Buckingham 'blazed forth'.[21] The Spanish ventured that matters might fare better if Lord Bristol was once again entrusted with them. Reduced to tears of frustration, the prince handed the reins over, causing a breach between Bristol and Buckingham that would never heal. Still negotiations floundered. Feelers were even put out for Princess Henrietta Maria as a means of spurring jealousy.

In England, James spent his nights in 'unbroken fury' and days surpassing 'internal agitation' over his son's absence.[22] The Venetian ambassador branded the king a 'laughing stock'.[23] King Philip sent James a gift of an elephant, prompting ribaldry that it was in place of the Infanta. Rather appropriately on St Swithun's Day, 15 July 1623, a weathervane at St James's Palace, bearing the prince's arms, was 'blasted' and 'beaten to pieces' during a storm.[24] It was later claimed that Charles had told his father that should he be imprisoned by the Spanish, the king should 'think no more of him' and settle affections on his sister.[25] Some even speculated that if Elizabeth was to land in Britain, then James would be forced to 'fly to Scotland' and leave his daughter 'mistress in England'.

The naturally optimistic Charles became sad and melancholy. As evidence of his love for the Infanta, he reminded the Spanish of the 'toil and peril' of his journey and conveyed his feelings in a 'very firm and erudite' paper drafted by Lord Bristol.[26] The Spanish continued taking him to bull fights or cane tourneys, where on one occasion he leaned out of a window and cast a glance to the Infanta. He also jumped over a wall in a bid to catch his beloved walking in a private garden, though Donna Maria screamed and beat a hasty retreat. By mid-July, Endymion Porter was writing to his wife that business here is 'not likely to hold. We are to come home suddenly'. It took another seven weeks before Charles accepted the fact that he could 'succeed no better than other negotiators'.[27]

He lavished parting gifts on his hosts; a sword set with diamonds for King Philip, and earrings with diamonds as 'bigg as a beans' for the queen. The Infanta received a string of 250 pearls. Even the royal pages were handed chains of gold, while the guard of archers and 'inferiour officers' received 8,000 crowns between them.[28] Philip gave Charles some Titians; *Emperor Charles V*, and the famed *Pardo Venus*, both of which were later hung at Whitehall. A fleet of seven ships, including two pinnaces and three transports, came for Charles and he boarded the *Prince Royal* at Santander on 12 September. Planning to spend his last night in the town, he set out in his barge. Seven months of adventure nearly ended that evening due to a 'tempest of rain and wind'. The quick-thinking master of the *Defiance* used casks and buoys 'with lights fastened unto them' to which the prince and his party clung amidst the storm.

On 18 September, Spanish delegates boarded Charles's flagship, which abounded with symbolic carvings; one displaying the royal arms was 10-foot-wide and another portrayed two pyramids with boys sitting on the top of them, representing peace and war. After feasting them with 'stalled oxen, fatted sheep, venison and all kind of fowls', the fleet finally departed.[29] Contrary winds caused a temporarily disembarkation on the Scilly Isles, and then Charles made it to Portsmouth on 5 October.

Chapter 11

Ecstasy of Joy

The prince's landing was signalled by a volley from the fleet to the 'comfort of all true English hearts'.[1] So momentous was the occasion, even for Charles himself, that he had the occasion painted in oil and hung at Oatland's Palace. From Constantinople, the English ambassador wrote of the 'universall joy of Christendome' over his safe return and that it 'resounded hither, eaven among ye Barbarians, as if ye care of yr Highs concerned the whole world'.[2]

Across London, timber-framed buildings quivered in the glow of celebratory bonfires, with one at Blackheath consuming forty loads of wood. Even the carts were broken up and used. People set off fireworks, beat drums, rang bells, fired ordnance and partied in the streets. Verses were composed and books written about the prince and his escapade. The king, who was indisposed, declared himself cured by the 'ecstasy of joy'. At Royston, Charles and Buckingham fell to their knees before James, whereupon all three wept, embraced heartily, and then spoke in private for three hours with much 'freedom and love'.[3]

The prince sported a neat beard in the Spanish style, but his time in Spain resulted in much more. Charles was brought closer than ever to Buckingham, who had shared the highs and lows, and their informality had shocked their hosts. King Philip's court had so appealed to the prince's sober, serious and shy nature that he went on to replicate the formality and splendour during his own reign. The Spanish government, closely managed by a royal favourite, left Philip to cut a supremely reverential and distant figure, above the day-to-day grime of politics. First-hand experience of this only legitimised Buckingham's extraordinary power and place. Powerful kings had powerful favourites – it was the way of things.

Stating that he would 'never match with Spain' until the Palatinate was restored, Charles was now set upon war and began working on his father.[4] He sent Elizabeth a casket of rock crystal and a 'most loving letter' that included a lock of his hair. It was a sign of encouragement, which she capitalised upon by adding the hair to a jewel and wearing it as an earring.[5] The prince was 'rousing himself' and spoke with ever more freedom, but his was a lone voice for the royal council did not 'differ one jot' from James. The old man, however much he was cajoled by Charles and Buckingham, still wore the crown.[6] To make matters worse, inevitable recriminations began.

Someone had to carry the can for the failure of the Madrid venture, especially following rumours of sell-out secret terms. When Parliament assembled in

February 1624, it hounded the duke, therefore James, Charles and Buckingham hatched a plan. When the king opened Parliament, many must have expected a clash. Instead, he expressed a desire to remove misunderstandings and cherish his people as the 'husband does the wife'. In the last session, James had railed at MPs, telling them that royal marriages were not their business, but now he openly solicited advice. He handed over to Charles and Buckingham to explain more. So far so good. The duke, however, wilted at the task and called upon the prince to 'assist and correct' him. An account was given of their reception in Spain and the negotiations, as well as the motives behind that trip. Next, they elaborated upon Spanish 'delays and artifices' and read out letters as evidence of deceit, which capitalised upon anti-Catholic sentiment.[7] When the outraged Spanish ambassador called for Buckingham's head, his intervention only served to assist the pair; Parliament exonerated the duke and called upon the king to end prospects of a union with Spain. In response, he asked what they would offer should he do so.

Speeches in Parliament praised the king for consulting them and the prince was deemed to have behaved with courage and wisdom, enabling him to handle 'councells and resolucions'.[8] When the Spanish ambassador sent Charles carts of hams, raisins and figs, he refused to allow its unloading and promptly gave it all away. Parliament had been brilliantly managed and the trio's seamless performance had saved Buckingham and put the monarch in line for a windfall. MPs even went so far as to call for an annual thanksgiving to mark the prince's return home, akin to 5 November.

The march to war was a popular move. Sir Benjamin Rudyard declared in the Commons that Protestantism was scattered and disunited. Britain's 'outworks' were the Low Countries, who had in their keeping Princess Elizabeth and her children, the 'jewels of this Crowne'.[9] In the House of Lords, Charles banged the war drum, declaring that if Britain did not begin hostilities, then Spain would. King James was talked around; the great peacemaker promised that any money granted for war would be overseen by parliamentary treasurers and that no peace would be agreed without consulting them. It was another declaration that flattered MPs and increased their standing. Cast into action, Charles set about clarifying details before committees and urging speed. But at this crucial point, James backtracked.

A parliamentary delegation arrived at Whitehall in mid-March, led by the Archbishop of Canterbury, who expressed relief that the king had seen through Spanish insincerity. James corrected them – he made no such inference and would not do so until he was granted subsidies. Dropping his facade, he called for his personal debts to be paid and gave an estimate of the grant needed for war. The king's words contradicted Charles and Buckingham, and the archbishop withdrew, feigning illness. Parliament became fitful.

Engaged in damage limitation, Charles urged his father to put personal debts aside for now. He told Parliament that the king's speech had been mistaken and made corrections to it which James went on to authenticate. Only two voices spoke out against war; the Lord Treasurer and the Catholic Earl of Arundel, but Charles protested that they should not 'hinder the common resolution'. The pair presented themselves to the prince at St James's Palace to excuse their intervention, and the Lord Treasurer was said to have been 'ill ever since'.[10] Charles and Buckingham certainly rounded on him and, within months, he was dismissed from office, leading one commentator to remark that Charles was merely resentful of any opposition.

By May, Buckingham was stricken with a tertian ague, and suffered a three-week-long fever, leaving Charles to lead the pro-war party alone. He persuaded his father to grant Parliament an extra week to pass the Subsidy Bill, and opposed the Spanish ambassador's requests for an audience. The Earl of Kellie admitted, 'that whitche I moste Dislyke is there is not that harmonye betwyxt the king's [majesty] & the prince as I culd wishe', though he accepted that Charles was acting out of a 'desire to have all things go well'.[11] The French ambassador labelled the prince too Puritan. Charles was so in step with MPs that they moved against the Tuttle Street brewhouses, regardless of profits and investors, because the smoke annoyed the prince when exercising in St James's Park.

Despite a fall when hunting at Enfield Chase and a bruised rib, word abroad was that Charles was the 'chief authority' in England.[12] James was even said to fear him. Yet the ageing monarch refused to make any declaration of war with Spain, despite subsidies being granted for a naval conflict. The Earl of Kellie summed up Charles's handling of the 1624 Parliament, noting that 'he has bean a lytill more populare then was fitting for him'. More prophetically, he wrote that James, and many 'of the beste & wysest sorte here' thought such popularity would haunt the prince whenever he came to 'governe these pepill'.[13] They were prophetic words.

While revenge was planned against Spain, Charles received a portrait of the young Henrietta Maria of France. The Venetian ambassador did not think the prince looked 'very favourably upon it', but he desired the match more than the king.[14] According to the Marquis of Hamilton, there was a desire to get Charles to the altar as soon as possible. Love letters were being carried across the Channel with Stuart jewels worth 200,000 francs. If this did not prove sufficiently grand, a second stash was sent. It was rumoured that an impatient Charles was ready to go and fetch Henrietta in person, obligated to show the same eagerness towards the French as he had done the Spanish. But this time he found an open door and Henrietta Maria expressed her great pleasure.

Marriage with France would provide Britain with a useful ally in the event of conflict with Spain. Parliamentary subsidies were so slowly collected that Charles offered an advance of £20,000. He also encouraged Ernst von Mansfeld, a commander fighting for the Protestant cause in the Low Countries and who was visiting England. Recruits were hastily scraped together for Mansfeld and hastened on their way before James could change his mind. Time was of the essence. But as if determined never to deviate from the path of peace, James fell seriously ill.

Chapter 12

Impatience and Love

Twelve miles from London, within the moated mansion of Theobalds, the king was bedridden with eight fits of a tertian ague. He rallied briefly, but soon suffered a relapse. Unwilling to leave his master, the Duke of Buckingham refused to go to Paris to discuss the royal marriage and Charles cancelled his review of the navy. By 24 March, twenty days into his sickness, the king's fits increased. He called for the prince and tried to speak to him, but 'had not Strength to express his Intentions'.[1] During a violent tempest, at noon on Sunday 27 March, King James died 'to the greife of all true hearts'.[2] In London, Westminster Hall was infiltrated by 3 feet of floodwater, while two parts of the shipping in Fife were destroyed. In Whitehall Palace, William Laud, Bishop of St David's, had 'ascended the pulpit much troubled' and cut short his sermon.[3]

The Privy Council requested permission to attend Charles, but he asked them to wait, 'being in sadness'.[4] The accession suffered no delay and between 5.00 pm and 6.00 pm, the new king was proclaimed at the gates of Theobalds. Similar events followed across the country. It was so quickly done that Sir John Oglander, on the Isle of Wight, heard about Charles's accession before news of James's death.[5] Elizabeth was assured that her brother would show a 'fatherly care'.[6]

Charles might have thought himself now free to be his own man, able to consider aspirations for his reign. Many others certainly pondered as Britain came to a pivotal crossroads. King James had failed to fully unite his kingdoms, either politically or religiously. Having considered it his divine mission, these policies proved extremely divisive. So, too, were the long-standing methods of government that he had furthered, such as lavish adoration of favourites, an innate belief in divine right and dubious taxation. During the space of ten years, he had ruled without a parliament for all but six weeks – yet this has never been singled out as tyrannical in the same way as Charles's similar period of parliamentary absence. All of this left many burning grievances, and the fact that James had never declared war on Spain, but had pocketed subsidies, sparked anger. There was much hope that the advent of a new monarch would drive change – facing vast expectations, Charles's reign had begun.

Elizabeth expressed grief over the 'evill newes of the loss of so loving a father'. It would have been worse had she not been left a dear and loving brother 'whome next God I have now all my confidence'.[7] Full of hope, she also waited on Charles with bated breath. Count Mansfeld, at the head of last year's raw recruits, offered to continue his service. But James's refusal to declare war had hindered their passage, leaving the soldiers unpaid and beset by illness. Thousands perished for no gain. To make matters worse, France had refused to support the force, despite Charles and Henrietta's forthcoming nuptials.

As much as Charles was different from his father in character, he truly believed in the old king's policies. The indoctrination had worked. Therefore, as he took the tiller, he steered the same political course, leaving significant sections of his kingdoms behind. The Earl of Melrose wrote to Sir Robert Kerr – Charles's old friend and Groom of the Bedchamber – of his hope and comfort in the new king's 'manifold and manifest vertues'.

The Earl of Rothes, by comparison, baulked at Charles's 'reserved disposition' and his obedience 'to all things which did pleas his lat father'. Rothes had opposed James's attempts to reform the Scottish Kirk and now lobbied Kerr on the matter. Should King Charles bring a 'mitigation of thos extremitys' of his father's policies, then the 'first fruits' of his actions would gain everyone's affection. But, Rothes urged, the king should act immediately, before 'the stamp of any bad impression' is made by negative and corrupt advisers of the old regime. The approaching chasm was stark; if Kerr could talk the king around, Rothes predicted 'the greitist afection a peopl can cary to ther Princ'. Sir Patrick Hume called upon God to give Charles 'that same mynd that [was] in King David, Salomon, Ezechias, Josias, etc'.[8]

All these men were disappointed in their hopes that Kerr might influence the king. There is no doubt that Charles was very close to the man, but he soon proved to be no pushover. Kerr was left apologising to another petitioner, Sir Thomas Hope, who lobbied for preferment, that despite teaming up with the Marquis of Hamilton, King Charles had 'refused us both'.[9] Just who did Charles favour? Three trusted leaders of his 1619 Scottish council were continued in their posts for life; Sir George Hay as Chancellor of Scotland, and the Earls of Mar and Melrose as Treasurer and Secretary. Sir Robert Carey became Vice Chamberlain. Apart from Robert Kerr, the king enjoyed a bond with the Marquis of Hamilton, who had lost his own father at the same time. Hamilton would go on to become a Gentleman of the Bedchamber and prestigious Knight of the Garter, which was a sign above all else of preferment. Naturally, the grief-stricken Duke of Buckingham was 'hugely high' in favour.[10]

A heavy Scottish presence surrounded the monarch 'almost in greater numbers' than the English.[11] This was nothing new. Prior to Buckingham, James's chief favourites had all been Scotsmen, as were the male attendants who departed with Princess Elizabeth after her marriage. Queen Anna had, at one point, described Scotland as 'her native land'.[12] So, when the Earl of Melrose wrote his first letter to the new king, he made a point of referring to Scotland as 'your native kingdome'.[13]

As Lucy Hutchinson wrote, 'the face of the court was much chang'd' in view of the temperate, chaste and serious king. 'The fooles and bawds, mimicks and catamites ... grew out of fashion'.[14] The Venetian ambassador echoed this, noting that Charles did not neglect his functions, nor attendance at church. The 'rules and maxims' of Good Queen Bess were brought back and each rank about the king had an appointed place.[15] The king was just as rigid with himself, setting timetables for the day; rising early, he would pray, exercise and do business as routinely as he would eat and sleep. Nobody was to be introduced unless sent for. For several hours each day he would read from a mysterious book, the contents of which were uncertain but were thought to include motivational quotations.

Travelling with Buckingham in the same coach 'as an equal', Charles moved to Whitehall Palace.[16] The embalmed body of his father was transferred to lie in state at Denmark House, watched over by thirty attendants. On 3 April, the Dean of St Paul's, John Donne, preached the first sermon to the new monarch. On that same day, the Mayor of Liverpool reported a maritime disaster off the coast of North Wales in which 350 soldiers, en route to Carrickfergus, had drowned. In France, plans were being made to convey Henrietta Maria to Britain. The bereaved Buckingham considered setting off in search of the Northwest Passage, and it would have been better for all had he gone, personifying as he did the grievances of the last reign.

The proxy royal marriage took place on 1 May in Paris's Notre Dame Cathedral, with Charles represented by the Duc de Chevreuse, dressed in black as a reminder that Britain was in mourning. That same day, the king granted a cessation of all pains and penalties towards Catholic recusants. Just under one week later, his father was laid to rest in Westminster Abbey after the greatest funeral ever known in England. Inigo Jones designed the hearse, behind which Charles walked in a long black robe and hood. The Lord Keeper then gave a two-hour sermon reinforcing the fact that James lived on in his son; a sentiment guaranteed to concern those wishing for reform.

With the entombment of *Rex Pacificus*, Charles sent Buckingham to France on a dual mission to oversee his wife's departure and shore up Louis XIII against Spain. Marriage to Henrietta was the 'greatest felicity which could happen to me in the world', but Charles's frustration grew over delays to her departure. Henrietta reassured him that she stood ready to 'cast herself into your Majesty's arms'.[17] In London, 'dying with impatience and love' the king held off mustering Parliament week after week, wishing them to assemble only when his bride was by his side.[18] Church bells counted ever-increasing plague numbers, while drumbeats recruited soldiers for war. Equally impatient to take up the 'cause of Christendom', Charles gathered 10,000 troops together from across England.[19] As usual, many were unruly and poorly armed, leading the French to estimate that only ten per cent would be effective. As Britain finally bared its teeth to the world, they appeared rotten.

Unable to restrain himself, Charles set out for Kent, covering 56 miles in one day. On 1 June he was at Dover, overseeing preparations for the queen's arrival and dining on board the *Prince Royal*. Two cold hours of one evening were spent on the battlements of Dover Castle, staring longingly into the night; Charles had an impulse to sail to France to meet his 'dear wife' and had to be dissuaded. Lord Brooke remarked that love must teach the king to 'suffer with patience'.[20] When Henrietta did arrive at Boulogne on 9 June, she stood at the water's edge and looked across to England, whereupon the sea did 'kiss her feet'.[21]

Finally, three days later, Henrietta arrived at Dover worse for wear after a six-hour crossing. The sea rarely treated her kindly. She took to a suite of nine rooms with her 'little army' of French attendants. Charles had gone to Canterbury to allow his wife time to settle, but next morning surprised her at breakfast. Nervously, she fell to her knees, but he raised her up. Thinking that Charles was pondering her height, and perhaps whether she was wearing platforms on her shoes, she assured him 'I stand upon mine own feet. I have no help by art. This high I am, and am neither higher nor lower'.[22] Warm embraces and kisses followed. Though Charles favoured formality, he could be extremely demonstrable and made no secret that he was smitten. Now they were together, Henrietta said she had her wish. They travelled to Canterbury, and after enjoying a banquet the couple retired to their bedroom, whereupon Charles locked everyone out. Next morning, in a light-hearted mood, he rose uncharacteristically late at 7.00 am.

After two blissful days it was back to business. Husband and wife, both wearing green – the colour of fertility – went by boat to London surrounded by 160 small crafts. They glided past the Tower of London, which fired its artillery in welcome, and Charles led his wife to the outside of the barge, 'that she might see the people and the city'.[23] At this point a heavy shower forced the couple back inside. Parliament finally got the go-ahead to assemble on 18 June, and despite the pestilence, hundreds of MPs and peers converged upon Westminster. The king was confident of their support, recalling his successful management of the 1624 session, and this time he was in the driving seat. From the throne, wearing his crown, he reaffirmed a commitment to war and pressed the Houses to do the same. At the heart of it all was a desire to recover the Palatinate after his loss of face in Madrid. To withdraw would 'dishonour both him and them'.[24] Parliamentarians, however, had their own priorities.

The sermon was preached by William Laud. It was a mark of royal favour to the man, who was perhaps already being groomed for the see of Canterbury. The 'little, low red-faced' son of a cloth merchant had studied at St John's College, Oxford, and became chaplain to the Earl of Devonshire.[25] His rise stemmed from Buckingham's patronage. Laud's Arminian beliefs acted as a red rag to Puritan bulls. The movement, named after Dutchman Jacobus Arminius, advocated ritual, ceremonial and the beautifying of holiness.

Feelings were running high over the terms of the marriage treaty, leading to demands for a ban on the hearing of Mass, restitution of penal laws and a new tax on the goods of Catholics. The queen soon grew concerned about the 'storm' breaking upon her co-religionists.[26] Sir Thomas Wentworth (later Earl of Strafford) spoke for many when he called for the business of the Commonwealth to be despatched before that of the monarch's. Without an injection of money, and with his father's debts supposedly at £1,000,000, the king was facing ruin. Since Midsummer, no officials had received a salary and the royal lands had all been mortgaged off. Nevertheless, Parliament sought, and secured, an adjournment until 1 August.

Parliament's refusal to vote money for war with Spain, despite demanding stricter persecution of Catholics at home, seemed contradictory. It presented Charles with a stark choice: Henrietta and their marriage contract, or his Parliament and war funds. Buckingham caused further complications by requesting that his wife, sister and niece be admitted to the queen's household. The last two were blocked on account of their Protestantism and as a result, the favourite 'spoke bitterly' to the queen.[27] During a coach journey to Windsor, Madam Saint George, Henrietta's childhood governess, was blocked from travelling in the royal carriage in favour of Buckingham's family. It was a dispute that Charles did not want or need. Some respite came when, in July, the king visited Woking and his wife went to Nonsuch.

Upon reassembling in Oxford, Parliament came out fighting and 'A great assault was made against the Duke of Buckingham'.[28] When one MP spoke in favour of the duke, he was forced to crave forgiveness on his knees. A stinging rebuke was also sent to Charles, who had pardoned a Jesuit at the French ambassador's intervention. Suggesting a winter session to deal with grievances, the king pushed the pressing question of finances. His predecessors had all received a lifetime income from Tonnage and Poundage levies, whereas it was being withheld from him. To Charles, it was his right, but Parliament needed a carrot to dangle.

Seemingly endless difficulties were grinding government to a halt and Charles considered losing half the fleet at sea preferable to having them rot at home. He informed Parliament of plans to support his uncle, the King of Denmark, who was targeting Catholic forces in North Germany. The English fleet would be deployed in an attack upon Cadiz. In a spirit of openness, the king laid bare his finances and stressed that he had married the queen's person and not her religion. It was to no avail, and under pressure, he reinstated penal laws, despite the marriage terms, which compromised his word abroad. Having dealt with domestic religious policy, Parliament simply moved to their next topic – Buckingham – and began to draw up charges. Charles rapidly dissolved the session, having gained nothing but the combined opposition of France, the queen and his Parliament. The duke's safety had prevailed over the needs of the Crown and public affairs. The king felt humiliated that his climbdown had brought no benefit, whereas Parliament saw it as reinstating basic statutes that were the bedrock of Britain's security.

Of the pressed 10,000 troops, one-fifth had now deserted, died or been discharged. Replacements were raised, the fleet was instructed to make ready, and Buckingham had Sir Edward Cecil appointed to command it – an experienced general, but no sailor. With the Spanish ready to take advantage of the political turmoil and threatening to 'make descent' upon Ireland, the English turned on each other.[29] Many poor countrymen attacked the soldiers that were billeted on them, while unpaid troops resorted to highway robbery.

At Southampton, conflict raged in the king's household. On 18 September, Henrietta and her ladies, deliberately making 'such a noise', walked through the middle of a sermon given by the vicar of Tichfield.[30] It was an attempt to assert themselves. On another occasion, as the royal couple dined together, Henrietta's chaplain began to compete with the king's over the saying of grace. Charles pulled the dishes towards him and began the meal, but once finished, another contest broke out. Grabbing his wife's hand, he led her from the chamber. The matter was highly embarrassing, especially as he was hosting Dutch commissioners, who had brought terms for an offensive and defensive alliance. Though the king and queen disagreed over religion, their love for one another was not seriously affected, and letters from Buckingham lay unread for three hours while the pair remained closeted together.

On 8 October, the fleet, supplemented by Dutch vessels, was finally ready to sail. Some crown jewels had been pawned in Holland to plug finances, and Charles, known to enjoy a wager, gambled away his wife's dowry on this naval expedition. If the Palatinate was not retaken, he was determined to continue efforts until he had 'not a drop of blood left'.[31]

In 1624, William Laud had heard Charles remark that if he had to choose a profession, he could not be a lawyer because he could never 'defend a bad, nor yield in a good cause'.[32] The king would live and die abiding by this maxim.

Chapter 13

Rights and Wrongs

November heralded bad news from the leaky English fleet off the coast of Spain. Entirely unprepared for a winter expedition, every man cried out for victuals and supped cider that 'stinks worse than carrion'.[1] Storms picked off the vessels – the *Long Robert* foundered with the loss of 175 men. When the seamen did see action, they only took the fort of Puntal after being driven to it by 'threatening and cudgelling'. The capture of 600 tons of wine sparked chaos, and the fort was soon abandoned, resulting in the slaughter of many drunken Englishmen. A 'great wrong' had been done to the king by assurances that the fleet had been ready to sail.[2]

The question was: who was responsible? Sir Edward Cecil, the commander, claimed to have anticipated these difficulties, but being commanded by Buckingham, he had faced no option but to set sail. As Admiral General – not content with one title – Buckingham's cards were marked. Settling at Hampton Court that Christmas, Charles made it clear that a second fleet would be readied in the New Year, and obstacles would be overcome by a well-timed coronation set for 2 February 1626. Four days after this, Parliament would assemble.

Having been continuously beset by problems since his accession, Charles's pending coronation created yet another. Aggrieved and slighted, the Scots called for him to be crowned in Edinburgh first and sent their council to London in January 1626. The king reassured them that he was born a Scot and would bear them the same affection as his father. Hoping that the New Year could bring a fresh start with Henrietta, as well as Parliament, Charles gifted her Denmark House, which led to a 'more intimate' understanding between the couple.[3] Two ships were also launched, one called *Henrietta* and the other *Maria*. Buckingham, too, treated the queen with more respect, speaking of her 'large heartedness and generosity'.[4]

Like the king, Buckingham was also preparing for the coming Parliament and their rabid MPs. In diplomatic circles, a secret circulated that he intended to marry his daughter to the eldest son of Charles's sister. He proposed a gift of 100,000 francs to help with Elizabeth's debts, most likely as a sweetener. The seamen also enjoyed the Lord Admiral's bounty, on paper at least, with an increase in their allowance. Nevertheless, hungry sailors and soldiers were still swapping their clothes for food. The fleet had limped back to England with barely enough men left to trim the sails, and ships were then abandoned. Sir William

St Leger warned that officers were desperate enough to 'pull out the throats' of naval commissioners to get money to pay their men.[5] General Cecil lay sick in Ireland. Though created Viscount Wimbledon, he was soon called 'General Sit-Still'.[6] But blame was primarily attributed to Buckingham. As if this was not enough to contend with, Charles had his sights on yet another crusade.

The French town of La Rochelle was a Huguenot stronghold, and after refusing to submit to Louis XIII's religious reforms, it was under siege. To raise his credit with the coming Parliament and firmly align himself with the Protestant cause, Charles entertained the prospect of a full breach with his brother-in-law. If the town fell, word was that King Charles would recover it in person, accounting it a matter of 'honour, interest and religion'.[7] The queen wrote directly to her mother, expressing anguish at this conflict of loyalties, but another juxtaposition loomed over the coronation. The French protested that Henrietta could not be crowned in a Protestant ceremony and suggested that one of their own bishops might take part. The king declined to make the 'smallest departure' from its sacred practices, leaving Louis to declare that a 'heavenly crown' was far better for his sister.[8]

The big day was a 'very bright sunshining' one.[9] For the serious-minded Charles, it was to be the most important moment of his life to date. Days earlier, he had viewed the regalia and tried on the tunic that had been worn ever since the days of Edward the Confessor. At 10.00 am he went by barge to Westminster Abbey for the five-hour service. Anointed on his chest, back, shoulders, the joints of his arms, and his head, he was then proclaimed by the Archbishop of Canterbury to shouts of 'long live the king'. Adorned with the crown, sceptre, sword and spurs, a series of oaths followed, one of which was to uphold Magna Carta. Many remarked that they had never seen such solemnity performed in 'so great an order'.[10]

Westminster Hall hosted the second half of proceedings. Upon ascending the steps of a wooden scaffold, Buckingham offered his hand to the king, who pointedly replied, 'I have more need to help you, than you have to help me.'[11] Nine men were given earldoms, including Sir Robert Carey, now nearing 70, who became Earl of Monmouth. Despite being a difficult man, there is no doubt that Charles valued him and never forgot Elizabeth Carey's devotion. As much as the king was willing to reward, he was also prepared to shun those deemed undeserving; John Digby, Earl of Bristol, who had been scapegoated for the Madrid fiasco, remained banished from court. Digby had hoped the coronation might benefit him, but Charles did not budge over the man he felt had much wronged his sister's cause.

At this historic moment, the Duke of Buckingham also received a petition. Many of Sir Thomas Wentworth's friends had moved him to 'procure' the office of Lord President of the Council of the North. The outgoing incumbent was Robert Carey's nephew. Wentworth threw his hat into the ring and assured Buckingham that he reposed under the shadow of his favour. The linking of these two men was prophetic. Both dominated Charles's life – Buckingham the first half and Wentworth the second. Buckingham's patronage would unwittingly lead to Wentworth becoming his successor, and an infinitely more able one at that.

Now crowned and confirmed, King Charles prepared to open his second Parliament. Divine backing would surely bring a new respect from MPs along with his Tonnage and Poundage income. To be on the safe side, he postponed his wife's masque and had some opposition MPs nominated as sheriffs, thus tying them to their counties like a 'Snail to his Shell'.[12] In Holland, the king's sister prayed daily for the happy success of this session, but the day began badly. The queen was to watch the procession from rooms accessible via a muddy garden. She refused to cross, despite the urgings of her 'much irritated' husband. When the French ambassador's entreaties procured compliance, Charles's jealousy was aroused and he ordered her not to go. After pondering what to do for the best, Henrietta went anyway, heightening Charles's irritation. The farcical situation, which saw the couple sleep apart for two nights, led Henrietta to observe that her husband had 'too many enemies' without adding France to the list.[13]

After this bumpy start to the day, the king processed to Parliament, where William Laud quoted Tacitus, and reminded everyone that in-fighting between Britons had given the Romans an advantage. The words had little effect. Charles found many MPs reeling with anger over the Cadiz expedition, and its effect upon trade and their pockets. Had he been given his rightful dues, the king might assert, then there would not have been such wants in the fleet. Instead, he kept his speech brief. 'I am not very good to speak much,' he candidly admitted, preferring actions to words.[14] The Venetian ambassador remarked upon the 'impediment of his tongue' or stammer.[15] Continuing on the monarch's behalf, the Lord Keeper pointed out the 'Supreme Height' of majesty compared to the 'Lowliness' of subjects. Yet in this highest court of Parliament, men of every status were called upon to toil with 'united Hearts and Minds'.[16]

The king did not advocate a prolonged session, but MPs filled their time with matters of small importance, aware that the 'knot will be untied' once the subject of money was broached.[17] Anticipating hostility, the Duke of Buckingham played every card. To tackle piracy, and avoid charges of negligence, he met with the Lord Mayor of London to raise money for a dozen patrol ships. But his use of a proxy vote in the House of Lords caused uproar. He was not the only one to do so, but on one occasion, he cast fourteen proxy votes, resulting in an urgent motion to limit the practice.

Emboldened by the Lords' stand, the House of Commons dipped its toe into the hot water. Most noticeably, it was Buckingham's former friend who did so. Sir John Eliot asked for an account of how the money granted by the 1624 Parliament had been spent. In this way, he hoped, they could determine the true causes of the ill success of the fleet. A noted orator, the disaffected Eliot had become a leading member of the opposition and nailed Parliament's colours to the mast – the royal favourite was fixed in their sights.

March saw the council of war appear before Parliament with financial accounts, which they did with royal blessing. Afterwards, the Earl of Totnes advised the king to 'regard his own ends' and suggested the council might be used as scapegoats to help smooth the passage of subsidies. Rather that, he said, than the continued breeding of differences between king and Parliament. What followed reflected Charles's true opinion of Parliament's motives, as well as the immense strain of the last twelve months. He thanked Totnes but asserted that 'it is me upon whom they make inquisition' through veiled attacks on ministers. Gold, he assured, should not be 'bought too dear'.[18] Charles did not understand the depth of feeling that had built up over the past twenty-three years, nor how to assuage Parliament without sacrificing his favourite. His insecurities were stoked by this wholly unexpected level of opposition, which felt intensely personal.

In a desperate attempt to fight back, Buckingham warned of a military build-up in Spain and across the Channel at Dunkirk. King Philip, he claimed, was a tyrant who 'aspires to universal monarchy'. This was not entirely a dodgy dossier – Britain was incapable of continuing its war, let alone defending itself. The king also wrote to the Speaker over the 'imminent peril' and MPs' unreasonable slowness.[19] Vulnerable and powerless, he promised to remedy all grievances that were presented to him in a dutiful and mannerly way.

Battles at home and abroad took their toll upon Charles. The Earl of Arundel received the brunt of it when his son secretly married the daughter of the Duke of Lennox and Richmond. Charles had already lined the bride up for the Earl of Argyll's son, to secure that family's loyalty. Buckingham also wanted the groom for his niece. Arundel, a regular voice of opposition, claimed not to have known about the marriage, but Charles did not believe him and committed the man to the Tower. The newlyweds were sent to the Archbishop of Canterbury. The reaction was high-handed, but Charles had had his fill of disrespect, perceived or otherwise. Despite royal assertions that the arrest was for personal rather than parliamentary reasons, protests arrived from an incensed House of Lords. The Commons also responded with a broadside against Buckingham. One MP ascribed all ills to the duke because the king's council 'rides upon one horse'. Sir John Eliot was instrumental in drawing up seven points against Buckingham and his 'mis-government'.[20]

1. The king had lost control of the 'narrow seas' (English Channel).
2. Money from 1624's subsidies had been diverted to private use.
3. Royal revenues were diminished by the late king's 'extraordinary gifts' to the favourite.
4. Evils were occasioned by the duke and his 'incompetent' clan.
5. The commonwealth had suffered from the sale of honours, offices, justice and ecclesiastical dignities.

6. Ill-conceived plans, and Buckingham's not commanding the fleet in person, had led to its failure.
7. The duke's mother and father-in-law were Catholic recusants. Might he be?[21]

The direct nature of these allegations greatly perturbed the king. Amidst the furore over Arundel in the House of Lords, he now did battle with the Commons, calling for MPs to punish the authors of these 'insolent speeches'. It was the behaviour of a panicked man who had lost control. Considering that he had been 'too patient' for too long, he then threatened to use his royal authority.[22]

King James would have had the men thrown into prison without hesitation, and routinely did so. Charles, in comparison, issued unequivocal commands and then undermined them by quickly resorting to hollow threats. This approach boxed him into many a corner. When Dudley Digges and John Eliot were eventually sent to the Tower, they were released days later when the House of Commons protested. Charles's knee-jerk reactions and subsequent retreats encouraged his opponents and highlighted a distinct lack of ruthlessness.

When MPs finally spoke of subsidies, they linked them to grievances and would only pay out after these had been addressed. Then they got back to the matter of Buckingham and summoned him to the House of Commons. Calling upon MPs and peers to attend him at Whitehall, the king intervened. Thanking peers for their care of the state, he told MPs that he could not extend the same message to them, and promptly asked the Lord Keeper to list their unparliamentary proceedings. Declaring it better to be destroyed by a foreign enemy than be 'defied in his house', the king refused to suffer any violation under the pretended colour of parliamentary liberty.[23] Never was any monarch more loving to his people, he assured, before reminding them that Parliament was entirely 'in his hands' to summon and retain. In contempt of his royal rights, they had 'set the Dice' to make their own game.[24] Suitably chided, and given a deadline on the matter of finances, many Parliamentarians left feeling 'utmost disgust'.[25] Hardly a brutal speech, it was more like that of a self-righteous and disappointed father, but next day the conscientious king hastily clarified that he did not intend dissolution and gave assurances that grievances would be heard.

From deepest Dorset came a timely protest. The Earl of Bristol, under virtual house arrest, complained that he had not received a writ to attend Parliament. It was a deliberate oversight and he knew it. Bristol petitioned peers that he was wronged as a result of Buckingham's malign influence and intimated knowledge of the duke's crimes. The king denounced this intervention as 'void of duty and respect' and warned he would proceed against the earl as a delinquent.[26]

An Easter break did not resurrect any understanding. The king had supposedly been talked out of dissolving Parliament by Buckingham, who begged on his knees. At the end of April, matters got a whole lot more personal. Struggling to evidence their charges against the favourite, MPs alleged that he had killed King

James by administering a 'plaister' and a mysterious drink during the monarch's last illness.[27] This was a step too far. It suggested the king was harbouring a killer, or even worse had been complicit. Parliament became 'practically inactive' over their pursuit of the duke, and the king stood equally determined over Bristol, who as a noble had to be tried by peers in the House of Lords.[28] Summoning the bishops, Charles instructed them to follow their consciences in the matter and to be 'led by proofs, not by reports'.[29] He would need more support than two dozen clerics.

On 1 May, the Earl of Bristol knelt before the bar of the House of Lords. In a shock move, he interrupted the charges of high treason and counter-accused Buckingham. This turnaround derailed proceedings. Bristol's allegations were enthusiastically taken up, specifically that the 'Popishly affected' favourite had conspired with the Spanish to take Charles to Madrid to elicit his conversion. Feeding rumours of murder, Bristol asserted that King James had agreed to hear his complaints against Buckingham, but then 'His Blessed Majesty' coincidentally died.[30] For good measure, while in Spain the duke had engaged in 'vicious pleasures'. Buckingham listened in complete silence and then called for restraint on the latter point to protect his wife's feelings. One of the favourite's rare supporters at this time was the queen, who 'strongly recommended' the king to preserve the man in moments of 'sweetest affection'.[31] His wife's understanding must have been a great comfort to Charles.

The favourite's every move was scrutinised. When he fell sick and was carried from Whitehall to Denmark House in a covered chair 'upon his servant's shoulders', the grandiose behaviour was seized upon.[32] With events spiralling out of control, a book arrived from Flanders, ascribed to a physician called George Eglisham, who had fled to the Spanish territory to escape Buckingham. Claiming that Buckingham was a 'Murtherer and Traytor' who had 'terrannized' the old king, it also accused him of finishing off the Marquis of Hamilton and two other peers.[33]

Eglisham had his own motives. Some put the allegations down to a Spanish faction who wished to cause 'public discord', and when France concluded a shock truce with Spain, it enhanced Britain's predicament.[34] The king's cause was further shaken when letters surfaced, appealing to leading Catholics for financial support to facilitate Parliament's dismissal. Henrietta condemned the authors for using her name and forging her handwriting. The whole country was at fever pitch and in the House of Commons, the duke was called a 'canker worm' that threatened to ruin them all.[35]

Finally recognising his impossible position, Charles released the Earl of Arundel. Ironically, when the peer returned to Westminster, he took up a seat next to Buckingham, but they were not to be neighbours for long. Four peers interrupted Charles's exercise in St James's Park and entreated him against dissolving Parliament, but this time he was of a fixed mind. He would not let them sit two weeks, nor two hours more. On 15 June, his second Parliament ended, along with the king's noble designs 'for the restoring of God's oppressed Church and Gospel in foreign parts'.[36]

Despite reneging on the terms of his marriage, the king by hook or by crook tried to secure the rest of the queen's dowry. More contentious still, he attempted to collect Parliament's conditional subsidies. Voluntary loans were requested, but only token amounts came in from those beholden to his court. As the months passed, there were proposals to recoin gold pieces with less weight, and the family silver – £15,000 worth of ancient and admirable workmanship – was sold off. By the end of the year, Buckingham's coachmen and grooms were wearing worn-out liveries. When the French ambassador took his leave on 4 December 1626, the king was reduced to plucking four diamonds and a large pearl from the crown itself as an obligatory parting gift. One pension that survived this financial freeze, at the king's express command, was 2 shillings per day for John Street – the man whose 'extraordinary service' included killing the gunpowder traitors Percy and Catesby with bullets 'shot out of his musket'.[37]

That summer, picking his battles more strategically, Charles decided to get his own house in order and declined the queen's candidates for her household. Henrietta wished for the same freedoms that the king's mother had enjoyed, but he was quick to reply that Anna was 'a different sort of woman'.[38] Henrietta agreed – a daughter of Denmark was not on a par with the French House of Bourbon, to which Charles retorted that his wife was merely a third-born daughter.

Henrietta's French household prompted her to avoid physical intimacy on saints' days, during which she would withdraw to small rooms 'built like a monastery' at the top of her palace. This particularly 'vexed' Charles, who was already slighted at home and abroad. He was certain the queen's French household was responsible for mistrust between the couple, and in turn, France and England. But in this matter, as with all of his troubles, Buckingham was also involved.[39] The favourite desired more influence over the queen, therefore to send the 'Monsieurs' packing would serve his purpose as well as the king's.

At the end of July, Charles grasped the nettle. Henrietta was in her apartments suffering from toothache when the king told her that the time had come for the French to go. The shocked queen wept as her trusted companions were ushered out of the palace. Watching helplessly from a window she suddenly smashed it with her fist and cried out to them, but Charles forcibly pulled her back. The following day, taking responsibility for his decision, the king addressed the servants personally. Apologising for his French, he assured them he meant no offence and promised that civility would be shown as they journeyed home. Henrietta declared herself a 'tyrannised princess' and that the suffering was killing her.[40] With the duke's mother, wife, sister and niece now shadowing her every day, unable to speak or write unless in the presence of one of them, it made for a discontented life. A string of reports mentioned the depressed queen who feared appearing in public in case she could not 'restrain her tears'.[41]

Victory brought the king little respite, and he may even have been on the verge of a breakdown. Access to his person had always been strictly prohibited, but it was further withdrawn when new locks were applied to the doors of the privy apartments in Whitehall Palace; only three keys, the king's, queen's and Lord Chamberlain's would now work. By mid-August, it was noticed that Charles was exhausted. A few weeks later, his distress was 'at its height'. Formerly punctilious in matters of government, he now shunned it and 'abhors all arduous business'. When his exiled brother-in-law, Frederick, sent an agent to discuss financial support, Charles struggled to know what to say and rid himself of the man in haste.

The Protestant cause took a nosedive in September 1626 when the king's Uncle Christian was defeated by Catholic forces. Guilt-ridden that he had not been able to support the Danes, Charles spoke with their envoy for four hours. The news piled on additional pressure, and he promised every assistance at the 'risk of his own crown' and life. By the end of the meeting, he was in tears, admitting his 'personal wants and household necessities'.[42]

When the new Venetian ambassador sent home initial impressions of England, he wrote that the kingdom was divided in two between the king, Buckingham and a few individuals on the one hand, and everyone else on the other. It was even claimed that Charles had been bewitched. Rumbles of discontent broke out in Scotland, whose ministers resolved to call their own Parliament to discuss the worsening situation. When the king protested that this wasn't possible without his presence, precedent was quoted; they had done so many times in his father's reign, adding tartly that James had been crowned in Scotland and Charles had not.

A state of paralysis brought 1626 to a close. It was Charles's *Annus Horribilus*. Intentions of sending another fleet against Spain or France were dashed and his troops now turned on him. The sailors of six ships intended to surround king and duke in great numbers, but were dissuaded by a settlement of wages. October saw 150 seamen destroy Buckingham's empty coach with bludgeons, before being bought off by money fetched post-haste from the Royal Mint. Charles went so far as to instruct the Lieutenant of the Tower to fire on mutinous sailors if they should make resistance against the trained bands.

Gossip spread as far as Turin that the king was behaving very imprudently. A man threatened to kill the duke and vowed if that did not improve matters, he would have done away with the king so that his sister, Elizabeth, could be sent for. A second plot to murder the duke came in the form of a French lute player, who was found with a pistol. There was a real danger that Charles would go down with Buckingham's ship. As a vulnerable and inexperienced young king, facing unprecedented demand for reform, he doggedly put his trust in Buckingham. Such unbending loyalty might be considered noble, but at the expense of his three kingdoms, it was foolish.

Chapter 14

Man of Seyaton

'love is greater then Majesty'
Duke of Buckingham

William Laud, Bishop of Bath and Wells, preached on Ash Wednesday in 1627. The night before, Laud experienced one of his many bizarre dreams; that he had been 'troubled with the scurvy' and lost all his teeth.[1] For the king, who had lost many a ship, England without a fleet was like a 'body without a head'.[2] Intending to replenish his navy for a second offensive, he had the clergy exhort congregations to contribute to his forced loans.

A trade war erupted with the French, and the continued siege of Huguenots in La Rochelle was symptomatic of the crumbling Protestant cause. Charles showed his support in one of the few ways he could; he awarded the Order of the Garter to Protestant champions King Gustavus Adolphus of Sweden and the Dutch Stadtholder, Prince Frederick Henry. Other knights were the Duc de Chevreuse and Earl of Holland, both of whom had been key to arranging his marriage, and close friend, Viscount Andover, who had been in his household for over a decade. The New Year saw Charles much recovered. One Secretary of State described him as continually at exercises, such as tennis, when the weather permitted, but ominous clouds continued to overshadow his government. The Venetian ambassador observed that the king 'commands despotically' and due to lack of money, he ruined friendly powers by 'hopes without deeds'.[3]

In May 1627, war finally broke out between Britain and France. Charles hastened munitions from the Tower before leaving for Portsmouth to review his fleet. He dined in high spirits with musicians and his jester, Archie Armstrong, but while transferring from ship to ship, his silver travelling utensils fell into the sea and were lost. Before the fleet, led by Buckingham, departed for La Rochelle, Charles had sworn that he would not negotiate peace without consulting his favourite. It hints at Buckingham's fear that in his absence, his master might be influenced into changing policy, and both the queen and Prince Rupert would later call for similar promises of constancy during the Civil Wars.

Buckingham's departure coincided with that of the queen, who headed to the waters at Wellingborough, noted for their health benefits as well as fertility. War with France weighed heavily on her, leading Charles to write expressing his regret over hostilities. Though Henrietta prayed for her husband's success, being more interested in him 'than for anyone else', she remained at a low ebb.[4] When her 18-inch-tall dwarf, Jeffrey Hudson, was injured after falling from a window, she 'tooke it soe heavily' that she didn't dress herself that day.[5]

The English fleet of over 100 ships arrived at the Île de Ré, near La Rochelle, on 12 July 1627. An attempted landing was heavily repulsed, and many were drowned in the retreat. Buckingham's force was successful the second time and took the town of St Martin, whereupon 2,000 French troops retreated into the fort. English sappers began to tunnel through the stony ground towards the walls, backed by eighteen battering guns. The fleet was arrayed in a half-moon, trapping the French like a 'hare in a purse'.[6] Despite daily services, Buckingham's prayers were not answered. He had counted upon an uprising in France to coincide with his arrival, and its absence was a serious blow.

The king threw himself into organising supplies and reinforcements, urging the Lord Treasurer 'let not my monies go wrong ways'. Ministers were warned not to hide anything that might result in false hopes till it be 'too late to helpe'. When a letter arrived at council marked post-haste, the anxious king, taking it for long-anticipated news, broke it open. Inside, he found a blank sheet of paper, which left him suspended between 'choler and wonder'.[7] His rage subsided when it was understood to be an innocent oversight, but such uncertain days made Charles turn to Henrietta and he desired to know the soonest date she could join him.

On 28 July, after finding that siege ladders had proved too short, Buckingham concluded that the only way to take the fort was by starving it into submission. Despatching a desperate letter home, he called for supplies. With much bravado, Charles declared that any who were found lacking over hastening them would 'make their end at Tyburn'.[8] Over two dozen ships were appointed to reinforce Buckingham and command was given to the Earl of Holland. As if one was not enough, Holland was described as a second favourite. This golden-haired deputy failed to deliver, held back by adverse winds and other unexplainable delays, despite continued royal entreaties.

From the Île de Ré, complaints continued that not even a fishing boat had arrived from home. The English grew daily weaker as their bellies, purses and artillery were left increasingly empty. Despite the duke's exertions, supposedly staying until the 'last bit of bread', he sailed for home on 27 October after the French and Spanish agreed an alliance against the English.[9]

Charles bore the blow well. As expected, he honoured Buckingham's actions and cleared him of all blame, while lamenting the loss of experienced officers. Of the 7,000 men that had set out four months earlier, only 3,000 returned. For Sir Simonds D'Ewes there was no question of the king's sincere motives to 'deliver the French [Huguenots] from apparent ruin'.[10] A victory may well have quietened English Puritans, but defeat left them baying for blood. In London, Buckingham's astrologer, Dr John Lambe, was stoned and clubbed to death by a crowd of apprentices. Nearby, in Fleet Lane, a melancholy man of few words was quartered. Lieutenant John Felton had returned from the Île de Ré a changed man. Reading offered him a retreat and he borrowed books from a neighbour, though he failed to return one about Mary, Queen of Scots. Having been wounded in the service of her grandson, and perhaps suffering from post-traumatic stress disorder, he would go on to play a crucial part in the conflict between king and Parliament.

MPs assembled once more in March 1628. As ongoing wrangles over royal finances continued to dominate debate, Felton reportedly followed its progress. He had his own monetary worries and was owed arrears of pay amounting to 'fourscore and odd pounds'.[11] A compromise was finally reached when Charles agreed to the Petition of Right, which enshrined Parliament's approval of all taxation and prevented imprisonment without due cause. As the king's signature dried, MPs approved £300,000 of subsidies. The thorny issue of Buckingham remained, however, and in the face of resumed attacks on the man, a temporary prorogation was ordered. A jubilant Buckingham prepared to ready the fleet for a second bout, and August 1628 saw both Felton and the duke leave for Portsmouth.

Money could not come in quick enough. Until it could be had, Buckingham warned, the mariners would remain discontent. The king, in high spirits and hunting furiously, passed order that sailors should be kept on board ship. By 22 August, the duke considered there could be no 'happy success' without God's especial blessing and instructed all ships to hold a solemn worship and communion. William Laud had come under fire from Parliament, only for the king to promote him to Bishop of London, and now he penned a public prayer for the fleet's success.

Sunday 23 August 1628 was the eve of St Bartholomew's Day, which in France was the anniversary of a Protestant massacre. That morning, in the Greyhound Inn, Buckingham expressed great joy at news that La Rochelle had been re-victualled and at 10.00 am, he prepared to go and see the king. John Felton, having arrived in town just half an hour earlier, entered the inn. In one hand he held his hat, under which was a cheap knife that he thrust into Buckingham's chest. The duke extracted the weapon and stumbled after his assailant, collapsing in the hall with blood 'gushing from his mouth'.[12] A cry went up that the murderer was a Frenchman. Felton surrendered himself and claimed to have done the deed for the good of king and country. Others ventured that Buckingham had Felton's brother or cousin killed over a charge of mutiny.

For the last month, the king had been staying at Southwick Park, half a dozen miles from Portsmouth. It was a fine new house in the shadow of an old priory – a base from where he could keep in touch with his fleet. Charles was at prayers when word of the murder reached him. Though suffering 'great mental distress', he did not budge until the service was over.[13] Remaining closeted in his chamber for the rest of the day, the king took the death very badly, but his first thoughts were to assume protection for the duke's family. The duchess was brought to a village nearby, and Charles committed to paying her husband's debts. Though the entire court was plunged into mourning, the king pushed ahead with the naval offensive, vowing not to leave Southwick until the fleet had sailed. The royal coach made regular trips up a steep hill to view the ships at anchor. The queen was still at Wellingborough, so one of Charles's closest companions at that moment was faithful Sir Robert Kerr, Groom of his Bedchamber for fifteen years. From Southwick the disillusioned Kerr wrote to John Donne, Dean of St Paul's, complaining about the 'new spheare of courtship' that had begun.[14]

The power vacuum needed urgent address because Buckingham had held so many offices of state. The Earl of Holland, as deputy favourite, cast his hat into the ring with indecent haste the following day, adding that the late duke would have favoured him. Numerous others, who had owed their places to Buckingham, scrambled for a new patron. Edward Nicholas, one of the few who showed themselves a 'true and faithful servant', concerned himself over Buckingham's family.[15] The king rewarded the man, who would work his way up the ranks to become a Secretary of State. The Marquis of Hamilton was made Master of the Horse.

If anyone did harbour a desire to replace Buckingham, their hopes would be dashed. It was made clear, even in these early days, that the king would never again place so much of his affairs upon any one person. On this he kept his word. Many of Charles's subjects hoped that Buckingham's demise would lead to better relations with Parliament. In the royal household, it certainly helped the king and queen's marriage. By October, one of Henrietta's ladies, the wily Countess of Carlisle, thought there was never 'more affection nor happiness' between them.[16]

> I doe not find that the kinge is likly to have [any] favorite but the queene, who is so observinge that they are seldum a sunder for when he goes to tennis she is ever with him all the time.[17]

So wrote Edward Sydenham. As Charles and Henrietta's relationship deepened, she naturally become 'a great courtier'.[18] Hoping to capitalise on this love, the Venetian ambassador mediated to end the war between Britain and France. He sought the queen's support, who 'dared to recommend' negotiations, despite assuring her husband that she had no wish to 'interfere' in state affairs.[19] At her nineteenth birthday celebrations, Charles ran at the ring in her honour and became a gallant wooer once more.

When officers carried the coffin of the fallen favourite out of Portsmouth, a salvo of artillery fire paid homage to him. At the end of September, the body was taken to London in a great train of coaches and horses, and privately laid to rest in Westminster Abbey. Apart from lack of money for a worthy funeral, there were fears it might provoke a popular tumult. For William Laud, Bishop of London, the murder of his patron was the 'saddest accident'. Within his diocese, reverent crowds flocked to the Tower to pray for John Felton, who went to the gallows with people drinking toasts to him. It prompted Laud to note these 'stirring' bad humours.[20]

Chapter 15

Rejoice

The relationship with Buckingham was the most influential of Charles's life. It shaped him as man and monarch, as well as the three kingdoms he ruled. In 1627, he told 'Steenie' that true friendship was the greatest of all riches and hard to find, extolling their own. But did Buckingham ever realise the extent of his claustrophobic influence? In the Northamptonshire archives is one of his most poignant speeches from June 1628, made before king and council. It came at the point when long-awaited subsidies were finally granted, and he ceremoniously offers up his soubriquet of royal favourite.

> Give me leave, I beseech you, to be an humble suter unto yor matie [your majesty]; that I who have had the honer to bee yor favouritt, may now give up [that] title unto them, they to be yor favouritte and I to bee yor servant.

Assuming 'them' to be Parliament or the people, it is a key reflection on a most critical moment. Admitting that there was not a union of hearts and affections between the king and his people, he describes the personal toll of being a royal favourite but public enemy, and branded an 'evill spiritt'.

> I must confesse I have longe lived in paine. Sleepe hath given me noe rest, favours and fortunes noe content, such hath beene my secrett sorrowes, to be thought the man of Seyaton [Satan].[1]

Despite being freed of their demon, when MPs reassembled in January 1629, they proved in no mood for conciliation – the previous year's Petition of Right had been broken and debate about it became heated. Employing all his tact and charm, the king made a speech that doused tempers. He asserted that he had no thoughts of collecting Tonnage and Poundage revenues by prerogative and would instead have it as 'the Gift of My People'.[2] This was Charles at his best. His words provoked great applause, but saw no furtherance on the financial front, and Parliament returned to their favourite topic: religion.

Sir John Eliot avowed that 'all evil' was contracted by the Bishop of Winchester and the Lord Treasurer, and accused the late duke of having sheltered papists, Jesuits and priests. Scathing speeches flowed freely until the king sent an arrest warrant, summoning Eliot and eight others to explain their conduct. Refusing to answer to any but Parliament, they were accordingly committed to the Tower. In the king's eyes, such seditious behaviour was unparalleled in 'any former age'.[3] With Buckingham gone, Charles felt more vulnerable than ever.

In the Venetian ambassador's opinion, the king was being 'too complaisant' leading his subjects to 'dare anything'.[4] Antiquarian Simonds D'Ewes thought Eliot and others 'fiery spirits' who 'too much swayed and carried' the pious and religious majority.[5] The king was not a vindictive man by nature, but the continuous opposition made him extremely bitter. Many personal matters that year weighed heavily and eroded his patience.

In January, Frederick and his eldest son travelled to Amsterdam to view the Spanish treasure fleet, which had been captured by the Dutch the previous year. Eleven vessels contained £184,000 of silver alone. Any victory against Spain and the Hapsburgs was welcome news, but this was especially glorious. En route, Frederick's ship capsized after being struck by a barge and his 15-year-old son and heir was drowned. The tragedy grieved all in Britain, but Charles most of all. He put his court into mourning and sent close friend, Sir Robert Kerr, to represent him at the funeral.

Pregnant Henrietta moved to Greenwich for her confinement in March. Being with child proved a 'great impulse' for reconciliation and a truce was agreed between England and France.[6] At Somerset House, two months later, she attended a celebratory Te Deum, but on returning to Greenwich misfortune befell the queen – contemporaries mention two different accidents. Her boat lifted as it shot the rapids of London Bridge and threw her to the planking, and then a fight at the palace between 'two great dogs' scared her.[7] Whichever was the cause, the queen went into premature labour around 10 weeks early. The king was in 'constant attendance' at the bedside showing 'great love'.[8] Despite the best efforts of royal physician, Sir Theodore Mayerne, the baby was 'cut down' the instant that 'it saw the light'.[9] The queen made a swift recovery and was soon full of strength and courage. Orders were sent to cancel the services of the midwife, who was tending to Henrietta's sister, Christine of Piedmont, but nobody dared tell Christine the sad news until after her own delivery.[10]

Though baby Charles's life spanned only two hours, it was enough to be immortalised in an epitaph.

> Long wish'd, then born, he had scarce cried,
> But he despis'd the times, and died;
> Whom Heav'n but show'd to th' age's scorn,
> And then resum'd ere hardly born.[11]

Parliament was also to end prematurely. When Charles sent orders for an adjournment, on 2 March 1629, a small band of MPs received the news with incredulity. As the Speaker read the royal order, they cried out and pinned the man in his seat. The doors were locked. Resolutions relating to religion and taxation were yelled out and voted on, while from outside, the House of Lords usher, sent by the king, was refused entry. This moment of opposition is replicated today at every state opening of Parliament, with Black Rod refused admittance to the House of Commons. It is a symbol of the balance of power between monarchy and Parliament. To King Charles, however, this was 'undutiful and seditious'. Visiting the House of Lords on 10 March, the king dissolved Parliament, unwilling to condone the behaviour of the nine MPs at the heart of the action. Having decided not to call the unruly House of Commons to him, for fear of another scene, Charles spoke only to peers. He exonerated them from his outrage, and recognised that the tumult was sparked only by 'some few Vipers'. Considering the Duke of Buckingham had been their previous target, Charles now judged that the duke 'was not alone the Mark these Men shot at'. This was personal.[12]

In August 1629, Henrietta repaired to Tunbridge to take the waters, but finding that she could not bear the king's absence, she came 'suddenly' to meet him at Oatlands Palace.[13] Six months later her pregnancy was announced. For a second time the midwife, Madam Peronne, was summoned, but her trip would not be plain sailing. Amongst the small gathering despatched to collect her was Jeffrey Hudson, Henrietta's dwarf, and 'a perfect imperfection of nature' much beloved by her.[14] News that the party had been captured by Dunkirk pirates caused as much uproar in Charles's court as if they had lost an entire fleet. Thankfully the prisoners were soon released, and just after midday on 29 May 1630, the queen gave birth to a healthy boy at St James's Palace.

With his 'desires fulfilled and the succession established', Charles was overjoyed.[15] He declared the boy a principal means of securing the peace and prosperity of his kingdoms. As the king went to St Paul's to thank God for the safe delivery, a star could be seen in the sky above. There was uncertainty over whether it was Mercury or Venus, though considering the future Charles II, the latter was more apt.

Henrietta's sister Christine had just become Duchess of Savoy, a state with whom the Stuarts had a long-standing friendship. Charles was equally attached to her husband, Victor Amadeus, and wrote to him that day of the 'happiness' sent by God in the form of a 'beautiful son'. He invited Victor to 'rejoice' in the news.[16] Madam Peronne was awarded £300 and a further £100 was given for the relief of the poor and plague stricken. It was on account of the pestilence that the christening was hastened, and though contrary to his marriage treaty, Charles had his son baptised a Protestant. The terms had been so spectacularly broken that it no longer mattered. Nor did Henrietta protest.

On Sunday 27 June, in the chapel at St James's Palace, a silver font was placed on a stage. Guests gathered around it, including the Lord Mayor of

London in his velvet robes, flanked by scarlet-clad aldermen. At 5.00 pm William Laud christened the child Charles. After the ceremony, the font was transferred to the Tower for safe keeping, where it attracted crowds of sightseers. The king and queen went often to see their handsome and lusty son, who nurses alleged 'never clenched his fists' but instead kept his hands open, auguring well as a sign of great liberality.[17]

> When private men get sons, they get a spoon,
> Without eclipse, or any star at noon.
> When Kings get sons, they get withal supplies,
> And succours far beyond subsidies.[18]

As long as Parliament went uncalled, money remained a problem for Charles, but the birth did bring infinitely more security. The death of his firstborn had caused all eyes to be 'firmly fixed' on his sister and her 'progeny'. His people were said to have clamoured for her.[19] But the birth of a second Charles pushed the Palatines down the line of succession and lessened their influence. When Frederick died in 1632, Charles felt secure enough to invite Elizabeth to settle in England. 'I entreat you to make as much haste as you conveniently can to come to me'.[20] By confirming the succession, Charles – who, as a baby, had not been expected to live – now fulfilled one of the greatest expectations upon him. God had demonstrably favoured his monarchy.

Chapter 16

Some Few Vipers

The 1628 Parliament had brought two men to the fore. Sir Thomas Wentworth and Sir John Eliot both spoke out against granting royal subsidies until Parliament was 'secured against our liberties'.[1] By May 1629, Wentworth, who held the 'greatest sway', had moderated his stance to advocate a middle course.[2] Eliot, however, remained opposed to giving the king a penny.

Wentworth had never truly been against the king, even when at loggerheads with the government. The wary monarch, however, had excluded him from the 1626 Parliament by making him a sheriff. Then, after refusing to contribute to forced loans, which Charles was employing as a means of raising revenue, he was imprisoned for a short time. Blunt and impatient, he was his own worst enemy. Even while soliciting aid from friends at court, he made a speech criticising his dismissal and vowing to 'wipe [the dishonour] away as openly'.[3]

Wentworth's eventual moderation led to Charles being granted Tonnage and Poundage for one year only, held like a king on probation. Nevertheless, it was a big step forward, leading to Wentworth's ennoblement as Baron of Wentworth Woodhouse and his appointment as Lord President of the Council of the North. Proving extremely efficient, he rapidly gained a viscountcy and was admitted to the Privy Council in December 1629.

By comparison, Sir John Eliot remained languishing in the Tower. Charles was notably prepared to forgive even his bitterest enemies, clemency being, he considered, a trump card in managing opponents and an integral part of majesty. But John Eliot was a most spectacular exception. The man was Parliament's 'ringleader' and the 'greatest offender' of the last seditious session.[4] More unforgivably, he had taken a lead role in Buckingham's demise, thus betraying his former friend. Though able to receive visitors, publish writings, study Virgil and play bowls, Eliot's freedom would never be granted. At his accession, Charles could never have imagined the stance Parliament would take with him. Having been constricted as a child by debilitating health, then controlled by his father, when he reached the pinnacle of power, he found himself restricted from exercising it. Parliament's attacks had become personal, unprecedented and humiliating.

As Eliot sickened with a persistent cough, he petitioned for release. Charles refused on the grounds it was not humble enough. When the revised document was submitted via Eliot's son, the Lieutenant of the Tower objected, insisting that such business should go through him. At this point Eliot gave up. He summoned an artist to paint him in his last illness, and when he died the family petitioned for his body. The king's reply shows an uncharacteristic depth of vengeance; 'Let Sir John Eliot be buried in the parish where he died'.[5] Eliot's body, as commanded, was laid to rest in the church of St Peter Ad-Vincula at the heart of the Tower. Even in death, he could not escape the bleak prison. To the executors of his will, Eliot left mourning rings engraved with the words 'Amore et Confidentia' or love and confidence.[6] Buckingham's murder had transformed the duke into a martyr in the king's eyes, and now the monarch gave Parliament their own.

Eliot departed this life on 27 November 1632. That same year, Wentworth was appointed Lord Deputy of Ireland. The strong character made friends and influenced until he became a force equal to any on the royal council. He formed a close tie with Bishop Laud and their watchword was 'thorough' – more ordered and effective government where personal motives were laid aside for the good of the state.[7]

As an uneasy calm settled across England, Charles's attention turned to his Scottish coronation. It had been pushed back year after year, not from lethargy, but lack of funds and political turmoil. Finally, on 11 May 1633, he practically retraced the journey he had made into England at the age of 3. It gave the king a chance to meet his people and their 'love and dutiful demonstrations' in every place made him 'most cheerful'.[8] He touched sufferers of scrofula to administer divine healing, but 'refused to hear' Puritan ministers. Worksop saw him feasted by the Earl of Exeter. From that house, where his love of the hunt had begun, he passed towards Grantham. Common people crowded around and he greeted them 'with a smiling countenance' and received their petitions.[9] A novel welcome beckoned at Richmond, where a woman was introduced who had given birth to quadruplets, and Charles gifted her 1 pound per baby.

Lord Deputy Wentworth was departing for Ireland when, on 15 June, the king reached Edinburgh. At Holyrood he was crowned in an elaborate ceremony. The bishops, including William Laud of London, wore glittering golden copes and there was prolific kneeling before altars and crucifixes – even by the king, which was unscripted. Such practices, deemed Popish, generated a wave of suspicion, but to the blinkered Laud, he 'never saw more expressions of joy'.[10] An English official had sent the length, breadth, and height of St Paul's Cathedral, so that Laud could assert dominance through some steeple measuring. At 520 feet, the archbishop was confident he would not find 'any such church in Scotland'.[11]

For the king, the coronation was an intensely devout and serious moment that he cherished and was a sign of his overriding attachment to the Church of England. A medal was struck featuring his crowned profile on one side and a 'growing thissell' on the obverse. Charles kept it on his person as a memento, or perhaps a lucky charm, and it was later inventoried as 'much worne in [your majesty's] pockett'. Another gold companion piece, employed in the same manner, portrayed him on horseback with the sun 'shineing over london'.[12]

When the Scottish Parliament gathered, the king attended every session, hoping to win support and align the Scottish Kirk to that of England, which his father had begun. As a first step, he used the royal prerogative to regulate ecclesiastical vestments, but this threatened to set a precedent that reform could be furthered at his will. Lord Balmerino, who led opposition, was arrested and the unfortunate man looked set to become a Scottish John Eliot. Imprisoned for nearly one year, he was left under the shadow of a death sentence. Luckily for Balmerino, his French wife petitioned the queen, hoping that their shared nativity might 'move her to more pity'.[13] Henrietta's intercession had the desired effect, but the matter damaged the royal reputation.

With his subjects north of the border, the king was equally as popular. As the royal progress continued to Linlithgow, Secretary Coke remarked how 'considerable' the king is held with 'his people everywhere'.[14] Charles visited Stirling and his birthplace of Dunfermline. As a robust and athletic 32-year-old, his childhood must have seemed like a lifetime ago. In England, Henrietta was a 'perfect mourning turtle' contented by her husband's 'frequent remembrances' and the fact that she was pregnant again.[15] As his visit came to a close, Charles was eager to return to his wife and, intending to surprise her, left his followers at Berwick and rode on ahead. The journey of 360 miles took just four days. Two weeks later, while on a summer progress, Henrietta returned to London indisposed. Charles galloped from Woodstock to the capital, and for three days he engaged in prayers for the pregnancy's happy progress, refusing to stir out of town until, on 14 October 1633, James, Duke of York, was born.

Between 1629 and 1641, there was no Parliament in England and during these eleven years the king introduced a raft of reforms, starting with his own court. The ceremony of the Order of the Garter, as well as divine services for touching scrofula sufferers, were both made more formal. Duelling was forbidden and the wearing of boots was banned from the presence chamber, while nobody under the rank of baron could approach the inner closet. At the height of his reign, the king was in the 'full flower of robust vigour'. Well-proportioned and strong, despite being just over 5-foot tall, he was described as 'more disposed to melancholy than joviality' and entertained a dislike of 'immoderate appetites or unruly affections'.[16] His deep love for the queen was such that there was not the 'remotest approach' to anything that might cause her jealousy, despite differences in religion.

While Catholics and Protestants battled it out in Europe – 20,000 people were killed at Magdeburg alone – the Church of England seemed an effective middle way between the two religious extremes. Eager for closer religious alignment in his three kingdoms, Charles made a start with England. Churches should be beautified in a distinctly Armenian way to better reflect God's glory, and Lord Deputy Wentworth was in perfect agreement.

> Conformity in Religion with the Church of England, is no doubt deeply set in his Majesty's pious and prudent Heart ... But to attempt it before the Decays of the material Churches be repaired [and] an able Clergy be provided ... were, as a Man going to Warfare without Munition or Arms.[17]

In 1631, Charles launched a flagship appeal to restore St Paul's Cathedral, whose fabric was being allowed to 'fall to the ground'.[18] It was so close to the king's aspirations that when a tenant of the cathedral refused to contribute, he gave a personal order not to renew her lease. Rather aptly, on St George's Day 1634, he explained the fund's aim was for the 'honour of the kingdom'.[19] When accusations spread that the king's zeal was pretended and the money would be spent elsewhere, he deemed it a slander to his princely thoughts and immediately donated £1,500 to repair the west end Slabs of black Irish marble 'six foote long at least' were ordered to form magnificent cathedral steps.[20]

Using the trip to Scotland as an opportunity to inspect churches along the way, Charles had doled out orders to local officials. Shocked at the houses constructed upon the walls of York Minster, he had stopped the practice, and one in the cross aisle was pulled down. No seating was to be set higher than the stalls in the choir, except for the archbishop's throne, to maintain 'ancyent Beauty'. At Durham, it had been a similar story over 'most unfitting' tenements in the graveyard.[21] As a serious-minded Defender of the Faith, church services were also tightened up to protect his subjects' spiritual welfare. Laud was instructed to reissue a declaration permitting Sunday sports after evening prayers, and maypoles were favoured, which was 'hardly digested by the Puritans' and stuck in their throats.[22]

It was not all bad. The small religious community at Little Gidding, near Huntingdon, received the royal seal of approval when Charles detoured to pay a visit on his way to Scotland. So impressed was he with the religious works the Ferrar family wrote and bound with care, that he returned in the summer of 1634. Borrowing a copy of *The Concordance,* he eventually returned it with an apology for the number of annotations added in his own hand, as was his wont. The notes were evidence of how Charles had taken 'such delight' in the book and perused it every day, and he commissioned them to make one for him. After one year, when the exquisite copy, wrought in gold, was presented to the king, he declared it 'not to be equalled'. The subject matter was, he judged, 'the richest of all treasures'. Professing himself to be greatly indebted to the Ferrar family, he promised that 'whatever is in my power, I shall at any time be ready to do for any of them'. A second commission covering the Kings of Judah and Israel and the Chronicles allowed the king to 'behold God's mercies and judgements: his punishing of evil princes, and rewarding the good'. It fitted Charles's aspirations to be a good king, rather than a great one.[23]

Bishops were the cornerstones of royal authority – Charles's enablers, who delivered his religious vision – and Bishop Juxon was even appointed Lord Treasurer in 1636. Once English church and state were 'united and knit together', they could defend one another.[24] During his troublesome Parliaments, the king had marshalled clerics to support him in the House of Lords. He drove them hard, expecting the same dedication to their duties as he gave to his. Bishop Goodman of Gloucester was told that lack of preferment was down to his record, therefore he must 'do the duty' of his place.[25] Archbishop Neile of York was a man after the king's heart, diligently attending to malpractices in his diocese, and in the margin of one of his lengthy reports, Charles annotated that 'neglect of punishing Puritans breedes Papists'.[26]

The king was no less strict with his ministers of state and 'so rattled' the Lord Keeper on one occasion that he became 'the most pliable Man' in England.[27] So equally precise was the king over his artwork, that the overworked keeper of his cabinet room, which housed much of his treasured items, was often left on tenterhooks. On one occasion, Charles and Abraham van der Doort entered the cabinet room and found one item out of its case. The king expressed concern and then commented with a note that van der Doort was one of the precious few with a key to the room. The Dutchman eventually committed suicide, reputedly so distressed at the thought that he may have misplaced one of the king's smaller pieces of art.

Though many spoke about Charles's infamous formality – his friend, Will Murray, once described the court as 'like the earth, naturally cold' – the king could also express great personal affection.[28] Such warmth was at the heart of his nature, though protocol meant that only those closest to him were likely to experience it. When an abscess the size of a 'Turkey Egg' grew in the Lord Treasurer's throat, oozing bloody water, Charles hurried to his bedside.[29] He gave comfort and hope of recovery, but the treasurer gradually choked to death. When the end approached, the king gave assurances that there would be no lack of assistance to the man's family and was deeply affected when he expired. At the funeral, Charles gathered the Knights of the Garter to mourn the passing of one of their number.

It was the same when the Earl of Carlisle fell seriously ill, and Charles stayed many hours with 'every sign of affection'.[30] Thoughtfulness was also shown to the bereaved; he cancelled entertainments upon the death of the Earl of Pembroke's son Lord Herbert. The young man's widow was Buckingham's daughter, Mary Villiers, who the king had raised like a second father. Lord Cottington complained that after his wife died 'in a whole Week [the king] never sent to take Notice of my loss'.[31] At this time, however, the king had suffered a serious fall from his horse at Newmarket and was wearing one arm in a scarf – or sling. The hurt Cottington expressed over this lapse suggests the omission was unusual, and that a degree of personal comfort was almost expected.

It fell to the meticulous William Laud, appointed Archbishop of Canterbury in 1633, to oversee religious policy. His friend, Wentworth, had once said that 'a Bishop above Fifty is fitter for his Ease than Labour'.[32] At the age of 60, with a hard-working and demanding monarch to contend with, a heaviness supposedly hung upon Laud at his appointment. It stemmed from apprehension that there was more expected of him 'than the Craziness of these Times will give me Leave to do'. Despite these private concerns, within months he was eager to settle the church 'whensoever the King shall think fit to do more than is done'.[33] The Venetian ambassador felt Laud was straining at the leash with a raft of anti-Puritan measures, and was only called to heel by the king who wished to bide his time.

Wentworth and Laud cared more for results than public approbation, and the prelate was even willing to go against the king if it was in the government's interests. On one occasion, he gave fellow councillors a tongue-lashing and marshalled them to oppose plans to enclose part of Oatlands Palace at a cost of £50,000. One of his tools was the dreaded Star Chamber, an ancient prerogative court that the Tudors had frequently utilised to reinforce their rule. Being 'star-chambered' was even a phrase for those who fell foul of it. As the 1630s progressed, and Wentworth continued to toil in Ireland, Laud was ideally placed at the king's ear. He took to bypassing the council and discussing business with the monarch in private, rapidly becoming esteemed 'above every one else in the realm'.[34]

Like Laud, there inhabited in Wentworth 'an infinite Zeal and Vigilance to serve my Master'.[35] Letters between Dublin and London reveal the relationship between Charles and his Lord Deputy. The king respected his 'assured friend', admiring the man's drive and ethos, yet was careful never to create a second Buckingham. Wentworth's 'free dealing' manner made for Charles's ease – if he needed an opinion, the Lord Deputy would readily give it.[36] Whereas other men had 'been faultie', he praised Wentworth's 'care and industrie'.[37] There was a depth of personal affection, such as when he wished Wentworth a 'good jurney this somer' and enquired after the man's poor health.

> I am sorrie to heare that ye have beene so sick, yet I hope that ye shall live to doe manie services, that nither you nor I have yet thought on.[38]

On the whole, day-to-day government of Ireland was left to Wentworth, keeping the king's hands suitably clean. There were exceptions, such as in 1638 when Charles stated, 'I can asseure you that ther is no intention to displace the poore laboring Tennants of Londonderry.'[39] When one earl came to Charles 'in a great fright' over the forfeiture of his Irish lands, the king quickly extricated himself from the compromising position. As a result, he requested details of the man's case from Wentworth 'that I may give him an answer to free my self from importunitie'.[40] But sometimes he would forget about promises made to suitors in a bid to escape them, excusing his memory to Wentworth over such 'Court-importunity'.[41]

After three years of viceregal rule, Wentworth prepared to visit England to give account of his achievements. Having been stayed for three weeks by easterly winds and a violent fit of the stone that laid him up for ten days, he finally kissed the king and queen's hands at Hampton Court on 12 June 1636. The following day he had a private audience with the king, assiduously recording it in a thirty-one-page letter. Humbling himself as much as he could, Wentworth gave a long account of Ireland's church, army, revenues, public laws and trade, demonstrating 'how much they were brought to the better'. The magic figure was that Ireland would be £96,450 better off due to his rule.

Very much impressed, Charles asked him to relay the report to the Privy Council, considering it a good way to 'sharpen the Edge of other Men's Endeavours in his Service'. When invited to speak before the group, Wentworth peremptorily began by suggesting the king might withdraw to save being 'wearied with the repetition'. Charles considered it 'worthy to be heard twice' and avoided being dismissed from his own session. As Wentworth recounted how the church in Ireland was now 'altogether conformable' to that of England 'in doctrine and government', it must have seemed like the Stuart dream was coming true.[42]

Two years earlier, Wentworth had made a bold request for an earldom. Considering it a foregone conclusion, he had even left a sealed document with his secretary which would reveal 'the Title, which I should with your Majesty's good Leave chuse'. Put off by this forwardness, Charles had responded 'for the present I grant it not', but made it equally clear that Wentworth's services had moved him more than any 'Eloquence or Importunity'.[43] Following the flying visit of 1636, Wentworth was disappointed for a second time, having expected this reward for his labours. Public opinion accorded him 'more credit and far more consideration' than reality, and as he commiserated with Laud over his neglect he returned to Ireland 'without any publick Mark of his Majesty's Favour'. An earldom clearly cost more than £96,450, but for Charles, Buckingham's demise was still etched in his memory.[44]

Wentworth knew that he was amassing enemies as fast as his financial savings, therefore public accolade was essential in making rivals 'less apt to undertake or trouble me'.[45] But no mark of favour could save Laud, who had already become a hate-figure in the eyes of the public. His dealings with just three opponents would cause him, and the king, irreparable damage.

Chapter 17

Monk, Rogue and Traitor

Three Puritans were pilloried at Westminster at the end of June 1637 after being condemned by Archbishop Laud in the Star Chamber. William Prynne, Henry Burton and John Bastwick had their ears cut. Spectators wept. Blood poured from each man and the crowd 'strewed' herbs and flowers before the trio.[1] The letters 'S.L.' for seditious libeller were branded on Prynne's cheeks for having published writings condemning both Laud and religious policy. Ear-cropping was not confined to Puritans – a Catholic called Pickering suffered the same fate after claiming the king was a papist at heart and all Protestants were devils.

At the other end of the capital, work continued on the restoration of St Paul's Cathedral, intended as a monument to the king's quest for beauty and order. For his opponents, it became a focal point for protest; libels were fastened to its gates condemning the archbishop, or 'Arch-Wolf'. While accompanying the king to Scotland in 1633, the Earl of Arundel had witnessed orders to restore reverence to Durham Cathedral. His prediction that the Scottish Kirk would 'not followe ye good example' was proved correct.[2]

By 1637, Charles's happy family of kingdoms looked harmonious, with Ireland obediently taking after England, the favourite. Attention therefore turned to Scotland. This had all come about by small steps. An unusually savvy Charles had made minor alterations to the liturgy in 1634, which were then replaced by a second change in 1636. The Archbishop of St Andrews and 'his Brethren' had even been given authority to stick to the first if they 'see apparent reason'.[3] But when the new 1637 prayer book was sent north to further align the Kirk, first readings of it ignited decades of resentment.

In Edinburgh, the Archbishop of St Andrews climbed a new stone altar in his cope to perform the liturgy. The congregation listened aghast. The ghosts of Catholicism, it seemed, were coming back to haunt them and they set upon the bishop, tearing off his offensive vestments. It was noted that women appeared most in the action, flinging their stools. As he fled outside, the prelate faced a hail of stones until the Earl of Roxborough took him into his coach and made a quick getaway. The entire kingdom erupted into violence with women and children even using 'teeth and nails' in protest.[4]

Charles was on his summer progress, hunting on the south coast. He and his courtiers were soaked in a downpour and the weather continued so extreme that 'scarce a room' in their house held back the rain.[5] When news of

Scotland's perfect storm reached him, the king remained steadfast, hoping that the tumults would pass over. To avoid feeding them, and stirring up revolution in England, the bad news was buried. In October, as the king suffered from 'a bile', advice from the Scottish Privy Council hardly helped his condition. They recommended he abandon the new prayer book and 'forbear the pressing of it' for three or four years.[6] Reasons were communicated via 60-year-old Robert Kerr, now ennobled as Earl of Ancram after nearly twenty-five years of service to the king. The influential Scot was a fitting intermediary.

A second attempt to impose the new prayer book failed as spectacularly as the first, and there matters languished. Instead, the king and queen attended the moonlit launch of a new flagship, the *Sovereign,* a name suggested by the Earl of Northumberland. Referring to it as 'the Great Ship', Charles had kept the dimensions a strict secret. A model of the vessel had been made for Prince Charles, 'completely rigged and gilded, and placed upon a carriage with wheels resembling the sea'. Much fun was had speeding up and down the long gallery at St James's Palace.[7] At 1,637 tons, the real vessel was equal to the year of its launch and with 144 guns and 11 anchors, it was said to be the largest and finest construction in England. This show of strength did not deter the Scots.

The words of his father must have haunted Charles. Within *Basilikon Doron* King James had blamed the Scottish reformation, with its sedition and instability, on a breach between monarch and Kirk. The Church of England, by comparison, was the bedrock of royal authority, and a model that father and son wished to replicate in Scotland. Though Charles's plans were unravelling with devastating speed, he did not permit the English Privy Council to discuss Scottish problems until October. Wentworth condemned this 'unhappy Principle of State' that confined Scottish and English business to their respective councils.[8]

The Scots began signing a national covenant against what was seen as Archbishop Laud's religious innovations. Protestants became 'suspicious' and Puritans 'desperate'.[9] From a Westminster tavern came another attack on the archbishop from closer to home; Archie Armstrong, jester to Kings James and Charles, 'railing' about the Archbishop of Canterbury, said, he was a 'Monk, a Rogue, and a Traitor'. Archie made it clear his attack was in relation to the Scottish business and was summarily dismissed from court.[10]

When the Lord Treasurer of Scotland visited London, he warned that if the 'book' was to be read, then an army of 40,000 must see it done. An army would also be needed to save the Archbishop of Canterbury, who was vilified everywhere. In council, an angry Charles led from the front by backing his prelate and declaring that everything happened from 'his motion alone'.[11] It was a noble, but short-sighted, act of loyalty. The prospect of a Buckingham-style clamour made the king 'very unsettled in his mind'.[12] Incorrectly dating a letter to Wentworth as 31 April 1638 was perhaps one small indication of how the tense days and weeks were growing longer.[13]

The purpose-built cabinet room in Whitehall Palace, which housed the king's prized collection of coins, medals, books and art, offered some solace. One day in 1638, when showing the 5-year-old Duke of York some of the treasures, father and son gravitated towards a set of three small paintings in black frames. At 7½ x 9½ inches, the first portrayed a prison with two prisoners chained at their legs, while the second, he gifted to James. Charles must have felt equally fettered by the spiralling situation. Yet, even at such a time as this, he read over and judged the script of a new play that was being proposed. *The King and the Subject* included a line 'Monies? We'll raise supplies what ways we please'. He annotated the line as 'too insolent, and to be changed' but the author, rather surprisingly, was not taken to task and Charles eventually gave the play the green light.[14] In reality, as far away as Lisbon, merchants were grumbling over Ship Money, claiming that Charles could not impose taxation on his subjects in 'forraine partes' without their consent.[15]

April saw a last-ditch mission of the Scottish Privy Council. The Duke of Lennox, in a speech to the king, warned of the road to ruin. The loss of his subjects' affections would be 'like to Christall glasses which once broken are hardly sett together againe'.[16] Stepping back from the brink, Charles confirmed he would abolish the new prayer book so long as the Scottish bishops remained in place. In the face of 400,000 signatories on the Covenant, it was an essential U-turn. What's more, those names included Scottish settlers in the north of Ireland. The contagion was spreading to Wentworth's shores.

On 23 May 1638, Wentworth was 'playing the Robin Hood' and chasing all the out-lying deer he could find. During this hunting extravaganza he was 'so damnably bitten with Midges' that his face was itchy and 'all mezled over'. Soon a swarm of panicked letters reached him from England. The Archbishop of Canterbury warned of 'extream ill' and, with a certain detachment, called upon God to 'bless his Majesty and the State'. The Scots were listing those who could bear arms and had counted 40,000 in Ulster alone. The Earl of Northumberland felt the English would be readier to join with the Scots, than to draw their swords in the king's service. The king, he warned, could only rely on £110,000 of credit and the magazines were 'totally unfurnished of Arms and all sorts of Ammunition'. As for Commanders, 'we have none, either for Advice or Execution'.[17]

Though Charles was resolved to 'not proceed in Rigour' against the rebels and offered mercy, Wentworth wanted Scotland's 'gallant Gospellers' to be thoroughly punished. He suggested fortifying Carlisle and Berwick, to 'pinch' Edinburgh, and then land 8,000 troops at Leith, who could ensure the prayer book was used 'without any altercation'. In October 1638, royal approval saw 500 soldiers secretly shipped to Carlisle under 'some other pretext'.[18] The king and Covenanters were heading to war over bishops.

Many closeted meetings with the Archbishop of Canterbury followed. The king was 'distressed at heart' and try as he might, he could not hide it. If anyone failed to read it in his face, the fact he indulged himself sparingly in hunting, tennis and pell-mell was a tell-tale sign.[19] As his go-between with the Scottish rebels, Charles chose the Marquis of Hamilton. Talks led to an offer of a synod to debate religious matters, which apart from refusing to sit in the king's name, predictably called for the abolition of bishops. Hatred ran deep and there were threats that women would 'beat out their brains' with stones.[20]

King James was said to have declared 'no bishops, no king'. Charles decided that the only thing left was to 'subdue the audacity'.[21] The Earl of Arundel, appointed Lord General of English forces, was ordered to raise 6,000 infantry and 1,000 cavalry. Burning doubts remained, as summed up by the Earl of Northumberland. There was:

> so much Want of Experience in those who manage this Business, and such Regards to private Ends, that I have little Hope to see any Design prosper that may tend to the publick Good, Honour or Safety of this Land.[22]

The king's resolution to march north with the army did much to stem antipathy. Keenly aware that his presence had a power of its own, Charles often led from the front, certain that he could turn events to his favour. Secretary of State, Sir Henry Vane, thought the king's person worth 20,000 men 'at a pinch'.[23] The king's intended journey north engaged the honour of all men – peers were commanded to meet at York, on horseback, in russet armour with gilded nails or studs and suitably armed servants. Though many sick notes arrived at the palace, some with money in lieu of presence, a good turnout ensued. Charles's determination and leadership galvanised a unity of purpose in England that had been deemed impossible. Scottish peers who had refused the Covenant were sent personal letters from the king thanking them for their loyalty. To ensure he looked every inch the divine monarch worth fighting for, £600 was assigned to the royal wardrobe and £10,000 sent ahead to York for soldiers' wages.

In Scotland, the Covenanters readied themselves with 'preaching, praying, and drilling'.[24] Pamphlets flew between Edinburgh and London in a war of words. Charles accused Covenanters of proceeding as if he were 'their sworn enemy' and that they sought to overthrow his royal power 'under false pretences of religion'.[25] It was a view backed by Wentworth, who thought it a universal conspiracy against the king and his English subjects.

When the day of his departure came, Charles left half his ordinary guard with the queen, from whom he parted very affectionately. He committed Henrietta to the Lord High Admiral's protection, calling her 'his jewel' and let it be known that in the event of his death, his wife should have £40,000 per annum.[26] A general census was taken of all French and Scottish persons in England as a precaution against any sudden disturbance, while a last offer of pardon was sent to the Covenanters.

Charles chose to move north on the anniversary of his accession. There was one man, however, who had no plans to go anywhere; Lord Brooke resolved to follow the king only if it was 'adjudged' he should by Parliament.[27] It was moved that Brooke should be apprehended, but Charles refused on account of the man's quality and would not alter his opinion. Like Brooke, many soldiers shared a reluctance to fight for the hated bishops, and those in Yorkshire and Durham demanded one month's pay first. At Boston, a woman presented the Earl of Lindsey with her husband's toe, excusing his presence on account of it.

When the king reached York, he met with loyal Scotsmen who had fled across the border. Robert Maxwell, first Earl of Nithsdale, was a close friend and had married a cousin of the Duke of Buckingham. Back in 1620, Charles had promised 'if I [live] I schall remember [your service] to your contentment'.[28] The vow was honoured when Charles gifted £10,000 from the exchequer of Ireland, much to the hard-working Wentworth's frustration. The money most likely went to improving Nithsdale's family seat at Caerlaverock Castle, but now, in the midst of civil conflict, it was attacked by the Covenanters. They dealt harder with Nithsdale than others due to his Catholicism and unswerving loyalty to the king.

Charles could sympathise with his friend; the Covenanters soon took his own house at Dalkeith after putting ladders to the stable walls and scrambling over. The issue wasn't so much the house but the contents, for the crown jewels of Scotland were seized amidst 'great Joy and Triumph' and reverently carried to Edinburgh. The castle then fell after a petard blew in the doors, barely three days after the Royalist governor had bragged he had six weeks' worth of victuals. The explosion was rapidly followed by 'the Peoples Acclamations'.[29] It was not all bad news, because the Earl of Essex occupied Berwick for the king, and on the west coast, Wentworth's 500 troops entered Carlisle.

Upon leaving York, Charles expressed thanks for the affection shown to him, comparing it to London, where he never found the like 'true Love'.[30] When he tore up a letter from the Earl of Argyll and vowed that he would have the man's head, some about him offered to kill any one of the rebel leaders. Apart from declining the offer out of hand, the king also refused to strike the first blow, but warned the Scots that if they came within 10 miles of the border, he would take it as an invasion. Joining his army in the Camp Royal, he stayed in his own pavilion but much time was spent at the head of his troops, riding 'all day from place to place', and on one occasion he 'wearied' two horses.[31] Better that he was out and about, for disorderly Royalists frequently shot stray bullets through their tents. The royal canvas was pierced on one occasion, as was that of the Earl of Westmoreland's brother three times.

Whitsuntide, 2 June 1639, was a hot day and the English infantry refreshed themselves by crossing the Tweed, while the cavalry advanced to Kelso where they spotted the Covenanters. Both sides fired off trumpeters, the Scots warning the English they had 'best to be gone'.[32] They readily agreed. Wentworth's advice had been proved correct once again:

> your Majesty hath no more to do this Summer, but to secure Berwick and Carlisle by strong Garrisons; to exercise your Army in the Knowledge of their Arms; prevent their Incursion into your Kingdom of England; and by all Means to avoid fighting this Year.[33]

Both sides only came together once more – in the tent of the English Lord General. The Earl of Arundel, with senior peers and ministers, hosted Covenanter leaders for talks. The Earls of Rothes, Loudoun, and Dunfermline (son of the king's former guardian), together with Sir William Douglas and Alexander Henderson, arrived at 10.00 am on 11 June 1639. The Scots, with their backs to the entrance of the tent, were surprised by the king's impromptu arrival without pomp or ceremony. Charles had come to clear himself of the notorious slander that he 'shut' his ears to the just complaints of his Scottish subjects, assuring them 'I never did, nor shall'.[34] Discussions continued for hours. A second session was scheduled and a truce agreed.

As part of the terms, all points of conflict were to be debated in Edinburgh. Charles hesitated at the border, considering whether he should attend in person to obtain the best outcome. The queen fretted with great impatience at the danger of such a move and with the council's backing, she successfully implored him to return to London. The cost of engaging the military machinery of England had been immense – it had whittled away the moderate royal reserves that had been painstakingly accumulated over the last ten years. No battle had been fought and a Covenanter-led Scottish Parliament simply ratified earlier resolutions against bishops. At a loss over what to do next, Charles turned to his last hope – Thomas Wentworth, who had advice aplenty.

> I am most confident we might and shall propound a Way to make [Ireland] considerably active to inforce those Gainsayers to due Obedience, and settle the publick Peace of all your Kingdoms.[35]

Chapter 18

Beggarly Nation

'Good Lord bless our King, and open his eyes.'

Covenanter Prayer

As the end of 1639 approached, the Venetian ambassador petitioned his master for relief from the English weather and London's noxious air. The capital's atmosphere was set to get a whole lot worse. After the king appealed to the Privy Council for advice, Wentworth, Laud and the Marquis of Hamilton recommended calling an English Parliament to provide funds for a second war with Scotland. Forced to conquer his 'repugnance', the king acquiesced.[1] Despite these serious doubts over letting the genie out of the bottle, and the decade-long gap between Parliaments, Charles had never entirely dispensed with the assembly, in his mind at least. They figured in plans for a new palace at Whitehall, drawn up that year by Inigo Jones, and were to be housed at the heart of the building.

Wentworth's arrival in England had seen his long-standing wish granted. Created Earl of Strafford and Lord Lieutenant of Ireland, all important affairs were said to derive their impetus from his 'prudent counsels'.[2] Deliriously happy, Strafford was cast into action. He returned to Ireland and summoned a Parliament there, which promptly voted the king £200,000 and sanctioned the levy of 8,000 soldiers. £10,000 was diverted from Irish revenues to buy arms and ammunition. The dog had been let off his leash.

Declaring to the king 'I shall chearfully venture this crazed Vessel of mine', Strafford made his opinions known with unbridled passion. Why had six local regiments been sent to hold Newcastle, he challenged, as this would burden Northumberland while the rest of the kingdom kept 'their Fingers warm in their Pockets'.[3] To Viscount Conway, Lieutenant General of the king's forces, he asked how the Scots had marched so long without one skirmish. Yorkshire's deputy lieutenants were 'foolish and so ingrate' and he threatened to give the leaders 'something to remember it by hereafter'.[4] Ten years after becoming a Privy Counsellor, Strafford felt indispensable.

For all that he was a man of the moment, Strafford held no military post. Nor was he well enough to do so, and this furious energy soon burnt him out. Despite suffering from a flux, he returned to England and attempted to make his way to London 'on short journeys' via a litter. The concerned king imposed a travel ban, urging the earl not to move until well enough to do so – but on that matter, Charles wrote, 'I must require you not to be your own judge'. Strafford's good health was necessary 'for us both'.[5]

With the English Parliament set to assemble on 13 April 1640, negotiations between king and Scots stalled. Both wished to see which way MPs would gravitate. As election results rolled in, headed by a series of opposition names, the king felt as isolated as the royal garrison of Edinburgh Castle, which was once again surrounded by Covenanter troops. As fortifications were thrown up around the Scottish capital, General Patrick Ruthven, within the castle, began firing upon them.

Intending to throw his own grenade amongst mustering MPs at Westminster, Charles readied his trump card. So confident was he, that an opening speech was barely given. The king merely warned that there was never a 'more great and weighty Cause to call his People together'. Scotland was distempered by 'Fluxes of factious and seditious Humours' and to demonstrate the fact, Charles produced a letter addressed to the French king. It was written by the Covenanters – 'our traitorous subjects' – to King Louis as their Sovereign.[6] The signatures and seals of the Earls of Rothes, Marr and Montrose, Lords Montgomery, Loudoun and General Leslie clung to the letter. The revelation had members transfixed. A large red spinel set in the king's crown had reputedly adorned Henry V's helmet during his war with the French. As Charles sat in state, he prepared for a battle royal with Covenanters and Puritans alike.

Some MPs called for grievances to be put aside in view of the danger 'at the Back Door'.[7] But John Pym disagreed. Nicknamed 'the ox' because of his relentless toil, the Puritan had powerful patrons and was rapidly identified as an opposition leader. Born in Somerset, sixteen years before the king, Pym summarised grievances as being innovation in religion and attacks on the liberties and privileges of Parliament. He proposed that the king's record over the last eleven years had 'disabled' MPs from granting financial supplies.[8] Characteristically, Charles attempted to personally resolve the impasse, calling all MPs to Whitehall Palace, where he sacrificially gave up Ship Money. Quoting the Irish Parliament as a loyal example to follow, he warned that a delay in voting subsidies was tantamount to denial. The Commons debated from 7.00 am to 6.00 pm without resolution.

Within the palace, Strafford urged the king to proceed with an offensive war, 'loose and absolved from the Rules of Government'. Parliament's behaviour justified this before God and man, and the army in Ireland was at his disposal.[9] Henrietta was in full agreement and, with spirit, pushed for the complete subjugation of the Scots. Dissolved after barely three weeks, the short parliamentary session cast long shadows. Placards immediately called for bishops to be expelled from the kingdom, while protestors named Laud and Strafford as enemies of the state. To the beat of a drum, a large mob – named by Laud the 'rascal riotous Multitude' – converged upon the archbishop's residence.[10] They proceeded to 'chase the foxes out of thair [holes]' and both ministers fled to the royal palace, whereupon the king doubled the guard.[11] Posters attached to the gates warned that royal authority was not sufficient to save the pair.

One Scot in London, Archibald Campbell of Glencarradale, observed the city was 'in a combustione'. Many Englishmen, he continued, shared a 'generall dislyke' of the king's proceedings.[12] This was the first serious disorder Charles had experienced and it shocked him, considering one of his divine duties was to unite. A few bad apples were one thing, but the love of his people was paramount. In this, and other mass public demonstrations, Charles put the safety of his family first, and as anarchy descended, he was seized with 'serious fears' about what this might lead to.[13] A handful of aldermen, incarcerated when the city had refused to loan £200,000, were now released and for good measure, persecution of Catholics was stepped up. These concessions had the desired effect.

July saw an array of tents spring up near the border as wary Covenanters began to gather. Strafford's health underwent a timely improvement and Charles seized the opportunity to make him Lieutenant General. In Edinburgh, General Ruthven, bolted up in the castle, fended off two mines and when served with a summons to surrender, he answered that he would rather 'sacrifice' himself and all his people. To prove his feisty determination, 'divers beeves' [beefs] were thrown over the castle walls to show that he had ample provisions.[14] The hard-drinking, gout-ridden commander, having proved his mettle, would go on to become Lord General of Charles's Civil War armies.

On 23 July 1640, within the Tudor palace of Oatlands, the king's latest child was privately christened. Henry was held at the font by his siblings, Princes Charles and James, and Princess Mary. Presided over as usual by Archbishop Laud, it made for a cosy family scene. Almost to the day, 100 years earlier, King Henry VIII had married his fifth wife, Catherine Howard, at the same palace. The spirit of the Tudor tyrant must have looked upon his successor with some scorn. Both men shared many similarities; youthfully athletic, with a love of the arts, they had grown up in the shadows of their older brothers, with controlling fathers who had sought to determine their brides. Both had been close to their mothers, and were not expected to be monarchs. But whereas Henry was vengeful and ruthless to the core, Charles was not. David Hume, an eighteenth-century philosopher called it a 'paradox in human affairs' that Henry was almost adored by contemporaries, while Charles with 'so much virtue' met with such a fatal catastrophe, to be thereafter pursued by 'falsehood and by obloquy'.[15]

Charles allowed the Covenanter leaders to come to London, despite his recent 'evidence' of their treason, and under his own roof they presented their demands, fermented opposition and undermined him. He listened patiently. Across England, many disaffected ministers urged congregations to use this opportunity to restore England's 'lost liberty' and praised the Scots to the skies as angels sent by God.[16] Henry, by comparison, would have hanged the Covenanters without a second thought, as he did the leaders of the Pilgrimage of Grace, a 1536 religious rebellion. Charles's flawed idealism simply encouraged opposition, emboldening dissenters and giving them an advantage over him. He failed to appreciate that some men did not share his own sacred beliefs and were prepared to double-cross him – in short, he did not possess the necessary character traits of a tyrant.

Days before his son's christening, he had written to his good friend the Earl of Nithsdale, who, in his Scottish home, was subject to 'daylie troubles and dangers'. Despite being stalled by a chronic lack of men and money, the delusional king nevertheless promised to come to his friend's aid.

> we shall take such order for your relief as shall testify how sensible we are of the good service you have done us.[17]

In August, emboldened Covenanters crossed into England, hoping to capitalise on the friendliness to their cause. The king was 'extraordinarily perturbed' and resolved to counter them, but the window of opportunity had slipped away many months earlier.[18] The trained bands refused to rally, while some of the fleet mutinied, and all across England protests sprang up over taxation. The Scots found little opposition and, mastering public relations, declared they intended no hurt to any except bishops and Catholics. Positioning themselves as liberators, they promised to bring about an English Parliament by force – the Covenanters were already aligned with English Puritans.

Reaching the River Tyne after 'marching on the hills', the Scots came in sight of the king's dispirited army in the valley below. Only the royal cavalry seemed ready for the coming conflict. The Scots placed artillery on the tower of Newburn church and other high points, leaving the Royalists so exposed that missiles 'bowled in' amongst them, causing great loss and confusion.[19] As the superior Scots waited for low tide – their cue for battle – the English infantry retreated in the face of the barrage. Leading reinforcements from York, Charles was saddened to learn of the calamity at Newburn Ford. Worse still, Newcastle surrendered without a struggle, turning the coalfields and their revenues over to his enemies.

General Alexander Leslie, the Scottish commander, attended a church service in Newcastle with four bareheaded men preceding him. He took up a seat 'in the same place his Majesty sat' the previous year.[20] There was a real fear in the royal council that 'Leslie the Great' might draw the English to the Covenant. The Scots attracted praise, promising not to restrict 'free traffic' of coal to Londoners and ordering their army not to steal 'the worth of a chicken' nor let their horses 'bite corn' without paying for it. The property of any Catholic or bishop, however, was fair fodder.[21]

Ignominious defeat turned Charles's thoughts to the Earl of Nithsdale, whose home was under siege in Scotland. Finally acknowledging that 'our affairs permit not to relieve you so soon as we had determined', the king sanctioned the noble's surrender. 'Take such conditions as you can get, whereby the lives and liberties of yourself, your family, and those that are with you may be preserved'.[22] Charles, though, had no intention of giving up and the Tower of London was earmarked as his last refuge. Inigo Jones had been drafted in to look at pumping water from an old well. The lead roof of the White Tower, riddled with holes from the test shots of nearby gunsmiths, had been patched up. The outlook was grim. The Earl of Northumberland, commanding north of the River Trent, feigned illness and never joined the king's army. The southern commander, the Earl of Arundel, was also sick. Though Strafford was designated as Northumberland's Lieutenant General, he was also indisposed and struggled to reach York. It was indicative of the king's dying fortunes.

When Strafford finally joined Charles, they proved a formidable double act. On home turf, the earl easily mastered the gentry of Yorkshire, accusing those who failed to open their purses as being 'worse than beasts'.[23] This forcefulness was balanced by the king's sacred presence. As Strafford slowly began to mobilise the north and the Irish, the king called a chapter of the Knights of the Garter and awarded Strafford the hallowed blue ribbon. But even the earl's herculean efforts could not change the king's fortunes, and Charles reluctantly called all peers of the realm to his northern capital for their advice.

Back in London, at 9.00 am on 16 September, the royal council assembled at Whitehall Palace. The Earl of Arundel proposed that the king should summon an English Parliament now, on his own initiative, rather than being forced into it later. The motion was supported; these men knew there was no alternative. To foreign correspondents, England had become 'useless' to the rest of the world and of 'no consideration'.[24]

On 24 September 1640, English peers met with the king at York. Charles rose to the occasion, as he so often did when backed into a corner. Swallowing his pride, he opened with a resolution to summon Parliament and posed three problems:

1. Maintenance of the royal army until parliamentary grants could be obtained.
2. Paying off mariners.
3. Means for setting out a winter fleet to guard coasts and shipping.

Speaking freely and graciously in a grave voice, Charles's performance drew much admiration. His 'familiar sweetness and ready delivery' provided many with hope and Secretary of State, Sir Henry Vane, felt he had never heard his master express himself better. Peers sent a delegation to treat with the City of London for a loan of £200,000 and for good measure, Charles let it be known that he would sell himself 'to his shirt' for the security of it, while the queen offered her jewels.[25] Now dealing with the lords of the realm, and their better credit, the city proved willing.

The Covenanters were driving a harder bargain. Charging £850 per day for the maintenance of their army, as a price for not living off the land, they nestled into Newcastle. Defences were upgraded and a stream of their blue-bonneted troops continued to flow into England, regardless of royal protests. A string of concessions was granted, including the release of Covenanter prisoners, and a promise not to refer to the Scots as 'rebels'. Archbishop Laud remarked with irony that the Scots desired to introduce their own innovations to the English church; the wheel had come full circle. For all this, the king behaved with perfect tact, but the queen felt certain such an approach would lead others to rebel without fear and secure advantages – even rewards – as a result.

By handing over all responsibility to peers, some of the strain was lifted from Charles's shoulders, and he expected the English Parliament to fall in line. Those imprisoned for refusing to contribute to the maintenance of his army were released to avoid a potential stumbling block. Quite tellingly, his patience gave way only when rumours spread that he had spoken reproachful words over a petition from the City of London. Such behaviour, he countered, was contrary to his 'mildness and sweet temper' and he took it 'much to heart'.[26]

During this crucial business, he was buoyed up by letters from his two eldest sons, the 10-year-old Prince of Wales and 6-year-old Duke of York. He also found the time to intervene in the care of Viscount Purbeck, the late Duke of Buckingham's brother, who was increasingly subject to 'distemper'.[27] The man suffered from poor mental health, and his marriage had crumbled decades earlier. Charles called for Purbeck to be kept from anything that might worsen his condition, specifically excess of wine and tobacco. Tending next to his nephew's cause, Charles despatched an honest message. Having already contributed a generous sum, he explained that further assistance was impossible. The young Elector Palatine would remark that the Protestant party in Germany was now likely to 'go to the pot'.[28] Charles's sister, Elizabeth, added her own voice to calls for a Parliament, writing that 'all true honnest hearts' wished it. Upset over the distractions of 'my own country', she kept a watchful eye on her pension.[29]

Charles arrived back in London at the end of October and, on 3 November, he opened his fifth Parliament with a distinct lack of outward show. Progressing by barge meant that Charles could not connect with his people and the majesty of his office was lessened, which could have influenced waverers. It was a fatal error considering everything was up for grabs and betrays a resigned acceptance of proceedings.

Archbishop Laud tried to insist that God – not the rebels – had put the idea of calling Parliament into the king's heart. Sitting on the throne, with the Prince of Wales holding the crown to his left, this was the king's chance to make a great speech, as he had done before peers in York. In the event, antipathy towards Parliament soured his better judgement. He asserted that matters would not have got this far 'had I been Believed' six months earlier and called for chastisement of the rebels. As his words fell flat, he attempted to inject patriotism by vowing to make England 'Glorious and Flourishing'.[30] It came too late. Following this ill-judged speech, he was, as usual, forced to climb down. In a second visit, which left him looking weaker than ever, he rescinded his words and apologised for referring to the Scots as rebels. His manner was effusive and submissive. There was good reason.

MPs' speeches condemned the lack of regular Parliaments, blaming this for all 'Mischiefs and Distempers'. Ship Money was branded destructive. Calls abounded for the dismissal of 'pernicious Counsellors' and 'disconscientious Divines', but the greatest vitriol was reserved for the Earl of Strafford, a 'grand Apostate to the Common-Wealth'.[31] It felt like a case of déjà vu. The Commons charged Strafford with treason and he was consigned to the Tower of London on their authority. MPs focussed on bringing every evil upon him.

Up until now, Charles had mistakenly assumed that the presence of the Scots on English soil would move Parliament to deal speedily with them. In the face of this avalanche of opposition, he called upon MPs not to allow innocents to perish and released the Bishop of Lincoln, a long-standing critic, from the Tower. He hoped to encourage clemency, but MPs were not bought off and they continued 'vindicating private spite'.[32] Seizing this crisis with both hands, Parliament used it as a means of furthering long-desired reform.

Puritans took matters into their own hands and stoned Catholics leaving the queen's chapel. A printing press capitalised on public opinion and began churning out seditious and libellous tracts. Prynne, Bastwick and Burton, who had their ears cropped some years earlier, were paraded as martyrs. A delegation would also be sent to investigate the death of Sir John Eliot, viewing 'the rooms and places where he was imprisoned' in an attempt to blacken the king's reputation.[33]

By way of compensation, the Scots demanded £50,000 per year for fifteen years from the royal revenues, and called on the defences of Carlisle and Berwick to be dismantled – yet continued fortifying Newcastle. Their presence was the English Parliament's *raison d'être*. The Stuarts had failed to secure unity between England and Scotland, but opposition to the king was now doing just that.

With Charles preparing to weather the storm, others refused to go down with the ship. One of his Secretaries of State, Sir Francis Windebank, fled to France with royal blessing. Henrietta even promised to take the man into her care. Still considering his troubles to be temporary, the king did not replace Windebank and instead anticipated his return at a later date. But when Lord Keeper Finch, a one-time Speaker, bolted to Holland, Charles began to consider the threat to his wife. Approaches were made to France to see if they would host the queen on the pretext of illness.

Chapter 19

Intestine Divisions

'Laudless Will of Lambeth Strand,
And black Tom tyrant of Ireland,
Like fox and wolf did lurk,
With many a rooks and magdepies,
To pick out good king Charles his eyes,
And then be Pope and Turk'.[1]

Christmas 1640 brought little peace and goodwill. Venison was shipped to Whitehall Palace for rather hollow festive feasts, to the number of 104 does, but in Northampton, the king's deer were being unashamedly poached. When caught, the trespassers were brazenly unabashed, assuming that they would be 'pardoned by this Parliament'.[2] It was a sign of the times. From the highest to the lowest, the king himself was fair game to all. From the Tower, Strafford passed through all sorts of 'afflictions' but clinging to a belief in God and his own innocence, he felt able to 'look through this foul Weather'.[3] That month, the king and queen's 3-year-old daughter, Anne, died.

When Charles finally fought back, he did not pick his battle well and made issue of a priest who was due to be hanged. It was poor timing and an extremely minor point on which to stake his reputation. The royal pardon heralded a barrage of criticism from both Parliament and city, the latter threatening to withhold their loan over it. Strangled by his empty purse strings, Charles backed down, but implored MPs to grant mercy so as not to induce a 'like severity' on Protestants abroad.[4] The queen offered never to protect another Catholic, save those of her own household. Once again, the king weakened his position by taking an ill-planned and rash step, only to be forced to backtrack.

Feeling confident enough to shake off 'the yoke' of the monarchy, the House of Commons voted in favour of triennial Parliaments, which could thereafter assemble independently of the king every three years.[5] The House of Lords considered it a step too far, but was unable, and unwilling, to resist it. Charles followed suit and gave his assent with a frank speech. Commenting that MPs had so far dealt only with matters profitable to themselves, he ventured that they had 'taken the Government almost to pieces' and 'off the hinges' like a watchmaker dismantling a timepiece. If one pin was left out at the reassembling, he warned, 'the watch may be the worse and not the better'.[6]

Time had run out for the Earl of Strafford. In a bid to save him, Charles paid court to a posse of opposition peers – the Earls of Bedford, Essex and Hertford, and Viscounts Saye, Mandeville and Savile were all made Privy Councillors. MPs launched a bid to impeach Strafford on charges of treason, which would see his fellow lords become his judges.

The courtroom drama took place in Westminster Hall. The king's seat was screened off from the court, though he tore the latticework down and made his presence, and support for the accused, perfectly clear. He also consulted with Strafford in private. This all served to aggravate the prosecution, as did Strafford's very able defence. Many were prepared to see the earl sacrificed to save their own skins and petitions came in thick and fast, calling for justice. But no matter how much public opinion was mustered against him, it was not enough to find him guilty. Nor could a 'hundred ffellonies make a treason' Strafford argued, imploring those assembled not to wake up any 'sleepy lyons' in these proceedings.

> I had commission to make warr as I saw cause for punishinge the
> rebells and securing the publique peace. And therefore how can
> I bee charged wth that which I had power to doe?

Certain that treason could never be pinned on him, and that nobles and bishops might fear the precedent of condemning one of their own, Strafford was secretly confident: 'I do with all chearefullness in the world submitt my selfe unto you [the lords] thinking that I have greate cause to give god thankes that I have you for my Judges'.[7] Grey-haired, prematurely aged and unable to stand, he cut a sympathetic sight, and upon finishing his long speech of defence, he broke down and wept. Yet, many of his enemies remained terrified of him even now. Mobs called for his head every day. The king sent to the Lord Mayor, calling on him to counter this tumultuary behaviour, but requested he keep this intervention secret.

The crux of the case against Strafford was an allegation that, at the height of the Scottish troubles, he had suggested the king use Irish soldiers to subdue 'this' kingdom. His accusers resolved that he had meant England. Strafford countered that he had referred to Scotland, specifically the Covenanter rebels. The evidence was minutes of a royal council meeting some years ago – a copy at that. The originals had been stolen from the desk of Secretary of State, Sir Henry Vane, by his own son, who transcribed and then delivered them to Parliament's leaders. The originals were promptly lost.

Called as a witness, the elder Vane stumbled over his words, deliberated and half-heartedly threw in his lot with the prosecution. Other delegates from the same council meeting condemned Vane's judgement. Lord Clare argued against it, asking what Vane and others had thought at the time. Strafford replied, 'If words spoken to friends, in familiar discourse, spoken in one's chamber, spoken at one's table, spoken in one's sick-bed … if these things shall be brought against a man as treason, this, under favour, takes away the comfort of all human society.'[8] Charles even sourced a written affidavit from Secretary Windebank in Paris that exonerated Strafford, but it was never needed.

The trial publicly collapsed when the Commons tried to amend charges to their benefit midway through proceedings. Much to their anger, peers then determined that Strafford could also add to his defence. As the court broke up, Charles and Strafford turned to one another and laughed. Doggedly continuing their attack, MPs introduced a Bill of Attainder to bring Strafford down. No evidence was needed – judicial murder could be carried out for the safety of the state, as long as the Houses of Commons and Lords passed it, and then royal assent was given.

On 16 April the Commons debated the Attainder. Strafford was accused of attempting to subvert ancient and fundamental laws, and introducing an arbitrary and tyrannical government. St Stephen's chamber had once been a royal chapel, but as its doors were locked in anticipation of the coming vote, Strafford's enemies needed no divine intervention. There were 204 who favoured death, while 59 bravely cast votes to save him. The latter were immediately named and shamed to the baying crowds that swarmed the city. The hot potato was passed to the House of Lords.

To stiffen faint hearts and force the issue, the City of London stopped the flow of money to English troops until Strafford paid the penalty. The fate of one man was causing a breach that threatened to break out in a 'terrible civil war' to the ruin of the monarchy and all those who intervene in it.[9] On St George's Day 1641, the king, considering his own honour to be intrinsically linked to Strafford, wrote to his fallen minister.

> I must lay by the thought of employing you hereafter in my affairs; yet I cannot satisfy myself in honour or conscience without assuring you (now in the midst of your troubles), that upon the word of a king you shall not suffer in life, honour, or fortune. This is but justice, and therefore a very mean reward from a master to so faithful and able a servant as you have showed yourself to be; yet it is as much as I conceive the present times will permit.[10]

On May Day, the king travelled to Parliament to plead for Strafford's life. He urged peers not to 'press upon my Conscience' by approving the Attainder, but then declared he could never consent to it.[11] The Lords had no intention of sacrificing themselves over Strafford – if the king would save him anyway, then why bother voting the Attainder down? In the event, only nine nobles rallied to Charles's call, while fifty-one condemned their colleague. The mobs now raced to Whitehall Palace.

As pressure mounted, news seeped into the besieged palace that the people were ready to 'secure' the royals. The din continued night and day. Charles and Henrietta were 'full of terror' and packed their bags, but when ready for flight a French minster arrived and argued against it.[12] There was no way out. A selection of bishops was summoned to provide advice, and the once-disgraced Bishop of Lincoln suggested a monarch had two consciences: one public and one private. It was argument enough to make the king consider the worst. With tears in his eyes, he eventually signed the death warrant, exclaiming that 'my Lord of Strafforde's Condition' was happier than his own.[13]

Even after consenting, Charles sent his son to Parliament with a call for Strafford's sentence to be remitted to life imprisonment. The wording was pitiful – calling for mercy, yet going on to say 'but if no less than his life can satisfy my people I must say *Fiat Justitia*'.[14] The postscript said it would be charitable to reprieve him until Saturday. Charles was a broken man with no fight left in him. To his dying day he never forgave himself.

The day before the sentence was to be carried out, he sent a last message to Strafford via the Primate of Ireland. 'If the King's own Life only were hazarded', he would never have approved the Bill. To have stood firm would have put the state in extreme danger, therefore Charles had to decide between his minister or people. Failing to keep his promise that Strafford would not suffer in life, honour or fortune, the most the king could manage was to make a new vow; that he would see his doomed minister's estate passed to the son. If that young man was to prove capable, Charles would 'take special Notice of him' for royal employment and preferment.[15] The latter fact would be revealed to nobody but the 15-year-old who, unsurprisingly, left England after his father's death.

On 12 May 1641, after refusing a blindfold and declaring that he took off his doublet as cheerfully 'as ever I did when I went to bed', Strafford was decapitated on Tower Hill.[16] Spectators were said to number 200,000. According to one diplomat, he deserved a better age and a happier fate, while Sir Henry Vane, after stabbing Strafford in the back, called on God to send a 'happy end' to the troubles.[17] In the aftermath of the execution, an eerie silence fell across London. At the Cross Keys Tavern, in the Strand, a group of men debated the day's momentous events and exchanged opinions as to Strafford's religion. One asserted that the earl had died an atheist, another a Puritan, and a third a Papist. A Mr Lambert expressed wonder over why the trio troubled themselves with the 'damned ffellow'. Finishing his wine, he avowed that as sure as the glass would break, so Strafford's soul was damned, and threw it across the room.

> it strooke against ye seeling or roofe of ye roome and fell against
> ye wall and so upon ye ffloore and broke not wch amazed
> Mr Lambert, & ye whole Company.[18]

Within the Wentworth papers is an undated prayer written by King Charles. It seems to have been penned at a time of intense difficulty, perhaps around the time of the Attainder or Scottish wars, and is worthy of being quoted in full.

> Gratius Father: The lyfe of a man being a Warfare upon Earthe, & his lyfe invaded with dyvers dangers; & none so obnoxious to those dangers, as those whom thou hast sett to keepe thy People from them. I humblie beseeche thee to assist me, in all the cource & passages of my lyfe espetiallie in my performing the dewtie of a King: Suffer no malice to hurt, no cunning to circumvent; no violence to oppresse; no falshood to betray me: I beseeche thee prevent what I cannot foresee; to maister what I cannot withstand; & to unmaske, & frustrat, what I doe not feare: that I may governe thy People to thy honor, ther saftie, & my comfort that being delivered from all dangers of soule & bodye, I may praise thee all my lyfe long, perceaving how happie a thing it is to make thee o'Lord of Hostes my helper against anye day of feare & troble. Grant this o'Lord.[19]

Archbishop Laud succinctly captured the king's response to the furore over Strafford's life. Charles was a 'mild and a gracious Prince, who knew not how to be, or be made great'.[20] It is further evidence of a chronic lack of ruthlessness in the monarch, coming from one who had first-hand experience. The king was usually perfectly clear in his ultimate desires, policies and aims, but frequently he proved too naïve, or even too nice to make the merciless decisions necessary to drive them through to delivery. This ensured the need for a single-minded and forceful enabler to plug the gap. Wentworth had proved the most able of them all, and this in Parliament's eyes, more than anything, necessitated his removal.

Chapter 20

Popish Hellhounds

Before the axe fell on Strafford's neck, Parliamentary leaders had considered how to protect their own. Though the king had agreed to triennial Parliaments, he could still proceed against opponents in one of his prerogative courts. For that reason, a Bill was passed to abolish the brutal Star Chamber – an 'intolerable burden' that could condemn any opposed to royal rule.[1]

Expecting immediate conformity from the king, Parliament was 'much discontented' at delays over royal assent. Charles, for his part, found this impatience 'strange' and replied that he would take a few days to digest the details. If MPs considered all he had so far sanctioned, he told them, then 'discontent will not sit in your Hearts'.[2] To safeguard Parliament's fundamental purpose, the king also agreed never to levy tax without its approval. The raft of revolutionary concessions began to balance the power between Westminster and Whitehall, but John Pym and his junto were far from finished.

During these difficulties, the king was conducting negotiations with Holland over a marriage between his daughter, Mary, and the eldest son of the Prince of Orange. The Dutch had previously given tacit support to the Covenanters, so a wedding promised the king a useful union. Princess Mary showed 'little pleasure' for the match.[3] Neither did the Spanish, who had expected her hand, therefore a Protestant match played in the king's favour.

While Strafford's fate was being contested, 14-year-old Prince William arrived in London where he and Mary 'sealed their affection' with a pre-wedding kiss.[4] As well as contending with Parliament, the king had to deal with a rupture in the family. His nephew, the Elector Palatine, had also arrived to drum up Parliamentary support for reclaiming his lands in the Palatinate and, more embarrassingly, made a rival claim to his cousin Mary's hand. It appeared the king could not even control his own kin, never mind his kingdom, for Charles Louis had not sought approval before making his trip. Nor was it a good time to host one who might be seen as an alternative monarch.

Prince William remained in England for thirty-six days, during which he duly married Mary. At his departure, 280 pairs of sheets, used by him and his entourage, were gathered up and cleaned by an army of washerwomen. Within weeks, more dirty linen would be aired in public after a plot was discovered. The king had bided his time and many moderates began gravitating towards him. Never one to give up on a good cause, nor abandon hope, Charles now undermined this growing goodwill through tacit involvement in a hare-brained plot.

The English army in the north was to have seized the capital and released Strafford, with the French called upon for further support. As more details were revealed, several courtiers linked to the queen fled to the continent. This was taken as evidence of guilt. Henrietta was said to have been at the heart of it, determined not to 'suffer meekly' while royal authority was pulled to pieces.[5] Henry Percy, George Goring and Henry Jermyn were the leaders; no worse men could have been chosen. Percy wrote to his brother, the Earl of Northumberland, with the 'basest and foolishest confession' in order to save his skin.[6] Goring spilled more details when examined by MPs, deposing that the Prince of Wales and his Governor, the Earl of Newcastle, were to have joined the soldiers. Goring escaped conviction by sparing neither person nor circumstance in his confession.

The king and queen, though unaware of the finer details, had most likely sanctioned the plot, which handed Parliament a vital propaganda victory just when their cause was beginning to flag. Small wonder that when Charles indicated his wish to go to Scotland and ratify the peace treaty, which would take him past the English army, Parliament strongly objected. With blame for the plot tagged to Henrietta and an escalation in attacks on Catholics, it was announced that she would depart for Spa (in modern-day Belgium) to take the waters. She would also deliver Mary to her new husband in Holland. The plan met with immediate condemnation, and at first the queen battled MPs, confirming she was willing to obey her husband, but not '400 of his subjects'.[7] When they suggested a review of her revenues and a hand-picked guard to protect her person, Henrietta changed her tune, graciously notifying them that she would put her health aside for their contentment.

Edward Nicholas, a clerk of the council, wrote that there was nothing that gave any rational and moderate man hope for the future. Henrietta believed that unless steps were taken to reverse the decline, Charles risked losing his liberty as well as his crown. The king, however, clung to hope that his presence in Scotland would transform all and the aptly named *Bonaventure* set sail for Scotland with his personal effects.

The Parliamentary leadership orchestrated a series of protests, one of which mobilised 20,000 protestors, and MPs even sat on Sunday 8 August to debate matters, but warned that nobody else should neglect the Lord's Day. A distracted Charles was equally 'troubled with business' and after being pressed to confer a knighthood, he granted the honour to the wrong man.[8] Then, intending to leave for Scotland at 4.00 am, he did not go to bed the preceding evening, only for MPs to scupper plans by summoning him to Westminster. Running on adrenaline, the tired monarch arrived at Parliament at 10.00 am sharp and was met by 400 protestors calling on him to stay. Side-stepping them with feigned gratification that his presence was so much desired, he concluded his work within an hour and then headed north.

Travelling with him was his nephew, the Elector Palatine. They passed the English army without incident and stopped at Newcastle to meet the Scots who presented themselves in a 'posture full of obedience'. Their commander, General Alexander Leslie, gave the monarch 'gallant entertainment' and hosted a dinner in his honour.[9] Such displays fed Charles's belief – with some justification – in the power of his presence and ability to transcend political boundaries. A rapturous welcome was repeated in Edinburgh. Acclamations were doubled when he took prayers according to the form of the Scottish church. It was a major concession, and an intensely personal one too, which surprised everyone. Speaking of 'Love to My Native Country', his visit was turned into a homecoming. Every morning he left Holyrood and travelled to the Parliament House: 'I need not tell you ... what Difficulties I have passed through and overcome, to be here at this present'.[10]

Charles's care and diligence ensured no time was lost and his afternoons were spent in 'continual agitation' directing and overseeing all affairs. On 31 August, the king was feasted by the Provost of Edinburgh and as glasses went liberally about, many people drank to the health of the royal family. The revelling was like 'a day of jubilee'.[11] Both former rebels and the king's trusted ministers celebrated together. Outwardly, they prayed for it too. In the royal presence chamber, Charles heard two sermons every Sunday, as well as weekday lectures. The Covenanter minister, Alexander Henderson, was in great favour and stood by the royal chair throughout. On one occasion, derogatory words were used to condemn bishops, yet Charles did not flinch. Capitalising on this royal goodwill, the Scots requested permission to henceforth choose their own ministers of state and Charles reluctantly agreed, going further still by making Argyll a marquis and Leslie an earl.

One of the king's trusted bedchamber staff observed how the monarch was caught between a rock and a hard place. Leading Scots 'knew how to handle him', having on their side the Marquis of Hamilton, the king's 'bosom friend' (so termed as in the manner of Brutus and Caesar).[12] Charles's tactic of gaining popular opinion was a double-edged sword. Just as the royal phoenix began to rise, it was shot from the sky. Worse still, it was a case of friendly fire.

In mid-October a plot was discovered. Details were sketchy, but the crux was that the Covenanter's political leader, the Earl of Argyll, was to have been abducted or murdered. Charles's friend, the Marquis of Hamilton, was intended as a second victim. Details of 'The Incident' did not add up. It was betrayed by John Urry, a soldier who would go on to become infamous for turning coat in the Civil War, and the trust Charles had worked so hard to foster was now in danger of being lost. The king, accompanied by 500 gentlemen, processed to Parliament on 14 October to discuss these serious matters. Hamilton and Argyll fled the city, and taking this personally, as if they mistrusted him, Charles was incensed. He protested that the plot was a design to cause 'division' between him and his people, but like the Army Plot in England, it is likely he had permitted it while remaining ignorant of the detail.[13]

At the start of November, news broke of a great revolt in Ireland. Catholics had risen up on 23 October and attempted to seize strongpoints like Dublin. Many Protestant settlers were massacred and horrific woodcuts circulated showing images of children skewered on the ends of pikestaffs. Blame was once again apportioned to Henrietta, and realising the impending calamity, Charles was impatient to learn more.

Edward Nicholas, clerk of the council, expected the Irish rebellion to cost many men's lives 'before it be quieted'. The slightest rumour was enough to cause mass panic. Catholics were termed 'Popish hellhounds' and Strafford was blamed for being too lenient on them in his lifetime.[14] In reality, now freed from his oppressive rule, the native Irish seized their chance, fearful of the increasing power of English Puritans.

Returning to London, Charles was advised to make a formal entry into the capital and 'shew yourself grac'ous to yor people'. Furthermore, if he should 'speake a few good words' to officials, it would 'gaine [affections] especially of ye vulgar'.[15] One London MP tried in vain to block the event, and for once King Charles scored a victory over 'King Pim' (John Pym).

On 25 November 1641, the king met the Lord Mayor and officials, who were dressed in scarlet with golden chains, while sheriffs sported silver-laced hats. Amidst a fanfare of trumpets, he stepped out of the royal carriage and mounted a horse to 'show himself better' to his subjects.[16] The Prince of Wales followed this example, while the queen, Duke of York and princesses, together with the Elector Palatine, accompanied the cavalcade. Railed-off streets were packed with spectators whom the king 'courteously saluted ... by the often puting off his Hat'.[17] It was a gesture aimed at everyone, no matter their status, which proved a huge success. He had even been known to doff his crown in a similar manner when processing through Parliament.

The Lord Mayor and Recorder of London were both knighted. A speech tendered their hearts and affections, and Charles responded with a promise to maintain the true Protestant religion 'as it hath been Established in my two famous Predecessors times' with his life.[18] This timely statement was received with hearty acclamations. After a banquet at the Guildhall, he was escorted to the palace by torchlight, and passing St Paul's, where sackbuts and cornets played, the choir sang an anthem.

From within the shadows of Westminster, opposition MPs grumbled that they had overnight lost the people's backing. Many felt that a good balance of power had now been achieved and further encroaches on the king's position looked excessive. Pym and his supporters decided to seize back the initiative and cast discredit on the king by listing every outrage of royal government since his accession. Over 200 points of contention were laid out, covering the 'evils and corruption of sixteen years'.[19] The wide-ranging document was termed the 'Grand Remonstrance' and made numerous requirements of the king, from removing the voting rights of bishops, reforming the Church of England, and giving Parliament the power to select ministers of state.

When one MP spoke out against the Grand Remonstrance, he was sent to the Tower. After a heated twelve-hour sitting, MPs approved the document by a narrow margin of 11. Some considered that Pym and his friends were behaving like the tyrant king they condemned and a group of moderates formed the nucleus of a Royalist party. As the tide changed in Charles's favour, he simply put the Grand Remonstrance aside and promised to look at it in due course, busying himself instead with a cabinet reshuffle. Secretary of State and Treasurer of the Household, Sir Henry Vane, lost both offices. The king's sister, who nicknamed him 'vanely', was not sorry to see him go and attributed his fall to the queen, who 'doth governe of all the King's affayres'.[20] Vane, however, had blotted his copy book by stitching up Strafford at his trial. The void was filled by Edward Nicholas, a man respected by many for his diligence and modesty, and who was as surprised as any by his promotion to the post of Secretary of State. He had been the Duke of Buckingham's 'Honest Nicholas'.

The king's cousin, the Duke of Richmond and Lennox – who had married Buckingham's daughter – was appointed Lord Steward. But the greatest promotion was that of the Earl of Bristol as a Gentleman of the Bedchamber – the man who had suffered so much at Charles's hands over the Madrid fiasco. The move is evidence of Charles's belief that he could win back any man with clemency and patronage. Bristol's position was cemented after three of his nominees were adopted as Privy Councillors. His luckless son, George Digby, a favourite of the queen, was also earmarked for high office. The lawyer Edward Hyde and poet-peer Viscount Falkland, both of whom had once spoken out against royal courts, taxes and Strafford, were now giving first-class advice to Charles.

With Charles unwilling to roll over any longer, both sides came to loggerheads. Secretary Nicholas felt that if there was not a 'hearty and perfect union' between the king and his MPs, then they would all be confounded.[21] The Venetian ambassador was sceptical that a solution could be found 'without bloodshed'.[22] Capitalising on the support of moderates, Charles ordered over 200 MPs to return to Parliament in the New Year. The soldiers that Parliament had stationed about Westminster were dismissed, despite their protests that Catholics were 'lurking in the Suburbs'.[23] Instead, Charles ordered the loyal Earl of Dorset to take command of some trained bands and replace the previous troops. Falling back upon the Grand Remonstrance, desperate MPs now published it 'to the world' before the king had responded.[24] This was seen as an act of provocation, and Charles angrily responded that his opponents had no cause to complain, considering he had made more concessions than any of his predecessors. The king had his artist, Sir Anthony Van Dyck, buried in St Paul's Cathedral with an inscription that the man had made many sitters immortal through his work. Though Charles was confident that he could weather the political storm that had engulfed him, it seemed that the court of Van Dyck's canvasses was also dead.

On 22 December, the king received an early Christmas gift when the Lieutenant of the Tower resigned. His appointment of Sir Thomas Lunsford as a replacement, a man with a brutal reputation, caused a backlash. The Lord Mayor warned that apprentices were ready to storm the Tower, and though Charles quickly swapped Lunsford with Sir John Byron, protestors turned out anyway. Insults exchanged included the term 'roundhead', an early reference to Parliamentarians on account of the short hair that many sported. With his patience exhausted, Charles took drastic steps and called out the trained bands to suppress the disorder, permitting soldiers to shoot on those few who 'persist in their tumultuary and seditious ways' in order to protect the good majority.[25]

At this very moment, the king was also engaged in a struggle with Parliament over his wife and family. Word reached him that during his absence in Scotland, the Earl of Newport and John Pym had discussed proposals that the queen and Prince Charles should be secured and separated from one another. Despite Newport's denials, the king would not accept his excuses. Charles's sanction of desperate attempts to restore order, at the same time as these threats to his family arose, was no coincidence. His loved ones were the king's Achilles heel. Their safety would often prove the final straw and cause him to knee-jerk, or take extreme measures, perhaps even stirring fears within him that stemmed back to Buckingham's murder. He would not, at any cost, have his loved ones endangered in the same way.

Another appointment was John Williams, a Welshman, as Archbishop of York. He had been promoted from the See of Lincoln after a history of opposition, including numerous spells in gaol. Now, he found himself fighting on the front line in defence of royal government, and as a hated bishop he was beaten by the mob. After detaining some of his assailants, Westminster Abbey was stormed by protestors, who forced the doors and released their comrades. They then proceeded to pull down organs and the altar. From the House of Lords, the bishops counter-attacked, declaring that Parliament was not free on account of the intimidating mobs surrounding it. The very notion cast into doubt the validity of all votes passed against the king. Outraged MPs had all twelve prelates clapped up in the Tower.

In the last days of 1641, many were hurt in the chaos that overtook the city, but the wintry capital saw no hail of bullets. Matters had, however, reached their zenith. A letter was sent to the Royalist Vice-Admiral of England with the opinion that if the king did not comply with MPs, 'a sudden civil war' must ensue.[26]

Three days into January 1642, Sir Edward Herbert, the king's Attorney General, addressed peers in the House of Lords. Acting on royal orders, he accused six men of 'divers great and treasonable Designs and Practice'.[27] A mutter of discontent spread as Lord Mandeville, the long-faced heir of the Earl of Manchester, was named. A sergeant-at-arms made his way to the House of Commons to arrest five MPs: John Pym, Sir Arthur Hasselrig, John Hampden, William Strode and Denzil Holles. As the men's trunks and papers were sealed up, the house rang to cries of 'breach of privilege'. At the palace, the king was dismayed to hear that those accused had resisted arrest.

Things rapidly went from bad to worse. Reports that six pieces of ordnance had been brought into the city, and that several people of mean quality had begun to hoard arms and ammunition, led the king to order searches of houses. The loyal Lord Mayor doubled the watch, chains sealed off the streets, and firefighting equipment was prepared. The palace was 'thronged' with supportive gentlemen and army officers. In the afternoon, Charles appeared in their midst and declared, 'My most loyal subjects and soldiers, follow me.'[28]

Entering a private coach, a military escort accompanied him into the street where passage was hindered by vast crowds. A stray officer also slipped out of the palace, reaching Westminster well ahead of the king to tip off the six targets. The Countess of Carlisle, one of the queen's ladies, had also sent warning. When the king's cavalcade finally arrived, he had his soldiers wait in Westminster Hall and then entered the House of Commons, accompanied only by his nephew, the Elector Palatine. The king respectfully removed his hat. The seats of the five MPs were still warm as Charles asked the Speaker's leave to borrow his chair. Glancing around the hundreds of faces, he apologised for entering the chamber.

> no King that ever was in England, shall be more careful of your Privileges, to maintain them to the uttermost of his Power, than I shall be; yet you must know that in Cases of Treason, no Person hath a Privilege.

It was clear to the king that his 'Birds are flown' but all the same, he asked the Speaker of their whereabouts.[29] William Lenthall was a quiet man who had tried to give up the job one month earlier, claiming that it 'exhausted the labours'.[30] He now fell to his knees.

> I Have neither Eyes to see, nor Tongue to speak in this Place, but as the House is pleased to direct me, whose Servant I am here.[31]

A scribe's scratching quill noted all that passed. Once again, Char[les] humiliated, but worse still, publicly and personally so. After lea[ving] chamber empty-handed, his opponents successfully portrayed his actions as the behaviour of a tyrant. It was certainly a misjudged move. That evening, the king summoned John Rushworth, clerk of the Commons, and asked him to write out a transcript of what had been said. Rushworth nervously cited the experience of another man, who had been incarcerated after recounting the words of MPs that were not to the king's liking. An exasperated Charles clarified that he asked only what 'I said my self' and remained with Rushworth until the job was done. The documented speech was sent to the printers.

Next day, the king set off in his coach again, this time to the Guildhall. Symbolic of the worsening situation, an ironmonger managed to throw a paper through the window of the carriage, bearing the words 'to your Tents, O'Israel'. Before the Common Council, the king declared his missing traitors were 'Shrowded' within London. He also addressed rumours that he was a Catholic sympathiser, if not a convert himself, by assuring the men that he would prosecute all who opposed the laws and statutes of the kingdom, whether 'Papists or Separatists'. With his life, he would maintain and defend that 'true Protestant Religion which my Father did profess'.[32]

After concluding, he began private discourse with some aldermen, but was interrupted by repeated cries for 'Privileges of Parliament'. These voices were countered by exclamations of 'God bless the King'. Silence was called for and Charles asked if anyone wanted to speak. One man told him to take his Parliament's advice. In reply, the king countered that he already did, and would continue to do so, though there was a distinction between that body and a few traitors within it. As opposition began again, Charles calmly asserted that 'no privileges' can protect a traitor from a legal trial.[33] It is significant to note that the king was willing to engage with protestors on such a level and that no arrests were recorded as a result.

As the days passed, royal heralds made proclamations against the harbouring of the six men, but the trumpet rasps were lost in the uproar. Parliament blamed the king's behaviour on his wife, who they alleged was conspiring against the 'public liberty'.[34] The image of a Catholic she-wolf in the king's bed was designed to discredit the king and provoke fear. For Charles, it created a fear that she would be targeted in the same way as Buckingham and Strafford. On 8 January he sent orders that his ship, *Bonaventure*, should upon the 'first opportunity of winde' head for Portsmouth and await further orders.[35] The intention was that the vessel might spirit his endangered wife out of the kingdom. On the evening of 10 January 1642, with violence threatening to erupt, Charles took Henrietta and their three eldest children, and fled the capital.

Hampton Court had not been prepared for the royal family's arrival, and they all huddled together in one bed for warmth. As dawn broke over London, the six Parliamentarians came out of hiding and processed to Westminster.

Celebrations were on a par with the welcome the king had received on his return from Scotland. Ships filled the Thames, apprentices lined the streets with supportive placards, and applauding crowds vowed to protect the heroes. The Puritan Earl of Essex was chosen as Parliament's ambassador and sent to search out the king. Concerned that Hampton Court was not safe enough, the royals moved on to Windsor Castle.

During this gravest crisis so far, Charles found solace in his family. Endymion Porter, a Groom of the Bedchamber, observed and remarked 'I envy their happiness'.[36] The king did not know what to do for the best, but was not at this stage shaken by events. Dismissing offers of mediation from the ambassadors of France and Holland, he also turned a deaf ear to his nephew, the Elector Palatine, who clung to his side like a limpet. Whereas Charles Louis urged a reconciliation with Parliament to better serve his own ends, Henrietta 'would not heere of it' for fear of dishonourable conditions.[37]

Displaying courage in the face of adversity, the idealist Charles dealt with matters as trivial as the order of precedence between two Scottish earls. Failing to grasp the seriousness of events, he remained fully intent upon returning to the capital once calm and common sense prevailed. There was no realisation that he had just lost London. But first, he decided to carry out his earlier intention and send Henrietta to safety by arranging for her to take Princess Mary to Holland. On the day that Charles's royal barge sailed out of the capital, the Dutch Prince of Orange wrote a letter to the king and queen. Giving assurances that their daughter would be treated with honour and respect befitting a princess of such 'high and eminent birth', he had no idea how much the standing of British royalty had fallen.[38]

The prospect of parting from Henrietta, who Charles loved 'beyond expression', as well as his eldest daughter, was said to be a cause of suffering to him. The family travelled by way of Greenwich and Canterbury to Dover. En route, the king parted with yet another prerogative power when he assented to the removal of bishops from Parliament, losing their loyal votes in the process. This he did to 'make it plain' that his wife was no obstacle to the gratification of his subjects. It was another decision where defence of Henrietta was a deciding factor.[39]

Beneath the shadow of Dover Castle, where he had first met his wife, Charles now prepared to leave her and did not know how to 'tear himself away'. Unable to restrain their tears, the couple engaged in 'sweet discourse' and affectionate embraces, and he watched her ship until it vanished over the horizon.[40] Henrietta's absence was optimistically anticipated to be two weeks at most, but it was to be one year before she saw England again. Lonely and deeply moved, Charles was now devoid of his greatest support, but for a moment, he came face to face with one who would fight for him as fiercely as the queen. The king's nephew, Prince Rupert, had been incarcerated for nearly three years after being captured by the Catholic forces of Emperor Ferdinand. He had briefly crossed the Channel to give thanks to his uncle, who had been instrumental in securing his release, and now accompanied his aunt to Holland. In this brief meeting, Rupert secured permission to serve his uncle; theirs was a chivalric union.

Since leaving London, Charles had been pursued by messages from Parliament. MPs demanded to know who had advised him to arrest the six members, going so far as to incarcerate his Attorney General. With his bluff called, the king abandoned his position and issued pardons to the accused men, assuming the matter would then blow over. As the Venetian ambassador termed it, this 'lack of firmness' fostered a cautiousness amongst Royalists, who feared being 'miserably abandoned' in the same way.[41] A pattern was becoming obvious to all; whenever Charles made a stand, no matter how high-handed, he was not merciless enough to follow through.

As he took stock of opposition, the king could still count some blessings. The Tower of London remained in Sir John Byron's safe hands. George Goring, though a notorious drunkard, was also holding Portsmouth. The pressing concern was Hull, which contained a vast arsenal of the kingdom's arms and ammunition. The next prerogative power under attack was Charles's control of the militia and the right to appoint governors of fortresses and towns. Parliament forbade all commanders from acting on royal orders unless countersigned by them, and sent Sir John Hotham to take command at Hull. In response, Charles issued secret orders to the Earl of Newcastle to seize the town first. With both men converging on it, a custody battle broke out over the northern fortress. Hotham and Newcastle arrived at almost the same time. The mediaeval walls, crowned with twenty-five towers, were reinforced by earthworks, angled bastions and an outer ditch. Presented with the two opposing commissions, the perplexed magistrates were faced with the choice of king or Parliament, and shut both out.

Upon breaking the seal of Newcastle's report, in which the earl described himself 'very flat and out of countenance', Charles was cast into action.[42] He would deploy his presence in the battle for Hull and headed north.

Above left: James VI & I, attributed to Lawrence Hilliard. 1600–1625. (Rijksmuseum)

Above right: Queen Anna, print by Simon van de Passe, after Henry Farley. 1617. (Rijksmuseum)

Below left: Prince Henry Frederick, attributed to Peter Oliver. 1604–1647. (Rijksmuseum)

Below right: Princess Elizabeth, by Alexander Cooper. 1630–1660. (Rijksmuseum)

Above left: Prince Charles, aged 5, by Danelo Yarnold, after Robert Peake. 2022. (Mark Turnbull)

Above right: Prince Charles aged around 20, by Peter Oliver. 1615–1647. (Rijksmuseum)

Below left: Frederick V, King of Bohemia & Elector Palatine, after Michiel Jansz van Mierevelt. c.1621. (Rijksmuseum)

Below right: George Villers, Duke of Buckingham; print by Willem Jacobsz Delff, after Michiel Jansz van Mierevelt. 1626. (Rijksmuseum)

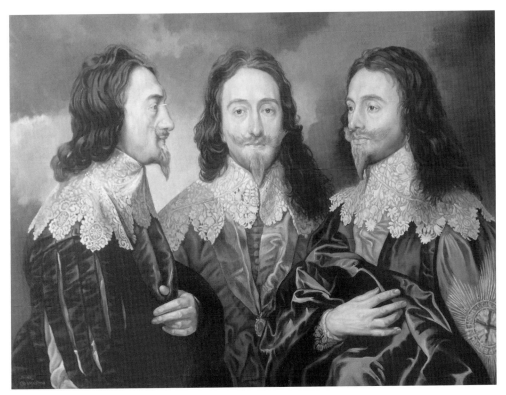

Above: *Charles I in Three Positions*, by Danelo Yarnold, after Anthony van Dyck. 2020. (Danelo Yarnold)

Below left: Henrietta Maria, by John Hoskins. 1620–1664. (Rijksmuseum)

Below right: Prince Charles, later Charles II, artist unknown. 1645–1655. (Rijksmuseum)

Above left: *Prince Rupert of the Rhine, in Combat Dress*, copy after Anthony van Dyck. c.1645. (Rijksmuseum)

Above right: Thomas Wentworth, Earl of Strafford; print by Pieter de Jode (II), after Anthony Van Dyck. 1628–1670. (Rijksmuseum)

Below: King Charles I and Henrietta Maria; print by Robert van Voerst, after Anthony Van Dyck. 1634. (Rijksmuseum)

Right: The Earl of Strafford on his
way to execution, being blessed
by William Laud, Archbishop of
Canterbury; print by Louis Pierre
Henriquel-Dupont, after Paul de la
Roche. 1840. (Rijksmuseum)

Below: Charles I, silver medal
signifying dominance of the seas;
by Nicholas Briot. 1630–1639.
(Rijksmuseum)

Henrietta Maria departing from Scheveningen for England; print by Balthasar
Florisz. van Berckenrode. 1643. (Rijksmuseum)

Above left: James Graham, Marquis of Montrose; print by Adriaen Matham. 1620–1660. (Rijksmuseum)

Above right: *King Charles I surrounded by Allegorical Figures and Historical Representations*, by anonymous artist. c.1650. (Rijksmuseum)

Below left: Miniature of King Charles I. On the back is a handwritten inscription 'Sat for by the King for Sir Bevil Grenville 1642'. There is some mystery to this piece. Bevil Grenville died in 1643, yet the king's long beard is unkempt, similar to how it was during his captivity in 1648. Before this point, paintings all show Charles with an immaculate beard and moustache. (James St Aubyn, St Michael's Mount)

Below right: King Charles on the eve of his execution with Princess Elizabeth and Prince Henry; print by Henri Van der Haert, after Gustave Wappers. 1836. (Rijksmuseum)

Above left: The king's execution – a hatchment painted by John Catlyn, vicar of All Saints, Burstwick, in 1676. Latin verses condemn rebellion and regicide. On the other side is the royal coat of arms. A much-forgotten treasure with a fascinating story, which is under threat – the church is newly closed and in poor repair. (PCC, All Saints, Burstwick)

Above right: Reverse side of above panel, shown hanging in situ. Royal coat of arms. For many years after Catlyn's time, this side was the one displayed and the execution scene was forgotten.

A detail of the execution scene from the hatchment.

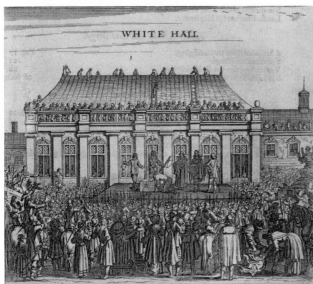

Above: Seventeenth-century view of the Palace of Whitehall; print by Israël Silvestre. 1631–1661. The Banqueting House is to the left. (Rijksmuseum)

Left: *Execution before Whitehall in London* by Salomon Savery. 1649. (Rijksmuseum)

Image of the Martyr King from *Eikon Basilike* (or 'Royal Portrait'), at least co-authored by King Charles I and written during the Civil War. 1649. (Mark Turnbull)

Chapter 21

Discord and Ruin

'A sharp sword always hinders starving'.

Charles to Henrietta

As hundreds of shipwrecked sailors struggled in the waters of the North Sea, the remains of a wooden baggage vessel slipped into the deep. Dead bodies bobbed on the surface. A leather-bound Bible, stamped with the golden Stuart crest, went to the bottom, along with damask dresses and all of Henrietta's chapel ornaments. Also lost to this watery grave was a fragment of the true cross, which had survived for 1,000 years in the Tower of London. Said to have been owned by St Helena, the loss of this item was a double blow. Henrietta lamented it not just on religious grounds, but also as a 'venerable antiquity'.[1] Having arrived safely in Holland, she must have considered the ill portents of the lost ship, which had been battered by cannon shot and storms.

Matters were also getting worse for the stricken king. While Henrietta pawned crown jewels, her husband met representatives from Parliament. Charles was 'overtaken with one weighty occasion on the neck of another'.[2] Considering himself beset by snares, he refused to hand over control of the militia. The Royal Navy had been lost already after the Lord High Admiral (Earl of Northumberland) had declared against the monarch.

Though Parliament's victories had brought them much security, the stumbling block was lack of trust on both sides. The delegation that pushed Charles over control of the militia warned that if he refused, they would assume it without his consent. 'By God, not for an hour', the king had declared, insisting that they had asked of him that which 'was never asked of a King'.[3] Having given up so much to so little effect, Charles felt it was time to dig in his heels. When Parliament justified their demand by citing apprehension for their safety, he asked them to 'Lay your hands on your hearts' and consider whether he too had cause to fear for his own.[4]

Secret appeals were made to Charles's groom, William Murray, a fair-weather friend from childhood. Presiding over the shady world of the backstairs, Murray was integral to, and relished, cloak-and-dagger politics. His attempts to intercede over the militia proved unsuccessful, but his report back to Charles's opponents is enlightening. The king apparently held fast to his coronation oath to maintain Crown prerogatives over which, in his own

117

opinion, he 'had already failed too muche'. To grant what was being asked would 'subvert it totally'. The king also felt his concessions had been met with nothing but 'publike reproche'.[5]

The long-anticipated breach came when Parliament published a Militia Ordinance, taking control of the kingdom's armed forces on their own authority. Facing an inevitable abyss, the king was 'much disconsolate and troubled' and especially so by his wife's continued absence. Prince Charles said so in 'sad Lines' to his sister, Mary, including his own desire for peace.

> Dear sister, we are, as much as we may, merry; and, more than we would, sad, in respect we cannot alter the present distempers of these turbulent times.[6]

Resorting to energetic action, the king made all haste to York and called a Chapter of the Order of the Garter. At crucial points throughout his reign, he often aligned himself and his actions with this noble order. The knights, after all, should have been his closest and most loyal supporters in times of need. After investing his second son, the Duke of York, and Prince Rupert in absentia, those knights who had refused to attend him were blacklisted. The Earl of Northumberland was dismissed as Lord High Admiral. The Marquis of Hamilton, desiring a better understanding between king and Parliament, became discontented over the growing division. Considering himself to be 'useless' to king and country, he left York on the pretext of tending to his estates.[7]

Volunteers were sought for a royal bodyguard to protect the king from any 'sudden violence or affront'. Parliament protested in the strongest of terms. William Murray found the king 'extreamly ofended' by the tone of their message, which was 'sharpe and personall'.[8] On 22 April 1642, Charles sent the Elector Palatine and 9-year-old Duke of York to Hull to 'sound the intentions' of the Parliamentarian Governor, Sir John Hotham.[9] When the royal party was admitted and treated with respect, the king's hopes were kindled. On St George's Day, Sir John's loyalty was put to the ultimate test in an epic showdown.

Accompanied by 150 men of his household, Charles gave a few hours' notice of his own journey to the town. Upon arrival, the drawbridges were found to be raised and gates firmly closed. Following demands for admittance, Hotham appeared on the walls and called out his apologies. Declaring himself a faithful subject, he nevertheless refused to compromise his orders from Parliament. The rasps of a royal trumpeter pronounced Hotham a traitor, but still nobody moved.

Though in a 'great wrath', Charles refused calls for the governor to be overpowered.[10] Instead, the check-mated king withdrew with his dignity in tatters. The power of his presence, once described as worth 20,000 men, could not even procure the lowering of a drawbridge. Inside the town, the Duke of York and his entourage were sent to their lodgings, and calls for their release momentarily fell upon deaf ears. The boy would later recall this event, blaming the humiliation on William Murray, who had conveyed a secret message to Hotham, tipping him off that the king intended to arrest him and try him for his life. The loss of Hull 'prov'd very ruinous' but Murray never lost the king's friendship.[11]

Another faint heart even closer to the king was his nephew, the self-centred Elector Palatine. Six weeks earlier, he had admitted to his mother 'I protest to God, I would not staye a minute in this Kingdome' if affairs could be better served elsewhere. As the king's position became ever weaker, so Charles-Louis grew ever more fickle. He resorted to asking his mother to intercede with Henrietta over some 'false tales' circulating about him.[12] Then fearing his presence at Hull might compromise him, and valuing Parliament's support more than his uncle's, the elector finally absconded. He claimed to have been 'inticed' to go to Hull and was 'totally ignorant of what was else intended'.[13] His mother also distanced herself from the king. Her son, she agreed, had been 'sorely catched in' over Hull.[14]

As rats abandoned the Royalist ship, the king gravitated towards Ireland. For some months he had harboured the idea of taking command of the army fighting to suppress the Catholic rebellion. The ever-sceptical Elector Palatine had professed 'but little faith' in such an idea, though the king thought differently, going so far as to promise Charles-Louis's brother, Prince Rupert, a military command in Ireland.[15] Together, uncle and nephew would conquer Catholic rebels and disprove slanders that the king had somehow encouraged them.

Declaring himself 'grieved at the very Soul' for his good Irish subjects, Charles let it be known that he intended to raise a personal guard of 2,000 to accompany him, and offered to sell or pawn any of his 'Parks, Lands, or Houses'.[16] Parliament warned that any who accompanied the king would be deemed enemies of the state. Playing to patriotic hearts, Charles asserted that to 'adventure his life to preserve his Kingdom' was necessary and worthy.[17] There could be no greater comfort to any Protestant in Christendom than seeing him lead the attack against Catholic rebels. The trusty getaway ship *Bonaventure* was ordered to sail to Newcastle and await instructions.

Ireland's Protestant Lord Justices thought this declaration indicative of the 'Greatness and Wisdom of so mighty a King'.[18] The Lords of the Council in Scotland called more coolly for mature deliberation and suggested the king's presence was needed in England more than ever. As for the English Parliament, they feared the king's true aim was to 'win the affection' of Irish rebels and enlist their support.[19] But in Westminster, only one-third of MPs and a quarter of peers were attending sessions. The assembly no longer appeared representative of the nation.

Both sides were already on an unofficial war footing. When charges were made that the king was intending 'to make Warre' upon Parliament, he countered that they were, in fact, moving against him.

> Horse is still leavied, and Plate and Money is still brought in
> against us, notwithstanding Our Declarations and Proclamations
> to the Contrary.[20]

Across the kingdoms a silent majority watched and waited. On 4 August Parliament made the phoney war official. Announcing themselves 'engaged in a Necessity to take up Arms', they resolved to proceed militarily against the malignant party surrounding the monarch.[21] The Venetian ambassador was clear; MPs do 'declare war against the king' and all those who embrace his party.[22]

Chapter 22

This Poore Kingdom

Nottingham Castle was rooted in England's history, built on top of a high rock just after the Battle of Hastings. The town was ideally located within the road system of the Midlands, allowing any army to march north, east, south or west as need arose.

On 22 August 1642, the king chose Nottingham to host a vital ceremony, beating off a bid from Warrington. From the castle's highest tower, a giant pennant was unfurled that portrayed the royal coat of arms. Embroidered onto its length was a hand pointing to a crown along with the words 'Give Caesar his Due'. This symbolic act is frequently given as the formal start of the English Civil War and quoted as the king making war on his people. In actual fact, it was a reactionary response to Parliament's declaration of war, which puts this key event into a wholly different context. The fact was that both sides had been mobilising and skirmishing long before they each cared to admit it. Their declarations were mere formalities, but Parliament's less grandiose action is rarely mentioned. It lends credence to Charles's claim, in the last minutes of his life, that his enemies began hostilities upon him first.

King Charles called upon loyal subjects to defend him against 15,000 rebels being led north by the Earl of Essex. Royalist recruitment had been far less successful given the king's record of concessions, and many avoided pledging support in case he backed down, as he was wont to do. With scarcely 1,000 troops, the monarch prayed this ancient ceremony would bring recruits in, but only a meagre thirty responded. There was also a push for donations to help 'settle the Distractions of this poore Kingdom, of wch Our Conscience beares us Wittnesse that Wee are not the cause'.[1]

The standard was hoisted to the heavens two times; the first had been in a field nearby, where twenty men had used knives and daggers to dig a hole for it. Trumpets had rasped and drums rattled in the presence of the king and his two eldest sons, along with nephews Rupert and Maurice. Sir Edmund Verney, the standard's bearer, had gripped the blood-red flagpole and swore that any who tried to wrest it from his hand 'must first wrest his soul from his body'.[2] A herald had read out a proclamation justifying the mobilisation, but stumbled over the script because of eleventh-hour amendments made in Charles's own hand. When the standard was blown down that night, it was decreed a bad omen.

Gathered around the king were his military leaders. The Commander in Chief was the Earl of Lindsey. A godson of Elizabeth I, he had seen service in the armies of Sweden and Holland, and was a Knight of both Garter and Bath. Prince Rupert, the king's nephew, was Lieutenant General of the Horse. Reporting directly to the monarch, he had also cut his teeth in Dutch service from the age of 14. The dragoons were headed by Sir Arthur Aston, a brutal Catholic who had fought for the rulers of Russia, Poland and Sweden. During a council of war, Sir Jacob Astley, the silver-haired Sergeant-Major General, let it be known that he could not prevent the king being snatched from his bed, so badly were they outnumbered. That evening, unsurprisingly, Charles slept little. The queen, gathering supplies and money in Holland, had written about the many rumours she had heard.

> They have made you dead, and [Prince] Charles a prisoner … For battles, there is not a day in the week in which you do not lose one … I need the air of England, or at least that in which you are.[3]

On 6 September 1642, Parliament declared that anyone who did not support it was a delinquent and their property liable to be seized. Ironically, this provoked a steady stream of Royalist recruits until ranks numbered 2,000 cavalry and 1,200 foot-soldiers. With the Earl of Essex and his army closing in, the king took his small band to Shrewsbury, from where he hoped to draw troops from Wales.

It was to hearts and minds that Charles needed to appeal, and he identified a major oversight on his own part: the church. Having been too lax in reinforcing the doctrine of the Church of England, the king acknowledged that he was now paying the price through his kingdom's calamitous condition. At York, he had taken steps to replace many rebellious rectors and parsons who had fallen in with his enemies, thus securing the revenues that accompanied these positions. He even put forward names of displaced Scottish clergymen, asking English bishops to consider them for any posts within their dioceses. In this way he rewarded loyalty, but also secured the church hierarchy, which was key to preventing flocks being led astray.

> Wee cannot but note that a Principall Cause of the said Rebellion hath beene the great Increase of Brownists, Anabaptists, and other Sectaries and Persons mistaken and misperwaded In their Religion.[4]

The antidote to these sects (and Catholicism too) lay in the hands of the bishops, and he called upon them to execute 'almost neglected' ecclesiastical laws. They should attend to their pastoral duties 'with all care and Vigilance' and 'doe your uttermost Endeavour in Reforming all Abuses, Correcting the ill lives of the Clergie, and ... Diligently preach Gods word'.[5] In Charles's mind, mustering his clerics would fight the rebellion just as much as armies in the field.

There was also the propaganda war. He ordered the publication and printing of his 'messages, declarations, propositions, answers and replies'. They were read out in 'churches, colleges, halls and other public places' and stored in Oxford University.[6] The growing records would evidence the treason he faced and perhaps went on to assist in the writing of *Eikon Basilike*, his reputed autobiography. For months both sides had shadowed one another, posturing and taking the odd swipe, but unwilling to engage in a pitched battle. It was the Lord's Day when matters came to a head. Both armies, claiming to hold divine support, drew up near the Warwickshire village of Kineton.

Chapter 23

Rabble Multitude

23 October 1642, Warwickshire.

A wintry dawn broke across the escarpment of Edgehill as Prince Rupert waited for the Royalist army. One month earlier he had been basking in sunshine at Powick Bridge when he noticed a detachment of the Earl of Essex's army. Without donning armour, the prince had ridden straight at them and secured a sharp victory. It launched the legend of his invincibility. Now, the first pitched battle of the Civil War would determine control of London, even the outcome of the conflict itself. Many predicted that hostilities would be over by Christmas.

When the king's army formed up against Lord Essex's Parliamentarians, both sides totalled 30,000 men. 'Go in the name of God and I'll lay my bones by yours,'[1] Charles told his Commander in Chief, the Earl of Lindsey, but the first conflict of the day was over troop formations. When Charles overruled Lindsey, the latter resigned on the spot, declaring that since he was 'not fitt to perform the office of Commander in Chief, he would serve [the king] as a Collonell'.[2] His replacement was the Scottish Earl of Forth, who had commanded Edinburgh Castle in 1640.

Within Parliament's ranks, Sir James Ramsey, a cavalry commander, prepared his troops and declared the enemy to be 'Papists, Atheists, and Irreligious persons for the most part'.[3] The king did the same and gathered his officers in his tent.

> Your king is both your cause, your quarrel and your captain. The foe in sight … With your swords Declare what Great courage and fidelity is within you. I have written And declared that I intend always to maintain and defend the protestant religion the rights and privileges of the parliament and the liberty of the subject and now I must prove My words by the convincing argument of the sword. Let heaven Show his power by this days victory, To declare me just … The best encouragement I can give you is this; that come life or death your king will bear you company and ever keep this place, this days service in his grateful remembrances.[4]

Adorned with blackened armour and a velvet coat lined with ermine, King Charles took his message to the rank and file, speaking to them with courage and cheerfulness, which caused 'Huzza's thro' the whole Army'.[5]

> You are called cavaliers and royalists in a disgraceful manner ...
> fight for your king, ye peace of the kingdom and ye protestant
> religion ... our Reputation has Suffered some diminution and
> been in the eclipse of royal splendour ... [he then calls upon his
> troops] To make it shine out Again with Clear resplendent beams
> of majesty.[6]

The royal standard fluttered 'larger than ordinary' so that the king's location could be known.[7] The glittering sight goaded Essex, who responded with a salvo of 12-pound roundshot. According to Sir Philip Warwick, Charles had given order that his army should not engage until the enemy 'should first have shot their cannon at our body of men'.[8]

As battle commenced, the king retired to the rear. His horsemen, led by Rupert, thundered across the field and routed the enemy cavalry, but eagerly chased after them, leaving the Royalist infantry 'so alone'.[9] Sergeant-Major General, Sir Jacob Astley, uttered a hasty prayer before commanding his 'boys' to march on.

> O Lord! Thou knowest how busy I must be this day. If I forget
> Thee, do not Thou forget me.[10]

Both sides slogged it out hand to hand. Musketeers aimed the 5-foot barrels of their firearms. Pikemen levelled 16-foot ash poles, each tipped with a steel spike. Essex, however, had kept a small cavalry reserve, which now emerged to the horror of the Royalists, and before long, many of the king's infantry blocks began to crumble. A footman in the royal presence was bowled from his saddle by a shot to the face. Preparing to rally his flagging troops, Charles instructed the Duke of Richmond to take his sons to safety, but the peer refused to leave the battle. The Earl of Dorset, delegated the task, replied that he would not be thought a coward 'for the sake of any King's Sons in Christendom'.[11] Finally, Sir William Howard was prevailed upon.

Parliamentarian cavalry spotted the boys taking refuge behind a barn, and taking it to be a fortified position, most of them steered clear. Prince Charles levelled his pistol crying, 'I fear them not!'[12] One enemy cuirassier, however, rode straight at the princes. Clad head to toe in armour and impervious to pistol shot, it took a poleaxe to finish him off.

The king's presence helped stabilise his army, but the fighting was grim. Word spread that a 'blue riban' – a Knight of the Garter – had been felled, soon revealed to be the Earl of Lindsey, who had hoped to personally engage the Earl of Essex.[13] Mortally wounded, his son, Lord Willoughby, stood over him fighting off the enemy until both were captured. Sir Edmund Verney, carrying the royal standard, killed several assailants and even used the point of the flagstaff to defend himself. Eventually overpowered and killed, it was said his hand retained a death-grip on the staff and had to be cut off. The prized pennant did not remain in Parliamentarian possession for long before being retaken.

With both sides exhausted and the onset of nightfall, 'as if by mutuall consent' they disengaged, fearful of mistaking friend for foe.[14] For some of the wounded, the freezing temperatures that night tended to them better than any physician. Sir Gervase Scrope, with sixteen wounds in his head and body, was stripped and left for dead for nearly two days until his son discovered him. Despite this ordeal, the cold stemmed his blood loss and he made a miraculous recovery.

Sir John Culpepper warned of ruin if the king heeded advice and withdrew from Edgehill. Charles was in agreement, declaring that he would not stir from the place and stayed all night in his coach. Had he not 'bin in the fylde', Sir Edward Sydenham concluded, then 'we might have suffired'. The king's conduct received much applause. Sydenham, a Royalist, thought him 'of the least feare and the greatest mercie and resolution'.[15] The more impartial Venetian ambassador heard that contrary to general expectation, Charles performed with spirit and 'established the devotion' of his troops.[16]

England's soil was stained by the bloodshed of Edgehill. The chilling reality scarred all who experienced it, and reports of ghostly sights and sounds began circulating almost immediately. Locals described seeing spirits of the dead fighting the battle in the sky. A horrified Charles would eventually send a delegation to investigate.

Left in control of the field, following Lord Essex's withdrawal to Warwick, the king now had an open road to London. Rupert was ready to gallop to the capital and overawe it, but the Earl of Bristol cautioned against the feisty prince, who might burn it to the ground. Charles concurred. He confirmed the Earl of Forth as Lord General so the man's 'white hairs' may serve to temper Rupert's 'ardour'.[17] As London braced itself, the king instead entered Oxford, putting his faith in the hope that the capital might simply come to its senses. He refused to alienate Londoners by conquering them; far better to let their hearts move them into shaking off the traitorous yoke within Parliament. His blinkered idealist tendencies and deep sense of kingly responsibility saw Charles throw away his first chance of winning the war. Perhaps the same outlook had led him to this conflict in the first place.

Only when the Earl of Essex led his army back to the capital did the king stir. The Royalists raced after him, hoping for a second contest, but Essex managed to evade them and reached London first. Parliament then proposed peace talks, but as commissioners travelled to meet the king, their army also began to approach. Almost cut off in hostile territory, with Lord Essex's soldiers closing in, Prince Rupert attacked Brentford to establish a foothold. Citizens of London watched as plumes of smoke spiralled above the town and heard tales of destruction and slaughter. The king was condemned for having unleashed his men while peace overtures were in progress and this unified opposition against him.

No excuses could erase the stain of Brentford. But in an attempt to ease apprehension, Charles let it be known that he was falling back to Oxford to perform the duties of a 'pitiful prince' where he would wait either for negotiators, or the Earl of Essex's army.[18] Christmas in Oxford was not an entirely melancholy affair. The Royalist Earl of Newcastle had relieved York and looked set to conquer the entire north. University students, once described as 'zealots' devoted to the 'religious exercise of copulation',[19] now threw off their gowns and took up arms, swelling Royalist ranks.

On 22 December, Charles took the opportunity to remind his subjects that the unhappy times had been fomented by a 'Malignant Party of ill Affected Persons' who had endeavoured to subvert the 'whole state of the church and religion established, and in steede thereof to bring in Schisme Haeresie and Confusion'.[20] Resolving to be a 'Glorious King or a patient Martyr', Charles admitted he was not yet the former and did not apprehend to be the latter.[21] It was his love for Henrietta that got him through these dark, winter days and plans were made for their reunion.

Chapter 24

Angel of Peace

As 1643's Twelfth Night festivities got under way, Prince Rupert led a force of cavalry out of Oxford. His nocturnal march saw 'strange fire falling from Heaven, like a bolt, which, with several cracks, brake into balls and went out, about steeple height'.[1] His destination was Cirencester, one of a trio of vital targets that would help maintain the Royalist war effort.

Influential leaders on both sides shared the views of Royalist Lord Saville, who did not wish to see the king 'trample' on the Parliament nor the monarch brought so low that the people 'rule us all'.[2] As he penned these views at the turn of the year, he also wrote of rumours that the queen had landed in England. She had been itching to return, and had bided her time until Lord Newcastle had secured the north. Having toiled in Holland physically, financially and diplomatically, she brought with her the culmination of these efforts; much-needed men, money and munitions.

Her nephew, the Elector Palatine, had refused to accompany her unless she went as an 'angel of peace'.[3] The Dutch had been eager to see the back of their inconvenient guest and agreed to escort her little fleet. After eight days 'tossing at sea', a furious storm forced Henrietta to abandon her first attempted crossing.[4] Though left in poor health, her stash of supplies was unaffected. Despite Parliamentarian warships and Dutch officials, who attempted to seize one of her vessels, she readied herself for another try and wrote to Charles.

> Adieu, my dear heart … if it happen that I could not come to you,
> it would be [due to] my death, since I can live no longer without
> seeing you. Believe this, for it is very true.[5]

A desire to hasten to her husband's side left Henrietta willing to face all dangers. There were more than she imagined, and some emanated from the Royalist side. Putting his faith in men of dubious loyalties, Charles charged the Earl of Newport and Lord Saville with his wife's safety. It was a shocking lack of judgement. Far from securing her passage to the king, it transpired they harboured an intention of handing her over to Parliament as a bargaining tool. The furore of 1641, when Newport had supposedly called for Henrietta's confinement, should have been warning enough. It demonstrates Charles's assumption that as king, he could reclaim the loyalties of any person at any time. Perhaps this near miss prompted Henrietta's call for her husband to 'be more careful of me than you have been'.[6]

After landing at the little harbour of Bridlington, on 23 February 1643, the queen had more direct threats to contend with. Parliamentarian warships had shadowed her and in the early hours, as she slept in a small cottage on the harbour front, they opened fire. With no time to dress, 'bair feet and bair leg', she hurried outside to get out of range.[7] Forgetting her dog, Mitte, the indomitable queen, at 4-and-a-half-feet tall, returned in the face of this barrage to rescue her. With shot whistling overhead, Henrietta leapt into a ditch and kept up the morale of those around her until the rebel ships departed. She had been more concerned about her munitions than her own person, and recounted as much to her horrified husband. 'I never till now knew the good of ignorance; for I did not know the danger that thou wert in,' the king admitted. His heart was full of affection, admiration and 'impatient passion of gratitude'.[8]

Having barely arrived in York, numerous visitors came to pay their respects. Sir Hugh Cholmley, Parliamentarian Governor of Scarborough, defected and turned over that important harbour. Sir John Hotham, the arch-rebel of Hull fame, and his son, both paid court and flirted with defection. On account of his influence in Scotland, Henrietta gave audience to the Marquis of Hamilton, despite an 'utmost dislike' of the man's ambitious pretensions.[9] Hamilton's rival, the Earl of Montrose, was regarded with equal suspicion. A one-time Covenanter, he had consistently warned against trusting Hamilton and approached Henrietta with hopes that he might assume charge of the king's Scottish business. Montrose was extremely able and charismatic, but he was no friend of the ruling Scottish junto. Duly holding him at arm's length, Henrietta complained that if only the king's supporters would 'not waste time' in disputes then all the trouble expected from Scotland would be avoided.[10]

Having the queen back on English soil caused a flurry of panicked plotting in London. The Earl of Holland, who had abandoned the royal cause, now tried to curry favour by proposing that Parliament send safe conduct passes so that she might join the king. MPs blocked the motion, reputedly exclaiming that if it wasn't for her encouragement, the king would never have managed to put himself 'in a position to resist' them.[11] They also feared she might talk her husband into more vigorous steps, suggesting his enemies recognised Charles's need for a determined adviser. Rather than welcome the queen, MPs voted to impeach her for high treason on account of the munitions she had in tow, having long branded her an 'incendiary'.[12] The prospect of despatching her in the same manner as the Earl of Strafford sent a signal that nobody could escape Parliament's justice.

At Westminster Abbey, rioters broke up organs and choir stalls, along with an epitaph that gave Henrietta the title of 'Majesty'. Her chapel at Somerset House was ransacked in an anti-Catholic frenzy, which spilled over to the Cheapside Cross and grand Maypole, both of which were destroyed. The queen knew what she was in for if ever she fell into Parliament's hands. So, too, did Charles. As protective as ever, he counter-attacked by declaring Parliament to be null and void, and that he, as monarch, was the last legitimate power in the realm.

By July, Henrietta was on the road with 3,000 foot, 30 companies of horse and dragoons, 6 cannon and 150 waggons of baggage. The queen had been given a tongue-in-cheek nickname of 'her she-majesty generalissima' by courtiers. Charles's newest commander joined him on 13 July 1643, when they were reunited on the site of the Battle of Edgehill. Simultaneously, news arrived of another Parliamentarian defeat. In the West Country, the Royalists had trounced William Waller's army on two occasions within the space of a fortnight – Lansdown and Roundway Down. Except for Hull, the Earl of Newcastle was now master of the north. In the Midlands, by far the most fought over territory, success at Hopton Heath had pre-empted Rupert's capture of Birmingham and Lichfield. On 26 July he added Bristol to the string of towns taken. The second city of England brought with it a port and a stash of ships that formed the nucleus of a Royalist fleet.

Royal victories all came at a cost. The Earl of Denbigh, brother-in-law of the late Duke of Buckingham, had been killed at Birmingham. At Hopton Heath, the Earl of Northampton had the 'hinder part of his Head' cleaved open by a halberd. Having been unhorsed and refusing quarter from 'such base Rogues', his face was subsequently slashed.[13] One of the king's longest friends, Northampton had died in a manner similar to Richard III. He was another double knight – of both Garter and Bath – and the loss of such key figures was a personal blow to the king. Casualties at Bristol had been particularly devastating, with 500 men killed in that one night's action. It was a number that haunted Charles.

At this high point in the war, rumours reached him that Gloucester would surrender if he appeared before the town. It was too good an opportunity to overlook. More so because it could be had without incurring casualties. When the king duly arrived with his forces, he found Gloucester firm against him like Coventry and Hull before it, thwarting the power of Charles's presence for a fourth time. The garrison resolved to hold out until 'the last gasp'.[14] Royalist commanders counselled Charles to storm the place, but Henrietta pushed her husband to focus his efforts on London while it quaked with 'disturbing humours' over the loss of Bristol. Charles refused point-blank to countenance another list of casualties and instead, Royalists dug in around Gloucester and prepared for a siege. No bombs, mines nor repeated assaults could shake the obstinate defenders and instead, the king lost time he did not have.[15] As days dragged by, a bored Prince Charles scratched his name into a windowpane of the house where he was quartered.

For a second time Charles spurned the chance of victory because it did not fit with his idealistic notions. It often seemed as if he was acting out a court masque, entering centre stage and hoping to vanquish treason and rebellion by his divine presence and chivalrous gestures alone. St George incarnate, killing off the dragons at the heart of Westminster. His seemingly eternal clemency made loyalty more transient; many picked when to support him, knowing that they could regain favour and prestige in due course – and perhaps even obtain more by doing so. A singular act of forgiveness came when Charles sent his own physician to the bedside of one of his leading opponents, John Hampden, who had been mortally wounded.

It was during the Gloucester campaign that seven leading Parliamentarians turned up at Oxford. The Earls of Bedford, Clare, Conway, Holland, Lovelace, Northumberland and Portland all protested that they were no longer aligned to Parliament's 'cruelty and insolence'. Having been duped by Gloucester, both Charles and Henrietta showed 'little satisfaction' towards the penitent peers and refused to see them.[16] It was Prince Rupert who, recognising the value of this mass defection, led them into the royal presence and earned a stinging rebuke for it. Brought face to face with the men, Charles barely acknowledged them as they kissed his hand, leaving them with no alternative but to return cap in hand to Parliament. The paradox of the king was that when he actually needed to show clemency, he sometimes stood firm.

The approach of the Earl of Essex, along with his field army, occupied attention that September. Unwilling to be caught between Gloucester and its relief force, the king was forced to lift the siege. Charles, at one point, despondently sat on a milestone and when the young Duke of York asked if they might go home, he replied, 'we have no home.'[17] Once again, as after Edgehill, the Royalists pursued Essex in an attempt to engage his army. While desperately chasing down their quarry, one evening the exhausted Rupert sought out the king, only to find him sitting at a table playing cards with Lord Percy. The difference could not have been more apparent.[18]

Both sides eventually did battle at Newbury. Royalist cavalry swept across the common in an attempt to capture the high ground, and their infantry fought valiantly through the hedgerows and up Round Hill. It was a bloody affair. The Parliamentarians made good use of the high ground, which the king's commanders had failed to secure, despite having arrived first. This unforgivable oversight finished off another tranche of Charles's closest associates.

The Earl of Carnarvon was run through with a sword, and as he lay dying that evening, Charles reputedly sat with him until the end. The Earl of Sunderland, Marquis La Vieuville and Viscount Falkland were also killed. Falkland's demise would wound the Royalist cause in more ways than one. Respected by both sides, and depressed over the war, Falkland all but committed suicide by galloping into a hail of fire and leaping a hedge. He most likely perished before his horse had even landed. The mild-mannered and intelligent man had been instrumental in moderating royal declarations, and now his role as Secretary of State fell vacant. Bestowing it upon Lord George Digby, son of the Earl of Bristol, the king unwittingly condemned his own cause by promoting a politically inept meddler-in-chief.

Chapter 25

Gallant Gospellers

The borders between Scotland and England had been subject to lawlessness for as long as anyone could remember. Even when the Stuarts inherited England, this troubled territory never healed. Livestock was regularly stolen and houses were set on fire by feuding families. In January 1644, a Scottish army headed for the borderlands after allying with the English Parliament. Some of those very families now burned their own homes so the Scots should 'not find any comfort'.[1] The king's northern commander, William Cavendish, Earl of Newcastle, ordered similar destruction across the North of England for the same reason.

Ever since resisting attempts to meddle with their Kirk, the Covenanters harboured hopes of embedding Presbyterianism south of the border. When civil war broke out, they had proposed to send commissioners to discuss religion with the king, but he blocked them and though he backtracked to avoid giving cause for offence, the damage was already done. By February 1643, these commissioners were petitioning Charles to come to an accommodation with the English Parliament, but he delayed his answer, unwilling to have his northern kingdom involved. Thus sidelined, they finally requested leave to go to London to consult English MPs instead, but the king 'dexterously contrived' to delay them, and then outright refused to sanction any trip to the capital.[2] From Edinburgh, Scottish leaders protested at these slights and lobbied for their own Parliament to be called earlier than scheduled. Another royal rejection simply distanced the Scots even more.

Scotland's delegates returned home in April 1643 in a dissatisfied frame of mind. Mistrusting their intentions, Charles sent several Royalists after them, charged with keeping that kingdom neutral. When the Scottish Parliament assembled in Edinburgh, without royal consent in June 1643, Charles hastily issued writs to give the impression it was by his command. The Covenanters, however, created their own and imprisoned anyone who objected. This move infuriated the king, who condemned it as an act of disobedience and rebellion.

As 1643 unfolded, the English Parliament became convinced that victory could only be gained through a Scottish alliance. Although of a like mind, the Scots pointed out that 'feeble hopes of reward' would discourage them.[3] It took much negotiation before a Solemn League and Covenant was signed. The Scots felt sure that this treaty committed MPs to the introduction of Presbyterianism in England, but Parliament made certain the wording was as open-ended as possible, allowing them to renege later. To counter the risk posed by this alliance, Charles turned to the third of his kingdoms – Ireland – and sought to bring back troops to reinforce his armies.

The Marquis of Hamilton had been the king's chief instrument in Scotland. After promising that he could keep the kingdom out of the war, he was given a dukedom. Characteristically, the king turned a deaf ear to all alternative warnings about the Scots and clung to Hamilton's vow, which the man had made on his life. As Charles once wrote to the Earl of Strafford, the mark of his favour was measured by the 'little welcome I give to accusers, and the willing ear I give to my servants'.[4] As such, inconvenient truths that highlighted Hamilton's failings, brought to Oxford by the Earl of Montrose, did not move the king, who responded with a dose of cold-shoulder.

By the time winter ushered in a temporary halt to the hostilities of 1643, Montrose's arguments against 'Captain Luckless' – the nickname he gave Hamilton – had been proved correct. It was clear that Scotland was mobilising and the cold reality dawned on the king. Humiliated and angry, he had Hamilton arrested. Attempting to exonerate himself, the duke even blamed the king, citing use of troops from Ireland as a trigger for Scotland's intervention. Now facing war with two of his kingdoms, shadows of suspicion fell across other Scotsmen at Charles's side. One, the Earl of Lothian, certainly had divided loyalties.

Lothian's father, the Earl of Ancram, had been one of the king's Gentlemen of the Bedchamber for the past thirty years. Upon the first of the Scottish wars in 1639, Lothian had espoused the Covenanter cause and became a leading and respected figure. In 1640, he had prayed that England might 'gett a reformation like ours'. Ancram, residing with the king, was in a difficult position. He rued his son's stance and had accused him of being in direct opposition to the monarch. Lothian disagreed – he was against the king's religious policy but not his person. The year before England descended into civil war, Lothian wrote to his father, 'I am sorry att the expression of your sufferings for me,' suggesting that his stance might have affected his father's standing.[5] Father and son nevertheless remained very close. At no point was Ancram shunned by the king, who could perhaps sympathise over family disunity, considering the behaviour of his own nephew, the Elector Palatine. In a stroke of irony Lothian had long demonstrated a 'constant affection' to the elector's 'person & Interest'.[6]

Having been engaged on a diplomatic visit to France in 1643, Lothian had returned to kiss the king's hand at Oxford that winter. Skeletal frames of charred timber littered the university town, because many brewhouses, bakehouses and malthouses had gone up in an inferno the month before. Once in the royal presence, Lothian was given an oath never to bear arms against the monarch – a result of the king's growing concern that Scotland was about to invade in support of his enemies. Lothian's hesitation appeared to confirm this, and the peer was imprisoned in Bristol Castle the next day. On 26 November 1643, Lothian wrote to his father protesting his innocence and assuring him 'the reasones of this [imprisonment] is unknowne to me'.[7] The fate of this well-respected leader was another nail in the coffin of Charles's relationship with the Scots, and just before their troops crossed into England, a petition preceded them calling for the release of the Earl of Lothian. Several months passed before he was freed in an exchange of prisoners.

The scales dramatically tipped against King Charles in January 1644 when 21,000 Covenanters crossed into England, nearly four years after their last incursion. Before their commander, the Earl of Leven, could consider his next move, an extraordinary snowfall blanketed the kingdom for eight days. As soon as he was able, Charles sent troops north with haste. Having offered a general pardon to MPs and peers at Westminster, the king had called on them to attend him in Oxford. As such, 1644 saw two parliaments in session, though the Royalists derogatively named the half-empty chamber at Westminster an 'assembly'. Speaking in Christchurch College to the hundreds who had answered his call, Charles warned of the miseries that would befall England by the invasion of the Scots, termed a 'foreign power'.[8] Secretary of State, Lord George Digby, ventured that the invasion might actually be welcome news if it forced a 'union amongst ourselves' and united squabbling Royalists in the face of a common adversary.[9]

The Oxford Parliament, which met on 22 January 1644, was a good publicity move. The king gave a rationale for calling MPs to him by explaining it was three years since he had passed the Triennial Bill. Parliament was therefore required to meet, and by quoting that legislation, which he had approved during the riots of 1641, he appealed to the heartstrings of every moderate. It was a powerful declaration that he would stand by commitments made and also undermined the legality of those left at Westminster. Numbers were increased when Charles ennobled his most loyal supports. Prince Rupert was made Duke of Cumberland and Earl of Holderness in preparation for a northern conquest. Westminster, however, remained unperturbed by their alter ego, confident in their new alliance.

If the Royalists thought the town of Newcastle might hold up the Scottish advance, they were sorely mistaken; the Earl of Leven bypassed it and searched for an alternative southern crossing over the River Tyne. On 19 February, Scots and Royalists did battle at Corbridge, where the latter failed to hold the bridge. Though the Earl of Newcastle's outnumbered army would be forced into a fighting retreat all the way to York, his letters to the king initially remained hopeful. In one, he wrote of his 'very good condition' and although the Scots had reached Sunderland, royal forces 'lie now almost round them'.[10] By March, updates became less frequent and unsubstantiated rumours abounded of a Scottish defeat.

The truth, however, was dire. As a result, Rupert began his northern venture, collecting men from the numerous garrisons he passed, until reaching the Royalist stronghold of Newark. It was besieged by 7,000 Parliamentarians with a 32-pound cannon nicknamed 'sweet lips'. In a brisk action, the prince crushed the enemy and lifted the siege, thus securing communication with his hard-pressed northern colleagues. The action was so spectacular that Sir Philip Warwick deemed the prince 'the life of the king's army'.[11]

The Earl of Newcastle, though vastly outnumbered, did his best to hold back the Scots. The slow passage of their allies made Parliament increasingly desperate for a victory to pin their hopes upon. Then Sir Richard Grenville, one of their senior officers, defected at the start of March, handing the king a cache of secrets, which revealed the enemy's hand just as they were about to play it. The key Royalist fortress of Basing House, a Catholic haven, was to have been betrayed while its owner, the Marquis of Winchester, was at Oxford. A Parliamentarian bribe had been delivered to his brother, who was to have deputised, but Grenville's intelligence scuppered the plan. Two other plots involving Reading and Oxford were also diffused. MPs were so angry that an effigy of Grenville was hanged in London, but it was only a matter of time before things began to look up.

Parliament's long-awaited victory came at Cheriton, in Hampshire, on 30 March 1644. Lord General Essex was ordered to capitalise on this and strike at Oxford, the king's headquarters, and the armies of the Earls of Manchester and Denbigh were assigned to join this 'enterprise of importance'. Without enough men to risk any encounter, the king left his base to prevent himself 'being shut in'.[12]

Similarly, Charles's northern capital of York was converged upon by the Scots and two Parliamentarian armies, leaving the Earl of Newcastle increasingly concerned that the king's 'great game' was endangered, if not lost.[13] With Rupert marching north, the king fired off numerous positive missives to buoy the earl up. As a former tutor to the Prince of Wales, Newcastle must have felt he was being instructed himself when, on 5 April, the king told him, 'Remember all courage is not in fighting, constancy in a good cause being the chief, and the despising of slanderous tongues and pens being not the least ingredient.' A hint of desperation slipped out when Charles later remarked that he was lost if the earl was ever to leave his service. One week later, another despatch noted the king's care for the north, but candidly admitted:

> you must consider that we, like you, cannot do always what we
> would ... if we [the king] fail, all you can do will be to little
> purpose; wherefore you may be assured of all assistance from

hence that may be, without laying ourselves open to eminent danger.[14]

This was Charles giving a dose of realism, venturing his opinion as a man, rather than a sanguine king. His own position must take precedence over Newcastle's, for if his royal army was defeated, then that would inevitably result in York's demise. Before Rupert left his uncle, he had secured agreement that a string of garrisons around Oxford would be maintained for its defence. Now, in the prince's absence, the council implored Charles to abandon these towns, gather the garrisons together and march west to draw the enemy away from Oxford. A novice in warfare, the king felt unable to oppose the move and wrote regretfully to Rupert.

> I confess the best had been to have followed your advice ... [we will] defend ourselves until you may have time to beat the Scots, but if you be too long in doing it, I apprehend some great inconvenience.[15]

As Charles's difficulties multiplied, so his commands became more contradictory. Rupert received an order to abandon his march north and rejoin the king, but this was rapidly cancelled. The Earl of Forth, Royalist Lord General, was forced to seek clarification on which enemy army he was to engage first. On another occasion, he received written instructions to march east one day, and then west the next. On 8 May, he was informed that the king would be with him at 9.00 am prompt the next day. A second letter explained that the monarch 'did not remember the Fast day' and would meet him at Abingdon instead.[16] Ever fastidious over religious observances, Charles tended to his cause by worshipping God, whose favour he sought, and led by example in observing such occasions. But the level of control exerted by him on military motions was enough to tie his generals in knots.

Authority was so fractured that some officers simply chose which orders to obey. After numerous attempts to have one particular colonel bring his brigade back to the field army, Forth resorted to calling upon the monarch to order it. This request reached the king after midnight, and 'as he was stirring' next morning, the Secretary of State secured the necessary permission and issued the command.[17] For Charles, the level of detail must have been overwhelming, especially while engaged in a game of cat and mouse with his enemies, all to buy time for Rupert. Nevertheless, the king maintained a stoic front.

York's walls and gates were now blockaded. The Earl of Manchester's army was camped on the northern side. To the east, Scottish troops united with those of Lord Ferdinando Fairfax, and were within pistol shot of the city. More Scots manned a captured fort. The besiegers recorded with pride that their best battering piece, a 64-pound cannon, was now ready. The noose tightened daily. While Rupert headed through Lancashire, gathering men to his banner, Parliamentarian sappers tunnelled under York. Mines were sprung, making a breach in the walls near St Mary's Tower. The Prestigious King's Manor was captured, where Charles had stayed during the Bishops' Wars, but this assault had been made without sufficient notice to the rest of the allied forces. Therefore, with no diversionary attacks to contend with, the garrison were able to concentrate their numbers and repel the incursion. York survived another day. When celebratory fires burned on the top of the Minster, it was observed that they were met by similar signals from Royalists at Pontefract Castle. The fiery Rupert, meanwhile, advanced by 'crooked and lengthy routes' and by this means both evaded and confused his opponents.[18]

The king's equally erratic march west, pursued by the armies of Essex and Waller, also left his enemies second-guessing his intentions. Some supposed he aimed to link up with Rupert. In reality, Charles was as equally uncertain of his goal as they were, and his purpose was solely to buy time. Panicked confusion was translated into print with more ambiguous orders for Rupert. He would keep the letter for the rest of his days, as justification for what transpired. Charles wrote that his nephew's successes were 'no more welcome to me, than that you are the means'. These words betrayed a desperate hope that Rupert could miraculously see off the Scottish threat.

> If Yorke be lost, I shall esteeme my Crowne little lesse, unlesse supported by your suddaine Marche to me, & a Miraculous Conquest in the South ... but if Yorke be relieved, & you beate the Rebelles Armies of both Kingdoms, which ar before it, then, but otherwise not, I may possiblie make a shift, (upon the defensive) to spin out tyme.

It was fairly clear so far; relieve York by defeating the armies before it. But the next line told Rupert that if he discovered the city was already freed from its besiegers, then he should 'immediately March, with your whole strength, to Woster [Worcester], to assist me & my Army, without which, or your having relieved Yorke by beating the Scots, all the successes you can afterwards have, most infallibly, will be uselesse unto mee'.[19] Had Rupert been instructed to simply relieve York, or did that include defeating the armies before it too? If he found that the allies had raised the siege, should he seek them out for battle, or return to the king without further ado?

Such doubts and anxieties were not confined to the king and his commanders. When Charles made a feint towards Worcester, Lord Essex gave up the chase and marched off to the south-west, deciding instead to relieve the town of Lyme. His bemused subordinate, William Waller, was left to shadow the royal force.

The Committee of Both Kingdoms, which directed the allied armies, were outraged at Essex's dereliction of duty. As much as the Lord General might claim to be commanded by the 'discipline of war and rules of reason', it was jealousy of Waller that motivated him.[20] It spilled from his pen. He told the committee that if they were intent upon confining him, then supreme command should be handed to Waller.

Left to single-handedly deal with the king, Waller veered between despondency and over-confidence. The war could never end, he opined, if the king 'be in any part of the land and not at the Parliament'. Should the royal army be defeated 'never so often his person will raise another' – an infamous remark similar to this was attributed to the Earl of Manchester, months later.[21] Though the king and his army outmanoeuvred Waller, there were some near misses. At Wallingford, only six others were aware of Charles's intention to inspect the town, yet an enemy force turned up and 'missed him' by a few minutes.[22] It was said that the Parliamentarians had orders to seize the king as the best means of ending hostilities, and from the start, they had claimed their intention was to rescue him. But at the beginning of 1644, a new option reared its head when MPs resolved to put the Archbishop of Canterbury on trial. They accused Laud of having amended the coronation oath to include the upholding of royal prerogatives, leading to discussion over whether the king could be deposed based on the oath's invalidity.

The three commanders besieging York were visited by Henry Vane, eldest son of the king's one-time Secretary of State. During the period of Charles's personal rule, Vane had avoided the sacrament for years because nobody would administer it without kneeling. As a result, he made a vow to spend the rest of his days in New England. Having long ago given over that intention, he was now termed one of the 'chief directors of the present machine'.[23] This influential player, so it was said, suggested deposing the king should he be taken prisoner or flee the kingdom. The Scots, however, opposed any such notion, leaving Vane to beat a hasty retreat.

If the king did refuse to come to heel, thought was given to fabricating allegations of the queen's 'unchastity' and then declaring their children 'suspect'.[24] The prospect posed the question of who might replace them. In March, at the height of such speculation, the Elector Palatine arrived in England and sent timely congratulations to Parliament and Scots upon their alliance. His letter was clearly prejudicial to his uncle, not that Charles Louis cared. He judged the king and his court 'Spanishly inclined' and as such, of no benefit to him.[25] Gossip was that the elector had been invited to London by a group of MPs, who aimed to establish him in a 'position of dependency' – a puppet. Charles Louis even addressed Parliament in person:

> his Wishes were constant for a good Success to that great Work
> [Parliament] had undertaken, for a Thorough Reformation;

and that his Desires were, to be ruled and advised by their grave Counsels: and being ready to serve them, [he] will with Chearfulness embrace their Advice.[26]

The son of Viscount Dunbar wrote that the elector's coming was for no good. The king thought likewise. A letter of rebuke to his nephew was intercepted. The Earl of Essex deliberated over the disrespectful action of breaking it open – but this concern stemmed from regard for the addressee and not the author. Perhaps aware of the elector's prospects, the Lord General forwarded on the unopened letter and asked that he be 'favourably mentioned' to the young man for it.[27] The king's letter read as follows:

> your coming at this time into the Kingdom, is in all respects much more strange unto me … First, Upon what Invitation you are come? Then, the Design of your coming? Wishing by your Answer I may have the same Cause and Comfort I have heretofore had, to be, Your Loving Unkle, and Faithful Friend.[28]

On 30 June, Charles and his army marched along one side of the River Cherwell, watched from the opposite bank by William Waller. As the king's troops became strung out, Waller seized his chance, very nearly securing a great victory. The Royalists quickly rallied, and a brisk action ensued around Cropredy Bridge that lasted until sunset. Contrary to expectations, Waller came off worst, losing eleven guns. After having the rug pulled from under him, the Parliamentarian commander was nearly killed when, at a council of war, the floor of his command post collapsed beneath him.

Two days later, the undefeated Rupert massed his troops in fields to the west of York. By taking a surreptitious route and crossing the river by a bridge of boats, his approach so surprised the allied armies that they lifted the siege. The triple army withdrew in dismay and were in headlong retreat to Tadcaster, aiming to block his union with the king. But unbeknown to them, Rupert once more considered his confusing orders; York would only be at risk again if he left, and in his mind, the king had specified the necessity of a battle, therefore he resolved to fight. With uncharacteristic patience, he waited several hours as the allies turned about and drew up on a corn hill to the south of Marston Moor.

At 7.00 pm, Rupert deemed the day to be spent and the Royalists settled down for the evening, delving into their snapsacks to partake of rations. Seizing their chance, the allies advanced beneath a thunderous summer squall. Marston Moor was the biggest battle of the war. The outnumbered Royalists almost clinched victory, and the three allied commanders even fled the field, but the Scottish infantry and Oliver Cromwell's cavalry went on to win the day. In the darkness, an elite Royalist regiment, termed the 'whitecoats' or 'lambs', fought in a last-ditch stand to the death. Their resolution, it was alleged, had been to colour their undyed coats in their enemies' blood. Attacked time after time, they held out until only thirty bloodstained men remained. Rupert's famed hunting poodle, Boye, was also dead on the field.

News of Marston Moor was as contradictory as ever. Celebratory bonfires were lit in Oxford upon early favourable reports. In the West Country, Parliament's Lord General heard of Royalist glee and robustly countered this 'impudence'. To the king's garrison of Exeter, he sent his 'word of honour' that their cohorts had been trounced, offering to surrender Weymouth and Melcombe Regis if he was proved wrong.[29] As part of this wager of war, Essex suggested that Exeter be rendered up if he was vindicated. But nothing would induce them to do such a thing, for within the town's walls was Henrietta Maria.

The warrior queen had caused a stir ever since her arrival in England in February 1643. Those servants around her vied for position and influence, becoming part of the continuous round of intrigue that proved such an unnecessary distraction. By February 1644, the queen was pregnant, but a fall in April sparked fears for her health. Rotund royal physician, Sir Theodore Turquet de Mayerne, excused himself and refused to attend, while the king's enemies circulated rumours that his wife had died. A request that her bed be despatched to Oxford met with some protest before Parliament relented. The month prior to Cropredy Bridge, when the king had been most troubled, the vulnerable queen had left Oxford for the safety of Bristol. No doubt her health and welfare contributed much to Charles's anxieties and the subsequent confusions that occurred. As her entourage passed Gloucester, the rebel garrison captured some of her baggage and would have taken Henrietta too, had her escort not been so alert.

While the king and Rupert were battling to keep the Royalist cause alive, the queen was struggling with poor health. Ensconced in Exeter for the remainder of her confinement, and suffering bouts of paralysis, she sent another request to Mayerne. In the end, it was a personal entreaty from the king that stirred the physician – for the love of me, Charles urged, go and find my wife: 'Pour l'amour de moy allez trouver ma Femme.'[30]

One day, walking to the north of Exeter, Henrietta heard some doleful cries and found a woman whose daughter was almost dead of starvation. Taking a 'small chain of gould' from her neck, the queen handed it to the distressed mother and bid her sell it. Her confessor chided such compassion towards 'hereticks' and when the king heard of it, he was said to have quipped that his wife had most likely been tasked to do a 'penance for itt'.[31] Even though the couple were separated, her influence remained strong; Secretary of State, Lord Digby, admitted her approbation to any petition was worth more than his.

The birth of a daughter on 16 June 1644 brought little relief to Henrietta. Discovering that he had become a father again, Charles wrote expressing joy over the happy delivery and asked for news of his wife's health. Thinking that she was dying, and gripped with paranoia that the enemy might besiege Exeter, Henrietta feared her fate should she be caught. Her friends and the king's ministers expended much energy trying to reassure her. Though Oxford and York were at serious risk, Charles's overriding concern was for Henrietta, and he assured her, 'I have taken and will take all possible means for thy safety.' His intention was to battle his way south to Exeter just as soon as he could.

Writing two weeks later, after his victory on 30 June, which Charles candidly recognised as the ugliest of the war, his thoughts were with his 'prettiest daughter'. He determined that she should be christened in Exeter Cathedral, but only if the health of 'my little baby' permitted it.[32] To eliminate any doubt, the king felt the need to specify that it should be according to the Church of England, the same as the rest of his children. This letter would cross with one of the queen's.

Unaware of her husband's victory, she revealed that 'up to this time, I was unwilling to trouble you with my complaints ... because that would only grieve you.' She went on to list her symptoms; paralysis of the legs, stomach and bowels that felt heavier than one hundred pounds, and a squeezing of the heart that left her suffocated and like a person poisoned. Yet her life, she asserted, was of 'very little consequence' compared to his preservation.[33] Before he could lead his army to her, she took matters into her own hands. Choosing rather to set out on the road than wait for the Earl of Essex to move against her, she left baby Henriette-Anne and headed to Falmouth. Boarding ship, she was chased by Parliament's navy all the way to L'Aber Ildut, near Brest. Decades later, she would rue ever leaving the king's side.

Charles arrived at Exeter in August and saw his daughter for the first and last time. Then the exertion of 1644 caught up with him. Relieved that his wife was safe, but sad to find that she had departed, he was indisposed with 'mental distress' for some days.[34] Perhaps the reality of Rupert's defeat also set in. Not only that, but the Earl of Newcastle, who he had once described as the 'principal instrument in keeping the crown upon my head' had also fled the kingdom.[35]

A few days was all Charles needed to pray, meditate and come to terms with reality. He promised to retain a gracious memory of Lord Newcastle's services, which he would recompense as soon as he was able. Then he was back in action, having cut off the Earl of Essex and trapped him in the south-west. As the enemy general fell back into Cornwall, so the king and his army advanced, gradually backing their prey into a corner over a two-week period.

On 31 August, with his troops failing to escape the Royalist stranglehold, Essex stepped into a fishing boat at Fowey. Leaving his men to fend for themselves, the Lord General sailed to safety. His cavalry managed to break out, but the infantry had no option but to surrender. Despite terms agreed, the vanquished Parliamentarians were plundered, though the king and his officers did their utmost to prevent it. Charles now had his great victory, and with it came 36 captured cannon and weapons for 10,000 men.

One other major battle was squeezed into 1644, at Newbury, proving that lightning could strike the same place twice. For the second occasion, both armies did battle there. The encounter highlighted a growing divide within the Parliamentarian leadership. In the absence of Lord Essex, who made a plea of ill health, responsibility fell upon the Earl of Manchester who dragged his heels and reluctantly joined forces with William Waller. The latter was also 'weary' of the war and declared he would submit to 'anything that may conduce to the despatch of it'.[36] As these lethargic leaders confronted the king, who was determined 'to conquer or die', the Royalists had the chance of ending the year in a much better position than anticipated.[37]

The encounter centred around Donnington Castle, held by the king, and Shaw House, a fortified Parliamentarian position. Following a trademark night march, Waller launched a surprise attack on the Royalists, but Manchester hesitated for hours before supporting him. Making the most of this disunity, the king's men rallied and even managed to rout Oliver Cromwell. The fighting went on into the 'Moon-shine' and at Shaw House, built by a clothier, the Royalist Sir George Lisle removed his coat and fought in his white shirt, so that his men could better see him.[38] When night finally put an end to proceedings, the Royalists stole away from the field, leaving their enemies to claim a hollow victory.

Chapter 26

Crying Blood

Every Knight of the Garter wore a prominent badge that featured the cross of St George within a sparkling star. Membership of this prestigious order was something to be proud of and the knights wore its insignia as part of their daily attire. Every day the king placed its blue ribbon around his neck to demonstrate his own intrinsic beliefs. Hanging from it was a medallion of St George on horseback, set with diamonds, and on the reverse was an image of Henrietta Maria. The queen was always close to his heart.

On 1 January 1645, Charles replied to one of his wife's letters, which he deemed to be 'a good augur' to begin the new year. After later deciphering a coded section of it, he might have wished to retract his statement. The secret lines chided him for not writing enough as well as referring to 'those at London' as a Parliament, therefore giving them legitimacy. Somewhat hurt, Charles went on to express his surprise and asserted that he had 'never missed any occasion' of writing to Henrietta.[1]

The royal couple's correspondence betrayed a growing frustration and anxiety. Forbear 'judging harshly of my actions,' the king urged his wife, 'before thou hearest the reasons of them from me.' As for his terminology of Parliament, 'if there had been but two, besides myself, of my opinion, I had not done it.'[2] The truth was that Charles often called his Parliaments by numerous names; last year's at Oxford turned out to be a 'mongrel'. Comparison to animals was a theme. Many years ago, he had complained to Strafford that Parliaments were 'of the Nature of Cats, they ever grow curst with Age' and also likened them to a 'Hidra'.[3] That January of 1645, the late Earl of Strafford was, as ever, very much at the forefront of the king's mind.

Parliament had charged the 67-year-old Archbishop of Canterbury, William Laud, with high treason. Accusing him of attempting to introduce an arbitrary and tyrannical government, the trial had collapsed due to lack of evidence. MPs then proceeded with a Bill of Attainder, just as they had with Strafford. Predictably, it passed through a depleted Commons and Lords, but the Earl of Essex questioned whether this ruthless act was truly indicative of the cause of liberty in which so many had fought and died. Nevertheless, on 10 January, under the shadows of the Tower of London, Laud's head was duly severed.

Within correspondence to his wife, Charles reasoned that guilt over Laud's 'crying blood' was entirely with the rebels: 'I believe it is no presumption to hope hereafter that [God's] hand of justice must be heavier upon them, and lighter upon us.' This subject of the Almighty's wrath had been brought up by Lord George Digby in a poignant conversation with the king. As they touched on the sensitive subject of the Earl of Strafford, Charles listened to Digby's 'superstitious observation' that the earl's death had been 'one of the great causes of God's just judgements upon this nation by a furious civil war'. Ironically, the king and Digby had a shared responsibility for that death. Digby had been one of the men who had voted in favour of Strafford's execution, declaring that the dangerous earl must be dispatched from this world. Having sanctioning Strafford's demise, that moment of weakness had played heavily upon Charles ever since.[4] With each defeat, he began to question whether he was the focus of divine punishment.

For all the strain of separation, the king and queen's love for one another remained strong. Charles assured her, 'I love thee above all earthly things,' and rued her ongoing absence. Lack of good company was a torture in his misery. Most of his companions, he complained, were either too foolish or fanatical, busy or reserved. Too wise, even. Perhaps, the king wrote, because their company could not compare to hers, it simply made him 'hard to be pleased'.[5] In the face of the previous year's military disasters, the king and queen now turned to their eldest son's marriage prospects as a means of restoring their fortunes. The eldest daughter of the King of Portugal was one option, with a proposed six-figure dowry. There was also the daughter of the Prince of Orange, in exchange for 'such succours' that would assist the Royalist cause.[6]

At the end of January peace talks opened at Uxbridge, less than 20 miles from London. Representatives of king and Parliament met to discuss terms, though neither truly desired it. The Royalists had been heavily briefed by the king, who made clear his red lines: 'I shall ever show my constancy in adhering to bishops, and all our friends.'[7] Parliament's terms called upon the king to hand over control of the army and navy, establish Presbyterianism in England, surrender up his evil counsellors, and allow MPs to handle the Irish rebellion. As if this wasn't enough of an ask, he was also expected to take the Covenant, and thus abandon his own religious principles.

Regular bulletins were sent back to Charles. These he would studiously annotate and return, as he always did with official documents. He branded his opponents stubborn over their inflexible manner. Secretary of State, Sir Edward Nicholas, was instructed to put the enemy commissioners in the mind that they were 'arrant rebels' whenever private discussion gave opportunity, and that their ends must be damnation, ruin and infamy, except if they repented. Unsurprisingly, talks broke down in February.[8]

Opinions from the queen's circle in France was that until London was 'humbled', the rebels would never be reduced to reason.[9] Henrietta had warned Charles against going to the capital unless Parliament was ended, or he was accompanied by a good army. There was one problem about the latter; there were scant resources left 'but from abroad'.[10] All through the Uxbridge discussions, the king had continued negotiations for foreign aid. There was talk of ships from his Danish uncle, or the Dutch, and even a French army. The Pope was called upon for money and munitions, and a Gentleman of the Bedchamber was despatched to Venice to plead for financial assistance. The Republic had long held a special place in the king's affections, but the Doge excused himself on account of his war with the Turks. Hope, however, sprang from a home-grown source.

Before peace negotiations broke up, news arrived from the Marquis of Montrose, the king's newly appointed Scottish general. He had won a third successive victory over the Covenanters in the space of six months. In August 1644, Montrose had disguised himself as a servant, and together with only two other men, had ridden into Scotland. Sewn into his saddle was the glittering royal standard, as well as his commission. By sheer charisma alone, Montrose slowly attracted men to his side. Expecting to meet up to 12,000 Irish troops in the Western Highlands, he found barely 1,500 commanded by the giant Alasdair 'MacColla' MacDonald. This man more than made up for the deficient numbers, and he and Montrose formed a winning partnership. A master of guerrilla warfare, Montrose successfully welded together a diverse force of differing clans and religions, while MacColla brought some decisive tactics.

Their first test had been at Tippermuir, on 1 September 1644. Lacking arms and armour, Montrose exhorted his men to pick up the stones from the ground and bash their enemies' brains out. Those few who did have muskets had only one shot. Throwing missiles and charging headlong into their stunned opponents, this tirade of aggression and unbridled fervour sent the Covenanter horsemen fleeing from the field. A second victory followed at Aberdeen, and then on 2 February 1645, Montrose struck at the heartlands of the Marquis of Argyll, the Covenanter leader. In Scotland, allegiance cut deeper than two-horse politics; civil war loyalties were divided between king, religion and clan. Montrose and MacColla dealt a knockout blow to Argyll's Clan Campbell. After covering 30 miles in thirty-six hours, the Royalists rushed down the slopes of Ben Nevis in a wild charge that swept all before them. Montrose and MacColla offered the king renewed hope. Through their efforts, all he had lost might be regained.

When Charles had written to the Doge of Venice, he had observed that a constant turn of events and fortune was usual in civil wars. But the summer of 1645, he predicted, would be 'the hottest for war of any that hath been'.[11] Even before the discussions at Uxbridge were ended, the king was proved correct. He lost Shrewsbury, the base of his Welsh recruiting grounds. Distressed at the dire news trickling out of England, the queen feared that without powerful assistance her husband would be prevented from maintaining an army in the field. Most of the small funds she received went towards paying the monthly interest on the pawned crown jewels. Henrietta scrimped and saved, begged and borrowed.

The Parliamentarians were battling themselves as much as the king. The House of Commons had long harboured a desire to assert their superiority over the Lords, and at the end of 1644 they had voted to remove wavering noblemen from all military commands. To achieve this, a Self-Denying Ordinance was introduced, whereby no Member of Parliament could hold a military post. The House of Lords, anticipating the move, voted it down. Peers were subject to immense pressure from protestors, while preachers exhorted them to ask forgiveness of God for opposing the motion. Reluctantly bowing to pressure, the Lords eventually approved the Ordinance and military command was transferred to Sir Thomas Fairfax.

A Yorkshireman, Fairfax was moderate and sober in both character and politics, and held the respect of a broad base. He was also decidedly uncontroversial. What did turn heads was the exemption of Oliver Cromwell, permitted by MPs to retain both his parliamentary seat and military baton. Was Fairfax's appointment a front, with Cromwell as back-seat driver? Within this New Model Army, officers of Independent religious beliefs were certainly promoted: men of Cromwell's persuasion. Favouring the freedom of each congregation to decide their own form of worship, they opposed the conformity of a national church.

In 1645, preparing to take the field in defence of Oxford, the king remained outwardly unperturbed about this new enemy army. He wrote to Henrietta that he was ready to 'put an end to Fairfax's excellency'.[12] But in reality, the precarious Royalist position led to the Prince of Wales being sent to Bristol to establish a headquarters of his own. This would lessen the chance of both monarch and heir falling into enemy hands, and cement loyalty in the south-west. It also split up factious counsellors, some of whom went with the prince. The Oxford Parliament had fizzled out after calling on the king to make peace. Charles light-heartedly expected to be 'chidden' by Henrietta, who had been 'vexed' by the assembly, which she considered had gone on far too long.[13]

Main advice now came from his council of war. During sessions in May, Rupert advocated striking north to reconquer that vital territory and, in turn, draw Fairfax away from Oxford. He was opposed by Lord Digby, the Secretary of State, who thought it dishonourable not to seek out and engage the new rebel army. As commander and politician clashed, the outcome was a middle course. A significant detachment was placed under Lord Goring and sent to oppose Fairfax, while the rest of the king's forces headed north. Digby predicted that when it came, the inevitable clash would be 'a battle of all for all'.[14]

No sooner had the royal army set out than Sir Thomas Fairfax laid siege to Oxford. Once more, Digby led calls to turn about and attack. For Rupert, the city was well stocked and safe enough – and the siege would most certainly be called off once the king's army took a town or two. Leicester was named as a first objective. This would not just offer a base, but also allow contributions to be extracted from the wider area. The Governor of Oxford was told to keep in regular contact and not to represent his situation more pressing than 'really and punctually' it was. Rupert's gamble was approved.[15]

On 10 May 1645, King Charles reputedly spent the night at Inkberrow Vicarage and utilised a book of maps detailing every town in England, Wales and southern Scotland. Though the Scottish Highlands had not been mapped, it was in that inhospitable and remote terrain that the Marquis of Montrose achieved a fourth victory the day before. Pounded by driving rain, Montrose and his men were chased through the night by a Covenanter force twice their size. As morning broke near the village of Auldearn, the Royalists lay in wait under cover of a thick mist.

Thinly deploying a few hundred infantrymen amongst farm buildings, Montrose had the prized royal standard hoisted above them. Tucking himself away on a hill to the south, he lay in wait with the rest of his force. Assuming the flag to be fluttering over the Royalist main body, the 4,000 Covenanters made for it. When Montrose swept down to encircle his foe, the shock of this pincer movement broke them. The marquis had been pushing the king for reinforcements; just 500 cavalrymen would make the difference, he urged time and again. In the aftermath of this victory, he made a further plea for cavalry, which if given, would allow him to lead an army of 20,000 into England. The king, facing a crucial battle, had none to spare.

On 31 May 1645, the Royalists captured Leicester by storm. Their jubilant and uncontrollable troops pillaged and killed. Back in 1642, Rupert had threatened the mayor, calling for a £2,000 donation to guarantee the town's protection. The king had disavowed his nephew's threat as 'very displeasing to us' and freed the officials from yielding to it – though he kept the first instalment of £500. Charles had gone on to declare that the menacing act was 'so far from our heart or intention ... as we abhor the thoughts of it'.[16] Three years later, he was powerless to prevent any outrages.

Militarily, Leicester had the desired effect. The Parliamentarians abandoned the Siege of Oxford as Rupert had predicted, and searched out the king. Charles, freed from uncertainty, was in good spirits. In April, grossly underestimating his predicament, he told the queen that her return to England might be possible in as little as two months. Echoing, and perhaps encouraging, his vulnerable master's delusion, Lord Digby proclaimed that if they won the inevitable battle 'we never had more cause to thank God'.[17] The Chancellor, Lord Culpepper, anticipated giving the '*Hoghen-Moghens*' [high and mighties] a bellyful of knocks.[18] When Rupert advocated striking even further north, Digby and his band of optimistic brothers prevailed. The council resolved to turn back and fight it out.

King and Parliament came to blows in the fields around Naseby, a small village 13 miles from Northampton. Scouts had reported that the Parliamentarians were falling back, prompting Rupert to hurry after them. It soon became apparent to the Royalists that they were outnumbered; the king had 10,000 men to Parliament's 13,500.[19] The opening moves followed a regular pattern. As Lord General, Rupert's place should have been at the king's side, overseeing the battle. Perhaps recalling Marston Moor, when he had left the cavalry to subordinates, he decided to take personal command of the right wing at Naseby. The northern horsemen were placed on the left under Sir Marmaduke Langdale. In the centre, the king's elite infantry stood ready behind Sergeant-Major General, Lord Astley. King Charles retained a small reserve of cavalry.

It was a gloriously sunny day. Rupert opened the battle and chased those enemy cavalrymen opposite him from the field. The king's infantry proved their mettle and pushed their numerically superior enemy back with grit and determination. The Royalist code-word of the day was 'Queen Mary'. Opposing them, Parliamentarians hollered 'God our Strength'.

Trumpets screamed as men were slashed by swords or bludgeoned with the butt ends of muskets. Musket balls, capable of leaving exit wounds the size of a dinner plate, blasted bodies apart. It looked as if the Royalists might snatch a stunning victory. Their cavalry left wing, however, did not fare well against Cromwell's well-ordered troopers and the latter's success threatened the flank of the Royalist infantry blocks. At this crucial juncture, and in the absence of Prince Rupert, King Charles made ready to lead his reserves into the fray.

Four years earlier, Parliament had attempted to prevent the king departing for Edinburgh to oversee a truce with Scottish Covenanters. The frustrated monarch had told MPs that he would not be held back. He would give any who threatened to lay hands on his horse's bridle 'cause to regret it'.[20] Now, with the most important battle of the Civil Wars hanging in the balance, the Earl of Carnwath dared to do just that. The Scotsman grabbed the royal bridle and 'swearing two or three full mouthed Scottish oaths', he asked if the king intended to go upon his death.[21] The motion caused confusion and panic. Before Charles knew it, the window of opportunity passed him by and his troops were in headlong flight. Had he been fiery enough to have brushed Carnwath aside, a clash between the king and Cromwell might have been a suitable finale.

As he fled the field, the king was pursued by his enemies, who had been ordered to put aside thoughts of plunder in favour of the ultimate prize. At Bloodyman's Ford, the king discharged both pistols. Being a first-class rider, he spurred his horse and escaped. As for Carnwath, some years earlier the Scottish Parliament had sentenced the man to death, but because he was with the king and out of their reach, they simply declared him officially dead. Thus, Charles's life was most likely saved that day by his undead peer.

Though thousands of Royalist cavalrymen escaped Naseby, the royal carriage did not. The troops who captured the coach gave the king a double defeat. Discovering the royal cabinet, stashed with thirty-seven personal letters between Charles and Henrietta, they could not have apprehended the devastation these papers would cause. The pen would prove just as deadly as the sword. Charles claimed there was nothing sensational in them, and that the dishonour of publishing them would do his enemies more damage. He considered 'virtue and nobleness' to be sacrosanct, incorrectly believing that this 'inhumane' attack on his privacy would foster outrage.[22]

Nearly a month later, Lord Digby tried to play down the situation. Writing to the queen, he warned she might hear 'much noise' from London. There had been, he assured her, many successes since Naseby, so much so that they had already lost the 'sharp sense' of defeat.[23] But on the question of the king's letters, he thought them unfortunately and needlessly lost, and considered 'how we should behave ourselves' when secret foreign treaties came to be exposed.

Parliament moved against those named and shamed in the letters. The Portuguese ambassador, Antonio de Souza, was targeted, and wrote to the king of the 'tumults of the people' against him.[24] Apart from discovering details about the Prince of Wales's proposed match with the Infanta, it transpired that the envoy had helped convey Charles's letters to Henrietta. To make matters worse, de Souza pranked Parliament. Aware that they were opening his correspondence, he put together a dummy packet, which included some spectacles. With these, de Souza suggested, MPs could better spy on his correspondence. The French ambassador, by contrast, was favourably entertained because the king had written in one letter that the man was not to be trusted on any account.

Wales and Ireland offered Charles the possibility of part-repairing the losses incurred at Naseby. He would recruit from Wales and ship back more of the English army from Ireland. But he had to act soon. On 7 July, from Raglan Castle, he realised 'the longer I stay, it will be somewhat the more danger'.[25] The Royalist cavalry had survived Naseby, and with them, Charles considered striking north to link up with Montrose. Rumours of this plan prompted Rupert to point out the unfeasibility of such a 'strange resolution'. In what condition would the king leave all behind him, the prince wondered, venturing his opinion that his uncle had no option to 'preserve his posterity, kingdom, and nobility' except by a peace treaty: 'I believe it is a more prudent way to retain something than to lose all.'[26]

From one so trusted, this must have come as a blow to Charles, and his honest reply reveals the split at the heart of his character – that of monarch and man.

> I confess that speaking as a mere soldier or statesman, I must say there is no probability but of my ruin; yet as a Christian I must tell you, that God will not suffer rebels and traitors to prosper, nor this cause to be overthrown.[27]

Chapter 27

Hunted Partridge

Across the English Channel in Paris, Queen Henrietta Maria's fragile health continued. In April, she had been seriously ill and confined to her apartment in the Louvre. Unable to write due to a lame hand, she had also suffered multiple fits. From a bed hung with red silk and embroidered with gold, the queen received messengers and closely followed events in England. The news worried her more than ever.

That summer, when much recovered, she heard about the disaster at Naseby and fretted over her husband's 'hazarding his own sacred person'.[1] Yet, despite the bleak news, her 'rule' was that the 'Game must not be given over'.[2] Now, more than ever, was the time to redouble all industry. Much-needed gunpowder and arms were shipped to the few seaports remaining in the king's hands, and she employed her trusty pen to implore all and sundry to follow her example. France was taking a closer interest, not least out of consideration for itself. Diplomats in Paris reported fears that a Puritan-led Britain might breathe life into a Protestant alliance.

Holed up in magnificent Raglan Castle, home of the wealthy – and Catholic – Marquis of Worcester, Charles came to terms with his situation. Not even Digby could ignore the circumstances. The low ebb that seized the Royalists was a 'perfect trial' to all men's integrities, he admitted, and the torrent of misfortunes momentarily overcame his sanguine nature. From Launceston, Edward Hyde determined that grief, anger and indignation had broken his mind, and left him 'not able to continue this life'. Commiserating with Digby, Hyde mused that they might die honestly.[3]

Charles was equally despondent, fearing that God's wrath might run deeper than he ever imagined, but these personal anxieties were hidden behind a veneer of majesty. The radiance of the crown could bring light to the darkest of times. Having acted in court masques from an early age, Charles was adept at playing the role of monarch, which instilled in him a dignified calm – an almost meditative state. Closeted behind Raglan's formidable walls, he examined his relationship with God.

The aged Marquis of Worcester had bankrolled the Royalist cause from the outset, and each time he played host to the king, a further injection of cash was requested. Dr Thomas Baylie, the marquis's chaplain, duly informed his master of the latest financial appeal. Worcester interrupted him, 'hold Sir, that's no newes.' When Charles was informed that the old man wished to meet him, he guessed 'my Lords drift, well enough' and wondered whether his benefactor meant to 'chide me, or else to convert me to his Religion'.

At 11.00 pm, Protestant king and Catholic noble met in the bedroom known as the Lord Privy Seal's chamber. Worcester's father had died in the room, and from that point it had been cleared and never used again. There, according to Baylie, the two defended their religious beliefs in a tense debate. Worcester talked so much that he left little opportunity for counter-argument. He mentioned the king's speech to his troops before Naseby, and a promise made to expel all Catholics from his army if the Lord granted a Royalist victory. Worcester alleged that God was angry with Charles for disgracing Catholics in this way. Why else would the king's sword have 'broke in the aire' when victory should have been assured?[4] With rambling rhetoric, the marquis called upon the king to take new resolutions regarding his religion.

Baylie's account was published in 1649, after both the king and marquis were dead. It was criticised by some of his contemporaries. But according to him, Charles vociferously asserted that the Roman Catholic church was offensive, being full of 'so many ridiculous stories' and lies. As for Naseby, 'God blest us the worse for having so many Papists'. At the end of the evening, Worcester got to his knees, kissed the king's hand and began to weep. Within the torchlight, preparing to be escorted back to his room, Charles expressed pity that Worcester was wrong. The marquis retorted it was a greater pity the king was not in the right. Somewhat shaken by the ordeal, Charles judged that the old man had clearly been 'a long time putting on his armour' considering the detail of his arguments.[5] The showdown continued in writing. Several papers were exchanged until the king withdrew from the contest, considering the many other matters weighing heavily upon his mind at that time.

On 5 August 1645, Charles warned his eldest son to 'prepare for the worst'. If ever the Prince of Wales risked falling into rebel hands, he was to make every effort to get to France, where his mother would have 'absolute full power' in all matters, except religion.[6] Two weeks later, however, he referred to miraculously good fortunes when cheerfully urging Oxford to provide for the coming winter like ants. The two letters are symbolic: one written as a man and a father, the other as a resolute monarch. At the end of August, King Charles had resolved:

> by the grace of God, never to yield up this church to the government of Papists, Presbyterians, or Independents, nor to injure my successors, by lessening the crown of that ecclesiastical and military power which my predecessors left me.[7]

The coronation oath was Charles's sticking point and he considered the long game. With every last card played, his determination grew. Vowing never to give over the quarrel, despite 'whatever personal punishment' God might inflict upon him, he stood ready to accept his fate.

> I cannot flatter myself with expectation of good success, more
> than this, to end my days with humour and a good conscience,
> which obliges me so to continue my endeavours ... God may yet,
> in [due] time, avenge His own cause.[8]

It was this dignified aura of majesty which captivated many, and had them battle on with the king to the bitter end. His opponents equally sought to break the spell. Throwing 'all respect to the winds', newsboys on the streets of London pedalled an extremely personal satirical sheet that was also distributed to foreign states. Reading like a wanted poster, it lampooned the king, branding him a traitor to his promises and perfidious in his words. Having absented himself from his parliament for four years to 'bathe his hands' in the blood of his subjects, it called for sightings of the monarch to be reported. To identify their king, people were told that he is 'a stammerer' who cannot speak the truth or 'talk plainly'. This was left to circulate for days before the printer was apprehended.[9]

Then, as if by divine retribution, the Marquis of Montrose secured two further victories in the space of six weeks – the Battle of Kilsyth was his crowning moment. On 15 August 1645, the last Covenanter army in Scotland was scattered. After a year of miracles, Montrose had fully turned the tables. Glasgow fell to him, and he issued writs in the king's name for a new Scottish Parliament. In London, MPs responded by calling for solemn public prayers – there was little else they could do. While jubilant Royalists praised 'the glorious Montrose', the Marquis of Argyll and other Covenanter leaders fled across the border.[10] The army that had entered England in 1644 was now recalled to deal with Montrose. The king was presented with a last roll of the dice.

Leaving his Welsh recruiting grounds, Charles struck north with his cavalry and then turned east, cutting across the Midlands. 'Like a hunted partridge', he was desperate to fly to Scotland and join Montrose.[11] The Parliamentarians assigned Colonel General Poyntz, commander of their northern association, to track him. The Scots ordered Lieutenant General David Leslie to do the same. Reaching Welbeck and then Doncaster, the king's enemies proved too strong for him to achieve his objective. Contenting himself with a raid on Huntingdon, Charles then withdrew, falling back to Wales and flitting from one garrison to the next. The problem was that they were falling like 'ripe figs'.[12]

Chapter 28

Farewell Harry

Not long before his death in 1641, Anthony Van Dyck painted a life-sized portrait of two fair-haired brothers. Lords John and Bernard Stuart were distant cousins of the king. Van Dyck's brush perfectly captured the essence of these stereotypical cavaliers. John appears in a golden doublet, fashionably slashed at the chest to show off his white shirt beneath. He went on to be cut down at the Battle of Cheriton in 1644. Bernard looks out of the canvas with the confidence of a self-righteous late teen. His is a swaggering pose, resting one foot on a stone step and a hand at his hip. The lining of his cloak is revealed, and ripples of silver silk engulf him. King Charles affectionately called him 'Barny'.[1]

On 24 September 1645, the king stood atop Chester Cathedral. Even as daylight faded, his troops remained engaged with the enemy; Rowton Moor had been a battle of three parts that had lasted all day. Though fighting with courage and resolve, the Royalists had been broken, and in this last phase had fallen back towards Chester. To support their comrades, the garrison sallied out beneath the king's watchful gaze. Engaged in this desperate fighting, young Barny was killed while leading the king's lifeguards, becoming the third of four brothers to perish in the war.

Conversing with a captain on the tower, the king looked on, unaware of the personal loss below him. Then, a stray shot 'gave him a salute' and struck the head of the officer beside him, who died on the spot.[2] This near miss could only have reinforced Charles's believe that God had spared him once again. As his cause went into its death throes, the question was for what? At the end of July 1645, he had given a stark warning to Rupert.

> He that will stay with me at this time must expect and resolve either to die for a good cause or which is worse to live as miserable in maintaining it.[3]

At the heart of his loyalists, a feud between Prince Rupert and Lord Digby had raged for years. Digby had begun the Civil War as an officer, achieving some success and displaying bravery. When wounded in the thigh, he transferred to politics, which was infinitely more suited to his devious character. His fingerprints could be found upon many strokes of misfortune. Attempts to take

153

towns by coaxing their commanders into defecting (notably Hull, Plymouth and Abingdon) all exploded in his face, wounding – even killing – others, but never himself. The second Battle of Newbury had been fought at his urging, ambitious to do something 'extraordinary in the absence of Prince Rupert'.[4] Sweet-talking, witty and with impeccable manners, Digby always knew what to say and how to say it.

Some Royalists saw through Digby. Sir Philip Warwick recalled the words of Lord Bacon when describing the man: 'there are some things which have more wonder in them than worth.'[5] William Legge once tackled him head on: 'you did both say and do things to [Rupert's] prejudice ... not in an open and direct line, but obscurely and obliquely.'[6] The king's sister considered the whole Digby family poor choices for counsellors of state, but most especially George. The king, however, would not entertain any criticism. A news-sheet, *Mercurius Britanicus*, captured the relationship in one line 'a Prince cannot be long without his Secretary, nor can Charles without his Digby'.[7] In the run-up to Naseby, attempts had been made to smooth out issues between prince and peer. Rupert led the military arm, and Digby the political. Rupert had gone on to suggest the king sue for peace, while Digby took great pride in overconfident bravado. The queen tried to do 'good offices' between both men and Lord Jermyn expressed hope that they could be friends.[8]

Digby and his supporters labelled Rupert's party 'the Cumberlanders' after Rupert's dukedom.[9] The prince had led the Royalist armies for a year with one eye over his shoulder, writing in the aftermath of Naseby, 'doubtless the fault of it will be put upon [me]'.[10] Digby's spies fuelled his animosity towards Rupert by a torrent of hate-filled intelligence. One letter warned that William Legge, Governor of Oxford – and Rupert's 'assistant' – was showing 'his teeth plainer' towards Digby. Others implored the Secretary of State to 'take the bridle out of Phaeton's hands' and prevent Rupert from burning the world for a third time.[11] Marston Moor was presumably the first occasion and Naseby second. The third was about to reveal itself.

Fairfax and his army arrived outside Bristol, England's second city, on 21 August 1645. Its heart was distinctly mediaeval. Numerous streets led down to the castle, where the buildings of this inner sanctum seemed to huddle together in apprehension. Plague had infiltrated the city, but Prince Rupert confidently asserted that he could hold the place for months – unless faced with mutiny. General Fairfax summoned the prince to surrender by declaring Parliament to be the 'truest Friends to your Family it hath in the World' and then went on to storm it in the weeks following.[12] Without enough soldiers to man the extensive perimeter, and unable to hold off his opponents, Rupert surrendered the port city on 10 September under good terms. He rode out dressed in scarlet with silver ribbons.

Having anticipated that many might peel away from his service, the king was concerning himself with those who had a spiritual loyalty. His fierce and charismatic nephew's shock surrender devastated Charles. Turning in on himself, he wondered who he could trust if not his own kin? The news sent Lord Digby and his spies into overdrive, one of whom claimed that the House of Palatines 'do think themselves assured of the crown' and quoted a line from astrologer William Lilly's 1644 prediction: 'Now treacherous kinsman act thy part.'[13] Lady Digby even waded in, calling for Rupert's dismissal.

Governor Legge was arrested, and all of Rupert's military appointments were revoked. Charles had looked upon the prince as a son, and termed his actions the 'greatest trial of my constancy that hath yet befallen me'.[14] He also sent a message to his councillors in Oxford:

> Tell my son [the Duke of York] that I shall less grieve to hear that he is knocked on the head than that he should do so mean an action as is the rendering of Bristol castle and fort upon the terms it was.[15]

In the power vacuum that followed, Digby reached out to the Marquis of Ormonde, the king's deputy in Ireland. 'Prince Rupert's removal from all military power hath made way for your Excellency' he claimed like some sort of kingmaker.[16] Though Charles supported Ormonde's candidacy, it was impossible for the man to leave Ireland. Grasping at straws after defeat at Rowton Moor, the king resolved to make another attempt to join Montrose in Scotland. Gathering his cavalry, he marched 'tattered and tired' to Newark with an elated Digby at his side, who asserted were it not for Montrose, 'we should almost despair'.[17]

Welbeck Abbey was the king's furthest stop on the road north. The bygone world of the monks had been linked with the current owners, the courtly Cavendish family. The aged limestone abbey, adjoining a modern array of square towers and symmetry, was a haunting and empty shell. William Cavendish, Marquis of Newcastle, had left England after Marston Moor and remained on the continent. A famed equestrian, the marquis's riding houses, where extraordinary feats were performed, had been the talk of society. As the king reviewed his few remaining horsemen, he prayed they might achieve a miracle for him.

The appointment of Lord Digby as Lieutenant General north of the River Trent shocked the band of brothers around the king. His 2,000 cavalrymen were top-heavy with officers, many of whom were better qualified than the political pariah. Then word reached them of Montrose's defeat on a misty morning at Philiphaugh. Deciding to stay put in Newark, the king delegated to Digby the task of leading half his cavalry north. Some accused Charles of being bewitched – a word that had also been used decades earlier, when referring to his relationship with Buckingham. Digby most certainly held a similar sway over Charles, and like a Stuart-era Rasputin, he oversaw the 'last stages of decadence'.[18] Ironically, both the royal council and church were now presided over by men who stemmed from opposition; Digby, as a teenager, had once defended his father against allegations of treason, while Archbishop Williams of York had spent many a period in the Tower at his majesty's pleasure.

At Sherburn-in-Elmet, on 15 October 1645, Digby met with disaster only days into his journey to Montrose. The men he commanded had not forgotten the blame he had heaped on them over their conduct at Naseby. Nor had he endeared himself to their commander, Sir Marmaduke Langdale, who he had once labelled a creature of Prince Rupert's. At Sherburn, and then again at Annan Moor, in southern Scotland, Digby split his troops and then failed to support Langdale at critical moments. The Royalists paid the price for his inept leadership. When the king's private papers had been captured at Naseby, Digby had condemned those who had left such precious items in the royal carriage. 'I thank God I lost none of mine,' he had unhelpfully written.[19] At Sherburn, Parliamentarians captured his coach, along with sixty-nine personal letters, which were all scrutinised.

With his last hope dashed, the vulnerable king remained in Newark. Plague stalked the streets. Prince Rupert, too, was heading directly for his uncle. Unable to put up with slurs over Bristol, one supposedly stemming from the queen that he had sold the city, the prince set off on a cross-country march to exonerate himself. Eighty volunteers from Oxford accompanied him, including his devoted brother, Maurice. The king forbade his nephews to approach Newark but they ignored the order, entering the royal presence on 16 October. Maintaining a dignified front, Charles responded with a few words to Maurice and stomached their presence all through supper.

Eventually a court martial acquitted Rupert, judging him not guilty of the least 'want of courage or fidelity'.[20] But even this, which the king approved, did not end matters. Resolving to return to Oxford, the king was concerned about leaving Newark in the hands of Governor Richard Willis, who had so enthusiastically greeted the princes. Willis, the king decided, was to be removed and given an alternative role. The decision reignited resentment. As Charles left church and went to dinner, his meal was interrupted once more by his nephews and their followers. Harsh words followed and after accusing Digby of treason, they were ordered from the room. The disgruntled band of men marshalled themselves in the marketplace and asked for permission to leave royal service. Though Charles would 'not Christen' this behaviour as an act of mutiny, he declared 'it looked very like'.[21]

Parliament's Committee of Both Kingdoms eyed Newark closely. It seemed a ripe time to assault the town while 'great discontents' were prevailing.[22] Relations between Charles and his nephews were not helped by news that Parliament had granted their eldest brother, the Elector Palatine, a pension of £8,000 part-paid from revenues that were once the king's.

Rupert was guilty of a quick temper, but not treason, and the sad scenes at Newark did not break the family bond. He and Maurice were given passes to go beyond the seas, but they continued serving the king until the war's bitter end. Though Charles judged that Rupert's passions 'may sometimes make him mistake', he believed implicitly in his nephew's 'honest constancy and courage'.[23]

As for Digby, de-facto leader of the king's council and army, the man ended up with 'neither 100 pens [scribes] nor 100 men' and fled to Ireland. Upon hearing of his defeat, Rupert expended little ink over his one-time rival, merely exclaiming, 'Alas! poor man.'[24] As the New Model Army closed up around Oxford, the embattled king was ready to 'sink under my present miseries'.[25] Any personal animosities no longer mattered.

Chapter 29

Conscience

27 April 1646.

Oxford's gates had been locked for five days. At 3.00 am the governor let three men out of the city and called after them 'Farewell Harry'.[1] Two rode with pistols at their sides. The other was dressed as a servant, wearing a woollen Montero cap, somewhat like a modern balaclava. This was King Charles. Disguise, he deemed, was essential after Parliament's forces 'came so thick' around his headquarters.[2] Having had his lovelock cut off and beard trimmed, he now rode across Magdalen Bridge with Jack Ashburnham, Groom of the Bedchamber, and Dr Michael Hudson, his 'plain dealing chaplain'.[3]

The men headed for London, with the king certain he could win over MPs and citizens by his presence. The fugitives travelled via Dorchester, Henley and Maidenhead, but at the outskirts of the capital, Charles reassessed his options. Fearful of the number of defeated Royalists in London, Parliament had expelled them out of concern that the king might come either 'disguised or openly' and provoke an uprising.[4] MPs let it be known that if the monarch did appear, they would lodge him in the Tower for his own safety. The Scottish army was Charles's second option. Jean de Montreuil, a French envoy, had been acting as an intermediary and negotiating with the Scots for months. Loose promises had been extracted that if the king placed himself under their protection, they would work for his restoration. But before Charles left Oxford, Montreuil had a shock change of heart and warned of Scottish evasiveness.

Eventually, Charles resolved to head for King's Lynn, from where he might take a ship to Montrose in Scotland, or head to Ireland, France or Denmark. The trio evaded numerous enemy sentries, were troubled by drunkards and when challenged by a man with a halberd, threw him sixpence and asserted they were Parliamentarians. Quartering at common inns, the king reputedly took on the guise of a parson, complete with black coat and cassock. Charles was never averse to a bit of acting, even in such moments.

On 2 May, in the dead of night, he made a private visit to the religious community at Little Gidding. Being very well acquainted with the Ferrar family, who founded the peaceful haven, it was a noteworthy decision. This was Charles's third visit and it followed a distinct pattern; in 1633, he had stopped off en route to Edinburgh for his coronation. Seven years after this, he did so on his way to make war with Scotland. Now, he changed his mind on his destination yet again, and resolved upon surrendering to the Scots.

Riding into Southwell, he put himself in the hands of his countrymen on 5 May 1646. Upon his appearance, the Scots repudiated everything discussed with the French for fear of upsetting their English allies. Charles was outraged at such 'relapsed perfidiousness'.[5] Nevertheless, as a gesture of his desire for peace, he ordered Royalist Newark to surrender. On 7 May, the Scots withdrew to Newcastle with the king riding in the vanguard of their army.

Hoping to foster an understanding with the Scots, Charles was heartened by signs of a rift between his opponents. Parliament was proving evasive over establishing Presbyterianism in England and the Scots knew it. Charles knew it too. He had written to Digby of an idea to draw either the Presbyterians or Independents to side with him, 'for extirpating the one or the other [so that] I shall be really king again'.[6] But after his intimate attendants were sent packing, and friends barred from his presence, royal hopes of enticing the Scots began to fade.

Devoid of his supporters, the queen's letters were Charles's only consolation. Her love, he assured her, 'preserves my life'. But the couple's ideological differences had become apparent even before he left Oxford. She urged him to come to terms, and once suggested doing so at any cost. It doubly grieved Charles that his wife was unable to understand the deep workings of his conscience.[7] How would she feel, he turned the tables, if asked to give up Catholicism?

Almost immediately upon his arrival at Newcastle, the king called in vain for an assembly to examine the settlement of church affairs. He had proposed a council of sixty divines, equally split between Presbyterians, Independents and twenty of his own choosing. Resorting to plan B, he invited the Presbyterian minister, Alexander Henderson, to discuss theology. A good old religious debate was true to Charles's father's style. Henderson agreed but declined a verbal contest, so for two months, the newfound pen pals sent papers back and forth. Charles opened by declaring himself to be at a disadvantage to Henderson's learning and profession, yet claimed his father had settled him right in religion – and nobody could question King James's fame. Henderson replied the late king's ghost would counsel against attempts to save the bishops. A piqued Charles retorted that he knew his father better.

On the matter of the Church of England, the king extolled the virtues of its reformation, which did not stem from mass protest, nor revolution. For Henderson, it had not yet been concluded; only the head had been changed, while the limbs of 'Anti-christian Heirarchy' had been retained.[8] The honour of finishing it was, he asserted, reserved for Charles, which would make him a great monarch.

There was discussion over the coronation oath, and whether Parliament could absolve the king from it, and thus ease his scruples over church reform.

Charles maintained that there was nothing in the word of God that approved of subjects forcing their king's conscience. He refused to perjure himself by extending Presbyterianism, and therefore knowingly permitting his people to sin. Henderson argued that it was not sinful or shameful to change for the better and considered that bishops and Presbyter elders were one and the same. The exchanges simply reinforced the chasm between them. With King James's declaration of 'no bishop, no king' in his mind, Charles firmly believed that the Presbyterian doctrine was not compatible with monarchy.

No longer at the apex of government, dealing with daily business or overseeing a war, the king was at a loss. There were no petitioners crowding him, nor any ceremonial duties. Every night, a distinguished Scot sat in his chamber under the 'guise' of service and honour.[9] This enforced solitude was to last for six months, and for a man who disliked being idle, it must have been infuriating. But it gave Charles the chance to reflect. The coming negotiations offered him the best chance of regaining his position, therefore every effort was made to snuff out the last flames of war.

Oxford was directed to surrender to General Fairfax, but the governor paid no heed, assuming the king was acting under duress. Parliament, too, attempted to ignore the royal order in hope of taking the town outright. When Charles wrote to Westminster, enclosing a second instruction for Oxford's capitulation, MPs voted 145 to 103 not to send it on. When the citadel eventually came to terms, they agreed to the king's desire that the university be protected. Another wish, that the Duke of York should join him in Newcastle, was refused. Instead, the boy was taken to London and held captive with his younger siblings, Prince Henry and Princess Elizabeth.

On 19 June, the king fired off a letter to the Marquis of Antrim, who, rumour had it, had landed a Royalist army in Scotland. Commanding him to stand down, the king explained this was 'absolutely necessary' for his service.[10] The Marquis of Montrose was twice ordered to disband the remainder of his infamous troops and make the best of it. That summer in Newcastle, amidst negotiations and sermons, the king filled his time by writing to the outside world, even if he had nothing much to say. The Prince of Wales was informed 'this is rather to tell you where I am, and that I am well'.[11] His cousin, the Duke of Richmond, was assured 'I doe not forgett you'. Charles wished it to be known amongst his faithful supporters that despite being out of sight, he was 'not of a changeable constitution'.[12] He was keeping his supporters warm. As the weeks passed, and with matters looking increasingly hopeless, he implored Lords Jermyn, Culpepper and Ashburnham not to undermine him by making any concessions to his enemies:

> I conjure you, by your unspotted faithfulness, by all that you
> love, by all that is good, that no threatenings, no apprehensions of
> danger to my person, make you stir one jot ...[13]

The two sticking points for the king were church and militia. Of the latter, he eventually relented to Parliament taking control for ten years, or if pushed, the rest of his reign. The proviso was that this prerogative power should be returned to his son. To his way of thinking, soldiers could never conquer hearts and minds, nor could a church, once lost, be regained with an army. Therefore, church doctrine and bishops became his last bastion. 'People are governed by the pulpit more than the sword in times of peace,' he avowed. The Independents would have English congregations subject to 'the foolish fancy of every idle person' and the church ruled by Parliament. Should Presbyterianism be planted in England, then the 'doctrine of rebellion' would be made 'canonical' sanctioning the Scots' past rebellions and, in turn, condemning the king's policies.[14] In his opinion, both were as bad as Catholicism. Without control of the pulpits any monarch was lost, and Charles declared he would not part with the Church of England 'upon any condition whatsoever'.[15] We see in this viewpoint just why Charles hesitated over marching on London in 1642–43 and winning the war by conquest; he knew that without his subjects' hearts, it would have been a hollow victory.

By September, Henrietta and Lords Jermyn, Culpepper and Ashburnham were submitting draft declarations to the king that altered his stance. Demonstrating his 'inexpressible grief and astonishment' that his closest allies should try and have him betray his conscience, Charles sent long letters reaffirming his views.[16] It can be difficult to understand his stance nowadays unless his concessions of 1641 are put into context.

At that time, in the face of civil unrest, he had granted away prerogative courts, the expulsion of bishops from the House of Lords, agreed never to tax without Parliament's consent and assented to triennial Parliaments. The royal assent for a perpetual Parliament had been given in state, at Westminster. Although in hindsight, Charles admitted to being surprised by this Bill in the aftermath of Strafford's execution, there is no reason to believe he would not have stuck by it. Even in the dark days of 1646, he considered irreversible anything made law by Act of Parliament before the war. Instead, it was these moments of weakness – of condemning Strafford and failing to support the bishops – that Charles felt had incurred God's displeasure, and as a result, led him to defeat.

By standing firm over the church following his defeat, he now hoped God's mercy might 'take place of his justice'. His unmoveable stance was not simply a 'foolish or peevish' conscience, less still that of a tyrant unwilling to compromise – he had given so much away already.[17] Holding fast was necessary to save his soul, as well as to secure the people of his three kingdoms in the eyes of God, which was his ultimate responsibility as king. A letter to Henrietta, declaring that she was 'free from my faults', hints at a feeling of being somewhat cursed by his pre-war concessions.[18]

Henrietta Maria was the daughter of the Protestant King of Navarre. Her father, on converting to Catholicism, became King Henry IV of France with the rumoured remark that Paris was 'worth a Mass'.[19] Charles and Henry were two very different men. With her father's example in mind, Henrietta could never quite grasp Charles's unwavering position over the Church of England. As well as chiding what looked like wilfulness, her exasperation grew to such heights that she threatened many times to 'meddle no more' with business and retire to a convent.[20] It was a threat that broke Charles's heart, certain that he and his children would be ruined if that ever happened.

Increasingly alone, both physically and ideologically, Charles turned to the only section of his supporters that truly understood him: the bishops. They were his most natural allies and fully understood his reasoning. So hated were these prelates that there was no fear of their defection and, like him, they were willing to defend the Church of England until the last breath.

To Bishop Juxon of London, who did not know 'what fear is in a good cause', Charles promised his protection and turned to him for advice – specifically whether a temporary change to the church was justified, if at heart he remained determined to reinstate the doctrine and discipline he loved.[21] As 1646 closed without any peace settlement, the Scots made ready to withdraw from England. Charles let it be known that when they did so, he expected to be subject to a violent force upon his person.

Chapter 30

Golden Ball

A golden treasure train of £100,000 began winding its way north, reaching York on 4 January 1647. Escorted by a detachment of the New Model Army, these troops were under orders to behave civilly and inoffensively to their Scottish brethren. The money was one instalment of a £400,000 payment to the Scots for their support in the war. Once settled, they would hand over the king and depart England. Charles claimed he was being purchased like a mere commodity. Two days later, an inventory was taken of loot plundered from Raglan Castle, a former Royalist stronghold. Amongst tawny petticoats and white satin window cushions were five jewelled Orders of the Garter. These insignias of England's highest order of chivalry were given a price tag of just over £1, symbolic of how low Charles's lot had fallen.

Eight months of close confinement had, by January 1647, turned into outright imprisonment for the king. It came after a foiled double escape attempt; the Duke of York was to have been smuggled to Newcastle, whereupon father and son would have fled by sea. From Jersey, Sir Edward Hyde mused about his master. How often have we heard him say 'if he could not live a King, he would die a Gentleman,' he wrote to Lord Culpepper.[1] In Hyde's humble opinion, if the king continued 'firm and unshaken [in his principles] … there will be a strange concurrence in all men, to return to their allegiance, and to a reverence of him'.[2] Lord Arthur Capel, who was preparing to return to England, certainly felt that the king's 'great courage and constancy' was an anchor that many clung to.[3]

After the king again refused their terms, the Scots took their leave of him, some with tears in their eyes. Charles gave a 'sharp reply' about having been sold and attempted to hand a secret note to one man in particular.[4] The coded missive, addressed to the French envoy, only exacerbated the mistrust of his new English captors. There were many familiar faces, such as the Earls of Pembroke and Denbigh. Parliament assigned a barber and physician, and Thomas Herbert was appointed a Groom of the Bedchamber, one of the few people who would go on to share the king's last days. Charles was then moved to Holdenby House, an estate his father had purchased for him. As the royal party departed Newcastle, the Marquis of Argyll prayed that God would give the king 'a heart to grant the desyrs of his subjects as the best cure'.[5]

Nobody was permitted to approach the royal prisoner as he travelled south, but crowds lined the roads to catch a glimpse. It must have heartened Charles, who had feared being out of sight might leave him out of mind. Almost as soon as his carriage drew up at Holdenby, Parliamentary commissioners laid their peace proposals before him, which had been almost the same for the last two years. A deadline of twenty days was allocated for his agreement. Following the capitulation of Harlech Castle on 15 March, the last Royalist stronghold, it was hoped the king might follow suit.

Listing the names of a dozen preachers, Charles asked if any two might attend him to discuss the terms, which cut right across his most intrinsic beliefs. The request was refused. Edward Hyde thought this isolation for the best, as nobody could be more careful of the royal conscience than the king himself. Left to his own devices, he could display much 'wit and natural understanding'.[6] In April, a petition was addressed to the king by elements of the New Model Army, in which they pledged to restore his honour, crown and dignity if he placed his person in their ranks. Though Charles issued a stern denial, stating that too much blood had been shed already, and refusing to 'engage our poor people' in another war, the seeds of discontent between Parliament and their soldiers was duly noted.[7]

Several attempts were made to penetrate security at Holdenby, in a bid to keep Charles in contact with loved ones and supporters. Letters from the queen came via a colonel disguised as a fisherman, and a woman was arrested after attempting to hand over a packet, leaving it instead behind a tapestry. When discovered, the cyphered message from John Ashburnham promised 'a good war' for the king's release – as ever, foreign support was being solicited on his behalf.[8] Between games of bowls and walking in the gardens and galleries, Charles continued his sober habits; just a few dishes at mealtimes and two drinks per day, either beer or wine mixed with water. In the outside world, Parliament attempted to disband the New Model Army, but arrears of pay caused a wave of mutinies. General Thomas Fairfax admitted he could not 'do the impossible'.[9] It was at the height of this discontent that a relatively low-ranking officer visited the king.

Following secret discussions at the house of Lieutenant General Oliver Cromwell, Cornet George Joyce was sent to Northamptonshire with the goal of securing the king's person. Arriving late at night on 3 June 1647, he confronted royal servants who refused him access. A commotion ensued. Ringing his silver bell, Charles enquired what was afoot, and then advised that he would see the newcomer in the morning. When king and cornet met, Charles requested to see authority for his removal from Holdenby, leading Joyce to gesture at the troops in the courtyard. 'It is as fair a commission, and as well written a commission as I have seen in my life,' was the royal response.[10] Having no alternative, the king wrote to Parliament that MPs should believe nothing said or done in his name, for it might stem from duress.

Representatives of Scotland lobbied Parliament to rescue the monarch. General Fairfax confirmed that Joyce's men had acted without his orders. He would describe the king as a golden ball, whose possession offered legitimacy and control of any peace settlement. For the army, packed with Independents, the king was a pawn that could protect them from a Parliament led by pro-Presbyterians. Charles, who now declined to return to Holdenby, must have secretly hoped events might lead to more palatable terms from Parliament.

The exchange of captors, from Parliament to army, led to a readmission of Charles's friends and attendants – such as the Duke of Richmond, and chaplains Dr Sheldon and Dr Hammond. Freedom of worship was restored, and the king was allowed to receive letters from his wife. He was even permitted to meet James, Elizabeth and Henry, his three children held in London, after Fairfax overruled Parliament on the matter. Overjoyed, Charles considered they might 'come to some convenient place to dine, and go back at night' and then tentatively suggested they might even stay one or two nights.[11] But he didn't push his luck. To allay any fears his children might have, he told them that Fairfax had promised their return to London would suffer no 'interruption or impediment'.[12]

The Greyhound Inn at Caversham was the setting for this reunion. When Charles fled London in January 1642, he had not taken his two younger children with him, having fully expected to return to the capital soon enough. From that moment, 18-month-old Henry and 6-year-old Elizabeth passed into Parliament's hands. During the war, Charles had attempted to negotiate their release, even suggesting he exchange the much-loved Covenanter, the Earl of Lothian, for his children. The three youths who arrived that summer's morning were now aged 13, 11 and 6. Henry, the youngest, did not recognise his father, and when Charles embraced him, he mournfully mused 'it is not one of the least of my misfortunes that I have brought you and your brothers and sisters into this world to share my miseries'. What followed was, in Cromwell's opinion, the 'tenderest sight that ever his eyes beheld'.[13]

Elizabeth's health was fragile, but she had a robust and intellectual mind like her father. Despite both her confinement and modesty, an array of books had been published with dedications complimenting her abilities. James, Duke of York, was the only one of the trio to have already met Fairfax. At the surrender of Oxford, he recalled in later life, the general had given a less than eloquent speech and was the only officer not to kiss his hand. If Fairfax had made no positive impression on the youthfully arrogant James, he succeeded in earning Elizabeth's full praise, and she promised to repay his kindness for permitting this family gathering.

In London, it seemed that his people also wished to be reunited with the king. Protestors stormed Parliament and called for the monarch's return to the capital on his own terms. The Speaker was forced out to address them. Crowds demanded he shout 'God save the king', but when he went on to do so in a 'very low voice', he was ordered to try again with more enthusiasm.[14]

Wartime loyalty had been split between king or Parliament, but the burning question was now Independent or Presbyterian? MPs sympathising with the latter, seen as more moderate, had taken control of the city's trained bands.

Recognising the ultimate strength of the army and unwilling to sanction the tumultuous proceedings, Charles condemned events in the capital. It was clear that Parliament, Scots and the army were all looking to secure legitimacy by making a deal with him, therefore he was careful not to make any sudden judgements. Telling former supporters to 'rest quiet and unengaged', his intention was to capitalise on discord between his opponents to extract acceptable terms.[15] After the army marched into London and restored order, they presented the king with propositions of their own. By far the best terms on offer, they included the retention of bishops, though with a freedom of worship that satisfied Independents, biennial Parliaments and ten years' control of the militia. The drawback was that the army had no legal standing. To deal with them would be to sanction the rule of the sword over that of law, something that Charles would never do.

The Scots, fearing that Presbyterianism would never take hold in England, made further approaches to the king. Eventually, his unique position led to Charles becoming far too overconfident, and he warned the army they would 'fall into ruin' if he did not sustain them.[16] Henrietta, meanwhile, recognised that Catholics would be the real losers in any outcome other than a full royal restoration, and protested to the Pope that it was not owing to any fault or 'want of good intentions' on her part.[17] Should Independents or Presbyterians prevail, she could never return home.

By November, the New Model Army was beginning to disintegrate through internal divisions. Levellers demanded voting rights for all men over 21 years of age, the abolition of the House of Lords, and the king's trial, increasingly referring to him as a man of blood. Their popular manifesto, *The Agreement of the People*, was worn in hats and widely distributed. Yet some of their number were also making overtures to the king for approbation. It was enough to give Fairfax and Cromwell grave concerns. In a bid to control the movement, Levellers were invited to St Mary's Church, Putney, to debate the future with army high command. Lieutenant General Cromwell chaired the sessions, and with his son-in-law, Henry Ireton, opposed key Leveller principles. In response to extending voting rights, Cromwell replied that only those with property interests should have the vote, not the common man simply because he drew breath.

Installed in his palace of Hampton Court, the king must have been increasingly heartened. His children stayed often, artists painted him, friends visited and due reverence was shown. There was a new royal carriage and plenty of fine clothing. When the Scots enquired after him, Charles confirmed the military were treating him well – the situation was 'tollerably good', he admitted to the Duke of Richmond on 1 October 1647.[18] Employing a Scottish proverb – 'ill bairns are best heard at home' – Charles told the Scots that they must redeem themselves after handing him over to the English.[19] Around this period, Edward Hyde, closeted away on the island of Jersey, marshalled his pen and began writing his epic *History of the Great Rebellion.* The task was approved by Charles. In June 1647, Hyde reassured the king that his work would tell the 'story of your sufferings'.[20] By August, 300 sheets had been prepared, and with the king's support, Hyde was receiving a steady trickle of documents from various Royalists that would shape the narrative. On one occasion, William Legge and Arthur Trevor even sought out George Thomason, a London bookseller, to obtain one particular pamphlet that the king so desired. Life at Hampton Court offered Charles access to materials, which he would forward on for Hyde's use. Hyde often wished he had never begun, but by November 1647, his job would get a whole lot harder.

Cromwell's cousin, Colonel Edward Whalley, was in charge at Hampton Court. One evening, while at dinner with the king, Whalley revealed a letter in which Cromwell broached rumours of an attempt on the monarch's life, and then asked for the guards to be increased. An anonymous letter, warning of an assassination plot, also reached the king.

That November, a sect of Quaker women at Southwark were said to 'swell, shiver, and shake ... to preach what hath been delivered to them by the Spirit'.[21] Downriver, within Hampton Court's turrets, cupolas and crenellations, King Charles did not turn up for his prayers on 11 November. Colonel Whalley regularly accompanied the fastidious monarch at 5.00 pm prompt, but found the royal apartments locked. Thursday was a day appointed for letter writing, the king's staff explained, and as such, their master had been closeted away for three hours. Whalley, a wool draper by trade, had fought at Naseby and was no fool. Yet, he permitted two hours to elapse before questioning whether anyone had a key, only to be told that the door was locked from the inside. Another hour passed. At that point, Whalley resolved upon an act of desperation; he peeped through the keyhole, but beheld nothing of note.

After 8.00 pm, when access was finally gained via back stairs, he found the king's cloak lying on the floor and his black greyhound bitch, Gypsey, whimpering in a corner. There were four letters, one addressed to Whalley, in which the king gave thanks for being 'so civilly used' before briskly charging the governor to protect household items and moveables. Gypsey was to be given to the Duke of Richmond and various paintings returned to their owners.[22] He was to take special care of the portrait of the queen.

The king's disappearance can't have been entirely unexpected, for in light of threats to his person, he had withdrawn his promise not to escape. It's uncertain if the army, and Whalley, encouraged the king's fears of an attempt on his life and then allowed him time to abscond, but as soon as news broke, the divisive talks at Putney ended abruptly. The royal fugitive was a threat that reunited the quarrelling sections of the army, allowing Fairfax and Cromwell the opportunity to deal with the Levellers once and for all. At Corkbush Fields, on 15 November, while attempting to reimpose their authority, a mutiny occurred. Three Levellers were made to roll dice. Private Richard Arnold, after securing the lowest number, was shot dead.

While Charles fled through the night, he was at a loss as to where to go. In all his escapades, he never once showed a real willingness to leave his kingdoms, knowing that this would invariably lead to his deposition. Alongside Colonel William Legge, Rupert's old friend, the king met up with John Ashburnham, who had accompanied him during his flight from Oxford in 1646, and Sir John Berkeley. A number of destinations were proposed: the West Country, Channel Islands, France or a wild card – the Isle of Wight. The last option was favoured. The Governor, Robert Hammond, was related to Charles's chaplain, but was also yet another cousin of Oliver Cromwell.

Ashburnham, sent to sound out Governor Hammond, overstepped the mark and brought the man to the king. When informed, Charles was overcome with regret that his location had been given away, whereupon Ashburnham offered to kill Hammond. Charles would not hear of it and reluctantly accompanied the governor to Carisbrooke Castle. It would become his gaol for the next twelve months. The captivity of 1647 had been one of majesty – Charles had stood firm and dignified, displaying a patient resolve and faith in God. In 1648, the aura of kingship would be stripped from him, leaving bare the man himself.

Chapter 31

Hellen

As inhabitants of the Isle of Wight rejoiced over the king's unexpected arrival, some might have recalled his visit to Carisbrooke Castle twenty-nine years earlier as a 17-year-old. Furniture was shipped over to the castle, along with books and the royal coach, but nothing could disguise the fact that the fusty old walls were more like a prison than ever. Robert Hammond's loyalty was to Parliament, therefore Charles was back in the hands of MPs.

Initially the king was permitted to hunt and make visits to the surrounding area. As one who always enjoyed physical exercise, he walked the castle's perimeter walls reputedly with a dazzling cane of 'Blue John' feldspar, and later bowled on a specially-made green. A gilded wooden hut offered shelter and sea views. Quieter moments were spent reading; the Bible, sermons of Bishop Andrews, Hooker's *Ecclesiastical Polity* and the works of Doctor Hammond, his chaplain. For lighter moments there was Shakespeare, or Edmund Spenser's *The Faerie Queene*.

Many Independents within the New Model Army still considered their fortunes better served by dealing with the king. Cromwell, who 'directed the action of Fairfax', prudently favoured this approach.[1] Scottish commissioners were also quick to track Charles down and offered military intervention for his restoration, should he commit to Presbyterianism. The English Parliament stuck fast to their long-standing conditions.

On 26 December 1647, the king finally threw in his lot with the Scots. An agreement was signed, sealed in lead and buried at Carisbrooke. Two days later, a message was read in Parliament in which Charles declared himself 'very much at ease ... for having fulfilled the Offices both of a Christian and a King'.[2] He would wait patiently for the good pleasure of God to incline their hearts. This double-dealing approach, of keeping many irons in the fire, was precisely what alienated many. Edward Hyde had begun the New Year wishing that the king would 'sadly apply himself to the part he is to act, that is to suffer resolutely, and to have no tricks'.[3] The fact was that Parliament, Scots and the army were all as equally fervent as the king in their beliefs, and as unwilling to shift their fundamental positions. In such a situation, no settlement would ever be possible until one of them conquered the rest, whether diplomatically or militarily. Charles was no different to them when he sought a favourable outcome for himself.

Unwilling to accept Parliament's terms, Charles consequently lost his freedoms, and in January 1648, he was placed under close confinement. Eight warships were assigned to watch the island. A Scottish declaration that Parliament's unacceptable proposals undermined royal authority came as no surprise – MPs were already preparing for a breach with the Scots. In France, Henrietta queued alongside ambassadors, waiting anxiously for a moment of the Queen Regent's time in the hope of raising Charles's plight.

Though his close attendants and friends had been sent away, numerous household staff remained to serve the king in his captivity, such as the intrepid Mrs Wheeler and her laundrywomen. The wife of an MP, Elizabeth Wheeler was a faithful Royalist. With her ladies, she rapidly formed a secret network that connected Charles to the outside world. He once gratefully acknowledged 'nothing will come amiss when it comes in thy hand.'[4] Most of the few letters that reached him in 1648 were conveyed through this network. A young illiterate girl called Mary helped smuggle them and was assigned various parts in the secretive charades that played out. Charles asked her to pretend to be sorry for assisting him and then befriend Governor Hammond's maid. By this means, she could become a mole in Hammond's personal household. If she ever had anything to say to him, Charles candidly assured her, then she was welcome to do so.

The bonds he developed with humble men and women such as Mary, or the crooked old man that tended his fire, were a result of the lack of deference. Treated like a gentleman prisoner, with no bowing and scraping, the man behind the crown came to the fore. With the veil of majesty lifted, the real Charles was revealed as remarkably down to earth and with a common touch. Several soldiers set to guard him were captivated by his charisma and secretly engaged themselves in his service. The equerry appointed by Parliament, Captain Silius Titus, became his 'most asseured constant friend'. To Sir William Hopkins, the king sent a humble apology lest he ever be 'the Occasion of the least inconvenience.[5]

The confined space and claustrophobic atmosphere left the king prone to bouts of depression. Murder, he knew, was usually the outcome of a monarch's incarceration. The year 1648 was also one of the wettest in living memory. As rain hammered against the windows, seeped into the stonework and hampered Charles's exercise routine, the desperation to escape grew stronger. Secret notes were passed in the fingers of his gloves, left behind tapestries, under carpets and in laundry. Charles disguised his handwriting and employed a wealth of signals, such as the dropping of handkerchiefs and use of verbal codewords – anything from 'artichokes' to 'asparagus'. He told one of his undercover supporters that they must not take it ill if he looked 'sowerly' upon them in public, as that was simply to fool the guards.[6]

Prior to the king absconding from Hampton Court, a redhead had turned up at the door of William Lilly, a notable astrologer. The plague had just killed his servant, leaving Lilly reluctant to see customers, but the lady was insistent, telling him that she feared pox more than plague. Upon admittance, Jane Whorwood consulted him over the place where the king might be safest and most hidden.

In her mid-thirties, 'well fashioned and well languaged', the tall redhead had a round face with pock marks.[7] She was determined, courageous and resourceful. Sister of the Countess of Lanark (who was, in turn, sister-in-law to the Duke of Hamilton), Jane's connections were impeccable. Her stepfather was a Groom of the king's Bedchamber. Literally worth her weight in gold, in 1644 she had smuggled 775kg of bullion to Oxford within barrels of soap.

Codenamed either 'N' or 'Hellen', Jane was the central figure in Charles's captivity, organising escape attempts, procuring ships and acting as a go-between. Like him, she was married, but her husband was a violent man. It wasn't long before the king was prefixing her name with 'sweet' and signing off as 'Your most loving Charles', desperate to catch but a few minutes with her.[8] Much energy was expended on ploys to achieve this, such as Jane working her way into the affections of an officer of the guard. That way, Charles could accidentally discover her in the man's room and then whisk her away.

Both Jane and Charles – in cypher 390 and 391 – were drawn to one another. He once revealed his intentions of getting her alone and smothering her with '407'. Despite the code, its gist is clear enough. Using his punctuality to maximum effect, Charles revealed that after dinner he always locked himself in his bedchamber for three hours to write or read. He penned a plan for how she could gain access to him at such times, as well as what might follow.

> I imagen that [there] is one way possible that you may get a swyuing from me (you must excuse my plaine expressions).[9]

'Swyving' meant intercourse. Unfortunately, we cannot be sure if Jane was successfully smuggled into the stoole room – or toilet – as intended. But her 'Platonick Way' had Charles obsessing over her, while at the same time on the mainland, men were fighting and dying for him in another civil war.[10] Could the real world have been too much for Charles to handle, or was he so closely confined that he barely knew what was occurring? Perhaps this frolicking was an outlet to the frustration of being imprisoned while such crucial events were taking place. Charles always wished to lead from the front, but on this occasion, he must have been keenly aware of his impotence. In France, Henrietta clung to a golden cup, her last item of value. Times were so difficult that she kept her youngest child, 4-year-old Henriette-Anne, in bed as long as possible. There was no money to buy fuel for the fire.

Many ideas were proposed to get Charles away from the Isle of Wight. One bid for freedom that got beyond theory was via his bedroom window.

At barely 15 inches wide, with an iron bar at the centre, the whole plan was a tight squeeze. Towards midnight on 20 March 1648, Charles became wedged between breast and shoulders as he attempted to escape. Waiting below, his servant, Harry Firebrace, heard groans as the king desperately tried to free himself. In the end, finally getting back into his room, he set a candle on the windowsill as a signal that the attempt had failed. In May, after using acid to loosen the bar, Charles backed out of a second attempt at the eleventh hour. Overseeing the minute detail of these plans, whether they came to fruition or not, gave him a sense of control and occupied his troubled mind.

Rather naively, he wrote, 'I cannot think any Man so great a Devil, as to betray me.'[11] Unbeknown to him, however, Parliament's committee in Derby House was well aware of almost every plot. Prone to indiscretion, Charles could often be his own worst enemy. During 1647, he had promised Henrietta 'upon my faith to thee' that his secrets were always written in cypher.[12] Long-term friend, Will Murray, had been assured 'upon the word of a Christian' that no private instructions had been disclosed.[13] At Carisbrooke, the king told Abraham Dowcett to have confidence in him and 'doubt not my Carefullnes'.[14] Quite astoundingly, from Carisbrooke, Charles also began to correspond with Lucy Hay, Countess of Carlisle, the same woman that had betrayed his attempted arrest of the six Members of Parliament in 1642.

Lucy's former lover, the Earl of Holland, was now stirring in support of the king. Though at one time he had been a favourite of the queen, Holland fell into insignificance after supporting Parliament during the war. The truth was that without royal favour he was a man of little note. He had tried, and failed, to worm his way back into favour in 1643. Now, five years after that, he was at the head of a Kentish Royalist rebellion, which broke out in May. In Essex, too, men took to arms. Two months earlier, uprisings had sparked across Wales, when New Model Army commanders declared for the king in protest at unpaid wages. The biggest threat came in July when Scottish Royalists (termed 'Engagers') crossed the border with an invasion force. Because there was little synchronicity, Fairfax and Cromwell managed to suppress each threat with relative ease.

Whether Charles knew about these disasters is uncertain, but as they played out, he was chasing after Jane Whorwood like a lovesick spaniel. On 13 August, the best 'caudle' – or medicinal broth – he could send her was a letter. If she would 'have a better' then she must 'come to fetch it' herself.[15] Such flirtatious behaviour was way out of character for one who had remained famously loyal to his wife since their marriage. Just days after his letter to Jane, Oliver Cromwell defeated Scottish and English Royalists at the Battle of Preston.

Six months of confinement had worn Charles down, as had his isolation from his family. It proved such a challenge to smuggle letters to Carisbrooke that the king rarely heard from his wife or eldest son, Prince Charles, eventually writing to the prince that he would take it unkindly if he did not receive regular correspondence. As early as February 1648, rumours had been rife that Parliament intended to move against him by way of a trial. In May, there were suggestions that the young Duke of Gloucester might be made king. It must have come as a surprise to learn that Parliament, after dealing with the numerous uprisings, wished to reopen negotiations. Charles's regular lawyers, chaplains, footmen, equerries and bedchamber staff were all returned. His favourite bishops and chaplains were a particularly welcome solace.

In *Eikon Basilike*, most likely co-written by Charles and published after his death, he described how his agonies were exacerbated by the barbarous exclusion of any 'Angell' – his learned, godly and discreet divines.[16] By 1648, many of these angels had fallen, which must have increased the perceived threat to his own person. The worst fate was that of Dr Michael Hudson. In June 1648, upon the surrender of Woodcroft Castle, he had fled to the top of a tower to escape the New Model Army soldiers. After being thrown over the wall, the chaplain clung to it until his hands were cut off. Falling to the moat, he was then dragged ashore where his head was smashed by a musket and his tongue cut out. Devoid of hands and tongue, with which he had worshipped God, Hudson's death was a sign of the brutal times. Dean Walter Raleigh, a nephew of the Armada namesake, had died while under house arrest in 1646.

> [As Raleigh sat] in his chair, [his captor] told him that a stool would better become him and with that drew the chair from him and run his sword at him … the Dean did avoid it twice with his hand [but] at last he hurt him in the belly and fortnight after he died.[17]

Doctors Sheldon, Hammond, Oldsworth and Wren, as well as the Bishop of Exeter, were all in custody when negotiations opened. But the faithful William Juxon, Bishop of London, joined Charles. New clothes were provided for the king, and even a canopy of state under which he could sit. Business took place in Newport, affording Charles a change of scenery. The Parliamentary commissioners included those he was well acquainted with, such as the Earls of Northumberland, Pembroke and Salisbury. During negotiations, all debate over the terms were conducted in writing, which eliminated error and kept Parliament firmly in control.

Initially, the king likened himself to a garrison commander, holding out with no chance of relief. He would stand fast and 'make some stone in this building my tombstone'. As letters flew back and forth from Newport to Westminster, Charles sipped his watered-down wine and wrote Latin proverbs on the back of his notes such as 'Never was liberty more acceptable than under a pious king'.[18]

Parliament declined most of his responses as being too equivocating, and in the intense to and fro, he was pinned down on every last detail. Moved to tears of frustration, he 'reasoned hard' for weeks and then gave way.[19] Parliament could control the militia and appoint ministers of state for ten years, with Presbyterianism as the national religion for three years. The latter point was a major personal concession that he would never have countenanced a year earlier. Progress was recognised, and after the forty days elapsed, Parliament granted a hopeful extension. From Windsor, army commanders watched warily. Cromwell's son-in-law, Henry Ireton, had already suggested the army might move against Parliament. The army council petitioned MPs against making any agreement with the king and called instead for his trial, but their remonstrance was laid aside.

There were still many stumbling blocks between king and Parliament, such as a complete ban on the Book of Common Prayer, even in the palace, and Charles would have to take the Covenant. Mass was not to be heard in any household, including the queen's, which would leave his wife with the choice of sacrificing her beliefs or being forever exiled. But on 5 December, MPs voted that what had been thrashed out was an acceptable basis for agreement. Charles was to be invited to London to finalise it.

Since his surrender, the king could have agreed to any terms put before him, and then rescinded on grounds of duress. The fact he did not do this demonstrates a degree of honest dealing in that respect. He said as much to MPs in 1646, during negotiations, when candidly explaining his objections to some particularly contentious clauses. At Newport, his acceptance of Presbyterianism for three years marked a shockingly significant change in his stance. On 29 November, he set out his rationale for this new position in a six-page letter to the Prince of Wales: 'Censure Us not for having parted with so much of our own Right; the price was great, but the commodity was security to Us, Peace to our People.'[20]

The king's fidelity to his newly made promises was never put to the test because the New Model Army stepped in. From Pontefract, on 25 November, Lieutenant General Cromwell wrote to Robert Hammond at Carisbrooke. Asserting the army to be a 'lawful power, called by God' that might oppose 'one Name of Authority, for [its] ends, as well as another Name', Cromwell was demonstrating tacit approval of a move on the army's part against Parliament.[21]

As darkness fell on 30 November, several thousand troops arrived on the Isle of Wight. Six days later, soldiers massed in Westminster Hall, lining lobbies, stairs and yards, and patrolling the streets. They barred over 150 MPs from taking their seats and arrested others, all moderate men, or those suspected of Royalist sympathies. Only 75 had the army's seal of approval. The purged Long Parliament became a 'rump' and proceeded to repudiate all that had occurred at Newport. Charles had steadfastly refused to escape the army's clutches as they overtook the Isle of Wight, instead prepared to accept whatever fate God had in store for him, even if that meant dying like a sacrificial lamb for the church and his son's inheritance.

Once in the army's grip, he was taken to the small, bleak fortress of Hurst Castle on 1 December 1648. Sited on the end of a shingle spit, it was battered by gales and never-ending rain. As well as the fallen monarch, three small artillery pieces were shut inside the castle, along with fifty hand grenades, ten barrels of powder, muskets and swords. No chances were being taken. The king made the best of it, laying out his silver bell, gold watch and the silver basin for his wax nightlight – candles struggled all day to light the dank rooms. His bedroom door was bolted on both sides for privacy. Thomas Herbert was the only man to attend him. Hurst, Charles was certain, was the place where regicide would be committed, but his enemies had more public plans.

On 14 December 1648, writing to his daughter, Elizabeth, the king excused his lack of letters as not being down to want of affection. Simply, he was 'loth to write to those I love when I am out of humour … lest my letters should trouble those I desire to please'.[22]

Now that Parliament had been dealt with, the king was moved via Winchester, Alton and Farnham to Windsor Castle. As ever, his subjects turned out in droves to cheer him along the way. Charles's last Christmas at Windsor was a quiet affair. He marked the day in his own way, perhaps with the Duke of Hamilton, who was also held there after his failed invasion that August. Little else passed except a chimney fire in the room next to the king's and the temporary loss of a diamond seal.

Pace picked up on 2 January 1649, when Lord Grey of Groby conveyed details of a vote taken in the House of Commons. Amongst the scattering of peers, flanked by tapestries portraying scenes from the Armada, Grey explained that MPs had just passed a vote to try the king for high treason. The Ordinance for a high court of justice was rejected by the disturbed Lords. The Scots also warned that 'no harm, injury, or violence' should be given to the king's person, 'the very thought whereof the Kingdom of Scotland hath always abhorred'.[23] Days later, the army's obedient MPs resolved that they could make laws on their own initiative: 'the People are, under God, the Original of all just Power'.[24]

Chapter 32

Deadly Blow

'A sadder spectacle then ever we thought would
grow out of it'.

Robert Kerr, Earl of Ancram

Rows of red baize benches had been erected at the southern end of Westminster Hall. Public galleries ran around it, and there was a dais, which would raise up 135 hand-picked judges. Nearly eight years earlier, the Earl of Strafford's trial had taken place here.

On 19 January 1649, the king was brought to Whitehall Palace and slept in his own bed. But Charles's chamber was no longer his inner sanctum, for two soldiers were stationed inside, permitted to drink and smoke in his presence. Twenty-five years ago, he had complained to Parliament about the stink of the city's brewhouses that marred his exercise in St James's Park. This was a new level of disrespect.

Next day, led by twenty officers brandishing partizans, the king entered Westminster Hall for the opening of his trial. Half of his judges did not turn up. After taking his place on a red velvet chair, Charles stood up again and looked all around him with a stern expression. The commissioners' names were read out and when General Fairfax was called, his wife cried from the gallery 'he has more wit than to be here'.[1]

Dressed in black, with his trademark cloak and its sparkling Garter star, the king kept his tall hat firmly on his head. To remove it would have been to acknowledge the court's authority. John Bradshaw, the 46-year-old Chief Justice of Chester, presided over the trial – all of his seniors had declined to do so.

John Cook, the fair-haired prosecutor, began by accusing Charles of being the principal author of the late war's evils and calamities. To gain the man's attention, the king tapped him with his cane. When the silver head dislodged and rolled to the floor, silence ensued. Nobody stirred, and Charles was forced to stoop and retrieve it himself. The charge resumed and all the 'Treasons, Murders, Rapines, Burnings, Spoils, Desolations, Damages, and Mischiefs' were laid at his door.[2]

When the time came, the king asked by what lawful authority he was brought here, stating there are 'many unlawful authorities in the world' such as thieves and 'robbers by the highway'.[3] Royalist Sir Philip Warwick observed that

176

'though [the king's] tongue usually hesitated, yet he was very free at this time' and spoke perfectly.[4] Ongoing questioning of the court's authority resulted in an adjournment for the day. Charles had recognised only eight of his judges.

On 22 January, as the court prepared for day two, the Scots presented a paper to the House of Commons. They protested that the king hadn't been delivered up to the English for the 'ruin of his person'.[5] Only a few corridors away, their monarch was being pushed to enter a plea. Should he refuse, John Cook warned, then they would proceed against him as if it was guilty. Once again, Charles cast doubt on the legal basis of proceedings, prompting Lord President Bradshaw to call him a 'High Delinquent'.[6] Unperturbed, Charles replied that 'if power without law may make laws, may alter the fundamental laws of the kingdom', then no subject could be sure of either his life or property.[7] After further exchanges, the clerk pushed the king to acquiesce. Charles declared a desire to explain the reasoning behind his stance. 'Sir, it is not for prisoners to require,' Bradshaw retorted.[8] The monarch countered that he was no ordinary prisoner, and soon enough the court broke up, still no further forward.

Day three followed the same pattern. Charles saw himself as an example to his people and therefore beholden to champion justice and law in their defence, as much as his own. A peace treaty had almost been agreed upon at Newport, he reminded everyone. Bradshaw, somewhat rattled, replied that the king had written his meaning in bloody characters throughout the whole kingdom. The following three days would be spent examining witnesses and drafting the sentence.

When the court reassembled on 27 January, the king found the Lord President dressed in robes of scarlet. The break seemed to have offered a period of reflection. Almost immediately Charles desired to be heard, expressing his hope to avoid an 'ugly Sentence' by addressing a fully assembled Parliament.[9] John Downes, one of the commissioners, broke rank and supported the king, asking whether his colleagues had hearts of stone, only to be put in his place by Cromwell. After a thirty-minute adjournment, a refusal was given and the king was told that his time had passed. The court proceeded to judgement and proclaimed Charles guilty of being a tyrant, traitor, murderer and public enemy.

A sentence of death was announced – his head was to be severed from his body. As the shaken king attempted to intercede, Lady Fairfax disputed that this was all done in the name of his subjects: 'Not half, not a quarter of the people of England. Oliver Cromwell is a traitor'.[10] Musketeers levelled their weapons at the general's wife while the king was ushered away. Soldiers cried out for justice and blew tobacco smoke in his face.

In 1624, the Earl of Lauderdale had expressed hope that Charles would 'never taste such adversity' as his late grandmother, but that if he did, many who flatter him would 'shrink and slip away'.[11] Twenty-five years later, as the astounding prophesy became reality, there is no doubt that Charles considered his grandmother's sufferings. But there were key differences between their situations; Mary had been put to death by Elizabeth I, a foreign queen, and not by her own people. Nor was she a monarch at the time of her death, having already abdicated. Proceedings against Charles were without precedent, and that, he wrongly assumed, was one of his greatest securities. Following the purge of Parliament, he should have realised that his opponents were willing to do what they wished. They were carving out a new world.

Sunday 28 January saw William Juxon, the Bishop of London, admitted to Charles's presence to help prepare him for death. Upon sight of the man, the king welcomed him 'open facedly and cheerfully'. Charles dismissed Juxon's sorrowful regrets, telling him 'Leave off this, my Lord, we have not time for it'.[12] The axe was schedule to fall in forty-eight hours.

An infinitely harder day dawned on Monday. Elizabeth, aged 13, and 8-year-old Henry were allowed to see their father for a final time. Charles's daughter could not hold back her tears, yet she committed to memory all that he said. Blessing them both, he was pleased they had come. While giving instructions to obey their elder brother and love one another, Elizabeth's pitiful sobs interrupted him.

'Sweet heart, you'll forget this,' he said, telling her not to grieve or torment herself. It would be 'a glorious death that he should die – it being for the laws and liberties of this land, and for maintaining the true Protestant Religion'. Revealing he had forgiven his enemies, Charles commanded his children to do the same. As for their mother, he declared that 'his love [for her] should be the same to the last.'[13]

Turning to Henry, who looked very steadfastly upon him, the king declared 'they will cut off thy father's head ... and perhaps make thee a king'. Warning his son never to accept the crown as long as his brothers lived, the response – 'I will be torn in pieces first' – moved him.[14] A few diamonds and jewels were the only items of value he had left to hand over. They kissed and embraced. As the children drew away, Elizabeth's renewed tears made him hurry back to hold them in a last close embrace. The ordeal took its toll. The moment they left, Charles collapsed and took to his bed in order to recover his strength. It was imperative that he should die with dignity.

The following morning, having walked across a frosty St James's Park, he was escorted into Whitehall Palace and left in private devotion with Bishop Juxon. Hour after anxious hour passed. Juxon suggested a little food and drink. The king refused. Having already taken the sacrament, he would not have anything pass his lips. Juxon protested, warning that the cold weather, and such a long fast, might trigger a faint. At last Charles gave way and partook of a little bread and claret.

Outside, unbeknown to the king, emergency legislation was being rushed through Parliament to outlaw the proclamation of a new monarch. Two Dutch envoys, sent to intervene for the king's life, were also stonewalled by the House of Commons. Upon first meeting Fairfax and all his officers days earlier, they had requested to speak to the general in private. After a short time, Lieutenant General Cromwell interrupted them without permission and showed no acts of civility. On the day of the execution, they again went to General Fairfax and found him 'touched by our animated and pressing entreaties'. The general was at his secretary's house in Whitehall and resolved to go to MPs to press for a royal reprieve, but they then discovered 200 troops stationed outside the secretary's door. The diplomats 'knew not in consequence, what further to do' as the streets, passages and squares were all blocked by the military.[15] Fairfax had withdrawn from the business of the king's trial, leaving Cromwell's strong hand firmly in control of the general himself, the army and that day's events.[16]

Four hours of anxious waiting came to an end at 2.00 pm when officers knocked on the door. Juxon and Herbert fell to their knees with tears in their eyes, but Charles helped the bishop to his feet. Soldiers lined the walls of the gallery as the king passed, footsteps being the only noise to break the silence. The famed ceiling of the Banqueting House had been painted by Rubens to capture the majesty of the Stuart dynasty and its divine right to rule. Charles now walked beneath it and to his fate, ready to spill his blood in preservation of all this iconic allegory encapsulated.

Upon stepping onto the black-draped scaffold, Charles saw numerous spectators in the windows and rooftops thereabouts. One noted that the king walked with the same 'unconcernedness and motion' as if attending a masque.[17] Two army colonels were present, along with a few soldiers and reporters. The executioner and assistant were disguised with ghoulish masks and false beards, dressed in similar apparel to that of sailors.

The block in the centre, just 6 inches high and 18 inches long, condemned Charles to an ignominious end. Scattered sand would soak his blood, while a cheap wooden coffin was ready for his corpse. Staples had been driven into the boards with iron chains and ropes that could hold him in place if he should struggle. Though Charles came freely to give himself up to God, he baulked at the height of the block. A request to raise it was refused.

Shops had been instructed to remain open as usual. With the public held back out of earshot by lines of soldiers and horsemen, the king took from his pocket a piece of paper 4 inches square, and addressed himself to Colonel Matthew Tomlinson and others. This was his chance to get a final message across – one that he could not deliver during his trial. Every minute of this crisp Tuesday afternoon was crucial. More lasting and powerful than any Naseby or Marston Moor. As he prepared to exit his stage, Charles played his last role: that of martyr. 'I could hold my peace very well,' he admitted, but silence would only lead some to speculate 'I did submit to the Guilt'.[18]

Declaring 'I never did begin the War with the two Houses of Parliament', he did not blame Parliament as a whole, but only a few ill instruments. He suggested that the dates of commissions be compared as evidence that 'They began upon me'. As ever, the Earl of Strafford was never far from his thoughts. His own death was punishment, he alleged, for an 'unjust Sentence that I suffered to take effect'. Soon the guilt that had tormented him, ever since signing Strafford's death warrant eight years ago, would be washed away. Turning to Bishop Juxon, who might bear him witness, Charles explained that he had 'forgiven all the world' and even those who were the 'chief Causers of my death'. The peace of the kingdom was worthy of his 'last gasp' and he prayed with all his soul that the right course might be taken in future, warning that conquest is never a just end:

> believe it, you will never do right, nor God will never prosper you, until you give him his due, the King his due (that is, my Successors) and the People their due, I am as much for them as any of you.[19]

On the question of his people, he asserted that their liberty and freedom went hand in hand with the law. If he had submitted to an 'Arbitrary Way' where laws were changed 'according to the Power of the Sword', then he need not have fallen to this point. Though subject and sovereign were 'clean different things', Charles declared he was putting his head on the block in defence of the laws of the land, which made him a martyr of the people.

Juxon interceded. Perhaps for the 'world's satisfaction' something might be said about personal beliefs. Charles thanked him – he had almost forgotten. 'I declare before you all, That I die a Christian according to the Profession of the Church of England, as I found it left me by my Father.'[20] Turning to the executioner, he explained that he would say some short prayers and, when ready, would thrust out his hands. Next, he put on a white satin nightcap and with Juxon's help, tucked his hair underneath. Juxon told him:

> This Stage is turbulent and troublesome ... it will carry you from Earth to Heaven, and there you shall find to your great joy the Prize; you haste to a Crown of Glory.

Charles replied:

> I go from a corruptible to an incorruptible Crown, where no disturbance can be.

Juxon responded:

> You are exchanged from a temporal to an eternal Crown, a good
> Exchange.

Removing his cloak and then his Garter medal, Charles handed it to Juxon with the word 'Remember'.[21] Then he laid his neck on the block. When his hair was adjusted by the executioner, he entreated the man to 'stay for the sign' and then continued in whispered prayer. 'I will, Sir, an' it please Your Majesty.'[22]

Upon stretching forth his arms, the axe struck a clean blow through the fourth cervical vertebra. The assistant, after holding the decapitated head aloft by the hair, threw it to the floor, leaving the face bruised. The military cleared the streets.

On the scaffold, soldiers dipped their swords in the king's blood, while others did the same with handkerchiefs. Locks of hair were shorn for mementoes and vile language used towards the corpse. Horsemen rode through the city, warning that any who showed sympathy for the dead king would be finished off next. The people's Commonwealth had begun.

At the outset of the Civil War, Parliament had steadfastly denied that it was opposing the king himself, but attitudes dramatically changed over the succeeding years. Charles's execution was not an act of cruel necessity, but one that was intensely personal. A 44-gun vessel named *Charles*, built at the height of the king's personal rule, had been launched exactly sixteen years earlier, on 30 January 1633. Following its namesake's execution, it was promptly rechristened *Liberty*. As if killing Charles was not enough, the authorities signalled a clear pride and belief in their actions by committing the same act – eighteen months later – upon the statue of the king at the Royal Exchange in London. The head was 'cutt off' and over the trunk, etched out in 'great gold characters', were the words 'The last Tyrant of Kings dyed in the first yeare of the Liberty of England'.[23]

In various parts of the kingdom, clergymen discreetly noted their loyalty for posterity, inscribing the date of the 'murder' in their parish registers.

Chapter 33

Who Killed the King?

One question that has remained unanswered is the identity of the executioner and his assistant. This historical whodunnit leaves a tantalising gap in Charles's story, despite the spectacle of his death playing out before the eyes of the world.

Many candidates have been proposed over the years. Hugh Peter, the radical army preacher, is one, on account of contested reports that the severed head was held aloft without the usual cry of 'behold the head of a traitor'. Silence, it is advocated, prevented his well-known voice from being recognised. But Peter was said to have been ill on the day. During the trials of Hugh Peter and the other regicides, when interrogators attempted to identify the executioners, nobody put him forward.

The strongest contender for the man who swung the axe is Richard Brandon, the city executioner. After inheriting the job from his father, he had killed many notables such as the Earl of Strafford. The blow given to Charles was clean and professional. Much evidence suggests that Brandon protested over executing the king, but whether he stood his ground and refused, or proceeded after appropriate threats, remains open to debate. There is an eyewitness sighting of him at Whitehall, and a 'confession' published after his death.[1]

At the regicides' trials, some relatively junior army officers were named as having carried out the deed on account of Brandon's refusal. Testimonies report that financial incentives were offered as inducement, but this would have carried many risks. The men might not have proved willing to follow through or could have lacked necessary skills, which might have provoked spectators. What we do know about the executioner is that he showed respect towards the king, which fits with Brandon. The assistant, it is alleged, did not.

While carrying out research, I came across an anonymous letter in Lambeth Palace Library. Addressed to the then Archbishop of Canterbury, Thomas Tenison, it is dated 30 October 1696. Being a personal letter directed to the archbishop alone, it's unlikely many people were aware of it, making it all the more fascinating. The man named as one of the executioners (the assistant was also termed so) has never since been advocated.

Your Graces pious predecessor Dr Juxon, and Mr Seymar were
told by K. charles the first, wn he came on the scaffold that one
of the Disguised Executioners was Grey of Grooby he Knew by

his hand. your Grace can not be Ignorant yt he was father to the present Earle of Stamford, that he was a great enemy to that King, helping to break the treaty at Newport. Directed the Army who to exclude the house of commons [vide Whitlock &c] sat in the Infernal high court of Justice, wch sentenced him to the block, and there Struck off his head. ought not your Grace knowing this to Dissuad the King from Intrusting, and preferring the son of such an Infamous Regicide? Especially considering he manageth matters in the West so much to the Distast of the Gentry, as will occasion complaint in parliament, and Both his Majestys interest and credit no little Damage, I presume to Suggest this to your Grace, In true zeal to the King, and church, whose Bowells are eating out by a Viperous Brood.[2]

The author seems to be relatively well connected and displays a fair knowledge about the king's last day. They refer to Bishop Juxon and Mr Henry Seymour as having conversed with the king. The evidence of Colonel Matthew Tomlinson, during the regicide trials, mentions Seymour's presence in Whitehall Palace on 30 January 1649 at the time of the execution. A trusted Royalist, Seymour had delivered a last letter to the king from the Prince of Wales. Juxon was present on the scaffold throughout, and both he and the king spoke between themselves at various points while Charles prepared for his end.

Thomas, Lord Grey of Groby, was a hard-line revolutionary peer during the Civil Wars, fighting for Parliament as a commander in the field, as well as from his seat in the House of Lords. He died in 1657. The letter attempts to implicate him, and though clearly seeking to blacken the Grey family, it is evidence that cannot be ruled out for that reason alone. Born in Leicestershire, Lord Grey was the second signatory on King Charles's death warrant, and the highest-ranking. He sat every day as one of the judges at the trial, having been at the forefront of key actions that had paved the way to the scaffold.

In day-to-day parliamentary business, Grey could be vociferous. May 1644 saw him fall upon Thomas Hasselrigg with 'reproachful' and 'threatening' language, and in a loud tone call him 'rascal and base fellow'.[3] This was in public in Westminster Hall. With roots in Leicester and having governed that town, the Royalist sack of the place in 1645 must have rankled. After a failed 1647 uprising in London, Denzil Holles, in his memoirs, names Lord Grey as one who 'sets on foot' the proceedings against eleven ringleaders.[4] The rising had been a real threat to Independents like Grey, Cromwell and Ireton. In December 1648, when Colonel Pride purged Parliament, it was Grey who stood at the doors judging who should be barred entry or imprisoned.[5] Such a momentous action needed a resolute leader to see it through, and in the absence of Fairfax, Cromwell or Ireton, it was Grey who led from the front.

The peer also viewed the war from a deeply religious angle. In 1648, he likened the invasion of pro-Royalist Scots to that which those 'brethren in iniquity, did upon the Shechamites'. He wished that men would bow before the Lord that hath 'smiten' them, and 'tremble' before his foot-stool.[6]

A House of Commons resolution, in January 1649, to form a high court of justice to try the king was, unusually, conveyed to the House of Lords by one of their own – Lord Grey. After the Lords rejected it, they adjourned for a week. A contemporary Royalist periodical *Mercurius Pragmaticus* claimed that a frustrated Grey had made a speech in Parliament asserting that to ensure justice is done, 'hee himselfe would be the Executioner'.[7] This puts him in the frame and lends weight to contemporary opinion of him as a radical and leading opponent of the king. In December 1648, he was appointed to a Committee for the Army.

During the trials of the regicides, Richard Gittens deposed that a Colonel Hewson swore thirty-eight men to secrecy on the day of the king's execution and offered 'an hundred pounds' to any who would fill the role of executioner.[8] Nobody was said to have volunteered. As a result, Brandon was cajoled to see through his duty, but his assistant, Ralph Jones, was nowhere to be found. There are no claims or counter claims over Jones's absence. In my opinion, the role of assistant was one that would have been ideal for Lord Grey, allowing him to be on hand to watch over a hesitating headsman. Or, if army officers had been recruited, it would have been unwise to simply leave them to carry out the sentence. The peer could have stage-managed this event from close quarters, on the boards of the scaffold itself, in the same way he had overseen other key moments.

In Holland, in the immediate aftermath, one print showed Thomas Fairfax holding up the king's head, suggesting that as general of Parliament's armies, he was to blame. But a French pamphlet sensationally claimed that the leadership had carried out the sentence themselves. *Relation veritable de la mort barbare et cruelle du roi d'Angleterre* asserts that Charles found three masked executioners, naming them as Fairfax, Cromwell and 'Milord Say'.[9] The author remarks that the ordinary headsman had been too horrified to carry out the act. Fairfax and Cromwell were seen in the immediate aftermath, proving they could not have been on the scaffold. But what of Lord Say? Viscount Saye and Sele was certainly not a leading Parliamentarian in 1649, nor was he in favour of the king's death. On top of that, he was 67 years old. Could the author have meant Lord Grey, and not Say? Might this exaggerated story stem from any truth?

Sealing off London, and staying all mail, shows how careful the king's opponents were being. Cromwell, in overall command of the army that day, went to prayers with Ireton while the deed was done. Having Grey on the scene would certainly have offered reassurance that matters were in safe hands.

If no words were spoken by the assistant, then that could also be attributed to the fact that Grey's voice would have been distinctive considering his many parliamentary speeches. After the axe fell, the king's head was retrieved and held aloft by the assistant. One eyewitness reported that it was then thrown to the floor.[10] Such an action could only have stemmed from deep irreverence and disrespect – a person firm in the belief that the king was nothing but a man of blood.

William Lilly, the pro-Parliamentarian astrologer, had been consulted by Lord Grey and Hugh Peter at the end of 1648, when they sought a celestial forecast regarding the coming January. At that meeting, Lilly reported Grey as saying if they were not fools and knaves 'we shall do justice'.[11] The astrologer later wrote his own verdict on the identity of the executioner, revealing, 'I have no permission to speak of [the executioners], onely thus much I say, he that did ir, is as valiant and resolute a man as lives, and one of a competent fortune &c.'[12] Richard Brandon was not a rich man, nor were any of the suggested army officers. The description does fit better with Lord Grey, who, after the execution, secured a place on the new Republic's Council of State.

Finally, the day after the execution, the House of Commons Journal details authorisation for Lord Grey to take £100 for the 'Service' of the Commonwealth, as he should 'think fit'.[13] This is a coincidental sum when recalling the figure reputedly used to entice officers to fill the two roles. Could it have been for Grey himself, as assistant, or payment to the executioner? If the latter, what might the lack of an extra £100 for the assistant tell us – if it was, indeed, money allocated for this purpose.

We probably won't ever know for certain the identity of the two men that carried out the king's death sentence, but I believe that Thomas, Lord Grey of Groby, is a strong candidate for the disguised assistant.

Bibliography

Manuscripts

British Library, London
MS/22591/ff.31r-39v. Alleged poisoning of James VI/I.
C/194/a/1114. *Lachrimae Lachrimarum* lamenting the death of Prince Henry.

National Archives of Scotland, Edinburgh
PA2/16/f.3r-7r. Account of the Gowrie Plot.
PA2/16/f.12r-v. Ibid.
GD40/2/13/20. Margaret, Lady Ochiltree, elder, to Sir Robert Kerr of Ancram.
GD124/15/27/56, 79 & 195. Viscount of Fenton, later Earl of Kellie, to the Earl of Mar.
GD124/10/113. Negotiations over Prince Charles's marriage.
GD40/2/19/1/7-8. Papers of the Kerr Family, Marquises of Lothian.
GD40/2/19/2/5-7. Papers of the Kerr Family, Marquises of Lothian.
GD112/39/79/14. Papers of the Campbell Family, Earls of Breadalbane.
GD406/1/11/134. Papers of the Douglas Hamilton Family, Dukes of Hamilton and Brandon.

The National Archives, London
SP/89/4. State Papers Foreign. Portugal.
PROB/11/162/692. Will of John Eliot.
SP92/17. State Papers Foreign. Savoy.
SP81/32/149. Queen of Bohemia to Secretary Conway.
SP97/9/71. State Papers Foreign. Turkey.
SP14/72. State Papers Domestic.
SP78/52. State Papers Foreign. France.
E/407/57/2. Records of the Exchequer.
SP92/18. State Papers Foreign. Savoy.
Various State Papers Domestic, Charles I & Calendar Cecil Papers accessed via http://www.british-history.ac.uk

Lambeth Palace Library, London
MS/3192-3206/f.231. Talbot family papers.
MS/3192-3206/f.233. Ibid.

MS/3201/f.115. Ibid.
MS/663/ff.99r-100v. Thomas Murray papers.
MS/663/ff.192r-193v. Ibid.
MS/663/ff.191r-192v. Ibid.
MS/663/f.164r-v. Ibid.
MS/663/ff.155r-156v. Ibid.
MS/664/ff.71r-72v. Ibid.
MS/665/ff.166r-167v.Ibid
MS/666/ff.120r-121v. Ibid.
MS/666/f.205v. Ibid.
MS/708/f.83. Earl of Shrewsbury papers.
MS/930/21 & 122. Miscellaneous papers.
MS/930/161/ff.2. Ibid.

Sheffield Archives
WWM/StrP/40/6a. Papers of the Earl of Strafford.
WWM/StrP/40/9a & 10a. Ibid.
WWM/StrP/40/23a & 24a. Ibid.
WWM/StrP/34/2a-2p. Ibid.
WWM/StrP/24/25/133a-d. Ibid.
WWM/StrP/40-60a & 61a. Ibid.

Glamorgan Archives
DTD/8-11. Charles I's letters to Captain of *Bonaventure*.

Christchurch Library & Archives
MS540. Laud's annotated Book of Common Prayer

Hull History Centre
U/DDEV/79/H150. Speeches of Charles I to his courtiers and Soldiers.
U/DDEV/79/G156 &159-160. Charles I to Earl of Nithsdale.

Isle of Wight Record Office
OG/BB/247. Saint Paul's Cathedral in disrepair.
OG/BB/70. Oglander & Accession of Charles I.
OG/BB/38. Oglander's opinion of the Duchess of Richmond.
OG/BB/32. Recorder of Portsmouth's Speech.
OG/CC/65. Death of Dean Raleigh.

Longleat Archives
PO/VOLII/f.41r. Prince Charles his guifts and presents at his departure out of Spayne.
PO/VOLII/f.8r. Letter of Elizabeth [of Bohemia] to brother Charles.

Hertfordshire Archives & Local Studies
DE/B761/65448. Correspondence of Doctor Henry Atkins.
DE/B761/65452. Ibid.
DE/B761/65435a. Ibid.
DE/B761/65447. Ibid.

Staffordshire & Stoke Archives
D(W)1778/I/I/66. Letter from Charles I to Duke of Richmond.

Lancashire Archives
DDTO/E/16/1. Journey of Prince Charles from Scotland to England.

Northamptonshire Archives
TH/2285. Duke of Buckingham's Speech.

Publications

Aikin, Lucy, *Memoirs of the Court of King Charles the First*, Vol I (London, 1833)
Akkerman, Nadine, *The Correspondence of Elizabeth Stuart*, Vol I & II (OUP, 2011)
Akkerman, Nadine, *Invisible Agents: Women and Espionage in Seventeenth-Century Britain* (OUP, 2018)
Barratt, John, *The Civil War in the South West* (Pen & Sword, 2005)
Bayly, Thomas, *Certamen Religiosum* (London, 1649)
Birch, Thomas, *The Life of Henry, Prince of Wales* (London, 1760)
Birch, Thomas, *Court and Times of James the First* (London, 1849)
Brotton, Jerry, *The Sale of the Late King's Goods* (MacMillan, 2006)
Brown, Michael J., *Itinerant Ambassador: The Life of Sir Thomas Roe*, (University Press of Kentucky, 2021)
Bruce, John, *Letters of King Charles the First to Queen Henrietta Maria* (Camden Society, 1856)
Bulstrode, Richard, *Memoirs and Reflections upon the Reign and Government of King Charles the Ist and K. Charles the II'd* (London, 1721)
Calderwood, David, *The True History of the Church of Scotland*, Vol VI (1678)
Carew Manuscripts, ed. J.S. Brewer (London, 1867)
Carte, Thomas, *A Collection of Original Letters and Papers: Duke of Ormonde*, Vol III (1735)
Cary, Robert, *Memoirs of the Life of Robert Cary* (London, 1759)
Cavendish, Margaret, *Life of William Cavendish*, ed. Charles Harding Forth (London, 1886)
Chambers, Robert, *Life of King James the First*, Vol II (Edinburgh, 1830)

Chancellor, Edwin Beresford, *Life of Charles I* (London, 1886)

Charles I/John Gauden, *Eikon Basilike: the Portraicture of His Sacred Majestie in his Solitudes and Sufferings* (1649)

Clarendon, Earl of, *State Papers*, Vol II (Oxford, 1773)

Clarendon, Earl of, *History of the Rebellion and Civil Wars in England*, Vol I (Clarendon Press, 1826)

Clarendon, Earl of, *The History of the Rebellion and Civil Wars in England*, Vol II (Oxford, 1732)

Clarendon, Earl of, *The History of the Rebellion and Civil Wars in England*, Vol VI (OUP, 1849)

Clarke, Jack Alden, *Huguenot Warrior: The Life and Times of Henri De Rohan* (Springer, 1966)

Cobbett's Complete Collection of State Trials, Vol V (1810)

Cornwallis, Charles, *Life of Prince Henry* (London, 1626)

Cornwallis, Charles, *The Life and Death of Henry Prince of Wales* (London, 1641)

Cowley, Hannah, *The Poetry of Anna Matilda* (London, 1788)

Cust, Richard, *Charles I: A Political Life* (Taylor & Francis, 2014)

Cust, Richard, 'Charles I and the Order of the Garter', *Journal of British Studies*, Vol 52, No 2, pp 1-27 (2013)

D'Israeli, Isaac, *Commentaries on the Life and Reign of Charles the First* (Paris, 1851)

De Lisle, Leanda, *White King: Charles I, Traitor, Murderer, Martyr* (Penguin Random House, 2017)

De Lisle, Leanda, *Phoenix Queen* (Chatto & Windus, 2022)

Denton, Barry, *Only in Heaven* (Bloomsbury Academic, 1997)

Devon, Frederick, *Payments Made Out of his Majesty's Revenue - James I* (London, 1836)

Doran, Dr, *Book of the Princes of Wales* (London, 1860)

Dugdale, William, *The Life, Diary and Correspondence of Sir William Dugdale*, ed. William Hamper (London, 1827)

Huntington Library Quarterly, Vol. 68, No. 1-2 (March 2005)

Edwards, Graham, *The Last Days of Charles I* (Sutton Publishing, 1999)

Ellis, Henry, *Original Letters, Illustrative of English History*, Vol III & IV (London, 1824)

English Historical Review, Vol VIII (1893)

Epistolae Ho-Elianae. The Familiar Letters of James Howell (London, 1892)

Evelyn, John, *The Diary of John Evelyn*, ed. William Bray (London, 1879)

Finch, Heneage, *An Exact and Most Impartial Accompt of the Indictment, Arraignment, Trial, and Judgment (according to Law) of Twenty and Nine Regicides* (London, 1679)

Firebrace, Cordell W., *Honest Harry: Being the Biography of Sir Henry Firebrace* (London, 1932)

Firth, C.H., *Transactions of the Royal Historical Society*, Vol VI (Cambridge University Press, 1912)

Flaherty, William Edward, *Annals of England* (Oxford & London, 1877)

Forster, John, *Sir John Eliot: A Biography* (London, 1872)

Gardiner, Samuel R., *History of England*, Ten Volumes (London, 1895)

Gardiner, Samuel R., *The Constitutional Documents of the Puritan Revolution, 1625-1660* (Clarendon Press, 1906)

Gardiner, Samuel R., *The Fall of the Monarchy of Charles I*, Vol II (London, 1882)

Green, Mary Anne Everett, *Letters of Queen Henrietta Maria* (London, 1857)

Green, Mary Anne Everett, *Lives of the Princesses of England*, Vol VI (London, 1857)

Gregg, Pauline, *King Charles I* (Phoenix Press, 2000)

Guizot, François, *History of the English Revolution of 1640* (New York, 1846)

Guthry, Henry, *Memoirs* (London, 1702)

Hakewill, George, *King David's Vow for Reformation* (London, 1621)

Halliwell-Phillipps, James, *Letters of the Kings of England*, Vol II (London, 1846)

Halliwell-Phillipps, James, *Autobiography of Sir Simonds D'Ewes* (London, 1845)

Harris, William, *Life and Writings James the First* (London, 1753)

Herbert, Sir Thomas, *Memoirs of The Last Two Years of the Reign of King Charles I* (London, 1813)

Hervey, Mary, *Life, Correspondence and Collections of Thomas Howard* (Cambridge University Press, 1921)

Hibbert, Christopher, *Cavaliers and Roundheads* (HarperCollins, 1994)

Hibbert, Christopher, *Charles I* (St Martin's, 2007)

Memorials of Affairs of State in the Reigns of Q. Elizabeth and K. James I, Vol II (London, 1725)

Holles, Denzil, *Memoirs of Denzil Lord Holles* (London, 1699)

Hopper, Andrew, *Black Tom: Sir Thomas Fairfax and the English Revolution* (Manchester University Press, 2007)

Hughes, Ann, *Politics, Society and Civil War in Warwickshire 1620-1660* (Cambridge University Press, 1987)

Hume, David, *The History of England,* Vol VII (London, 1818)

Hutchinson, Julius, *Life of Mrs Hutchinson* (London, 1806)

James II, *The Life of James the Second*, ed. J.S. Clarke, Vol I (London, 1816)

Journal of the History of Medicine, Volume IX, Issue 4, October 1954

Keenan, Siobhan, *Progresses, Processions & Royal Entries of Charles I* (OUP, 2020)

King James VI & I, *Meditation upon the Lord's Prayer* (London, 1619)

Kippis, Andrew, *Biographia Britannica* (London, 1789)

Kitson, Frank, *Prince Rupert: Portrait of a Soldier* (Constable, 1996)

Knowler, William, *The Earl of Strafforde's Letters and Despatches* (London, 1739)

Laing, David, *Correspondence of Sir Robert Kerr, First Earl of Ancram,* (Edinburgh, 1875)

Laud, William, *Autobiography* (Oxford, 1839)

Letters to King James the Sixth, The Maitland Club (1835)

Lilly, William, *History of his Life and Times from the Year 1602-1681* (London, 1822)

Lilly, William, *Monarchy or No Monarchy in England* (London, 1651)

Lipscombe, Nick, *The English Civil War: An Atlas and Concise History* (Osprey, 2020)

Matusiak, John, *The Prisoner King: Charles I in Captivity* (The History Press, 2017)

Memoires of the Life and Death of Henrietta Maria (London, 1671)

Mercurius Pragmaticus (Dec 26 – Jan 9 1649)

Morrah, Patrick, *Prince Rupert of the Rhine* (Constable, 1976)

Mulryne, J.R. and Shewring, Margaret, eds. *Theatre and Government Under the Early Stuarts* (Cambridge University Press, 1993)

Noble, Mark, *The Lives of the English Regicides* (London, 1798)

Old English blood boyling afresh in Leicestershire men (1648)

Oppenheim, M., *A History of the Administration of the Royal Navy* (London, 1896)

Page, Nick, *Lord Minimus* (HarperCollins, 2001)

Partridge, Robert. B., *'O Horrable Murder. The Trial, Execution and Burial of King Charles I* (The Rubicon Press, 1998)

Peckard, P., *Memoirs of the Life of Mr. Nicholas Ferrar* (Cambridge, 1790)

Perrinchief, Richard, *The Life and Death of King Charles I* (London, 1676)

Perrinchief, Richard, *The Works of King Charles the Martyr* (London, 1687)

Petrie, Charles, *King Charles, Prince Rupert and the Civil War* (Routledge & Kegan Paul Books, 1974)

Pett, Phineas, *The Autobiography of Phineas Pett* (Navy Records Society, 1918)

Porter, Linda, *Royal Renegades: The Children of Charles I* (Pan Books, 2016)

Radcliffe, Sir George, *Earl of Strafford's Letters,* Vols I & II (1739)

Raymond, Joad, *Making the News: An Anthology of the Newsbooks of Revolutionary England, 1641-1660* (The Windrush Press, 1993)

Rees, John, *The Leveller Revolution* (Verso Books, 2016)

Reeve, L.J., *Charles I and the Road to Personal Rule* (Cambridge University Press, 2003)

Relation Veritable de la Mort Barbare et Cruelle du Roi d'Angleterre (Paris, 1649)

Ross, Josephine, *The Winter Queen* (St Martin's, 1979)

Rushworth, John, *Historical Collections of Private Passages of State*, Vol I–VII (London, 1721)

Sainsbury, W. Noel, *The Life of Sir Peter Paul Rubens* (London, 1859)

Sanderson, William, *The Life and Raigne of King Charles* (London, 1658)

Scott, Eva, *Rupert, Prince Palatine* (New York, 1899)

Seton, George, *Memoir of Alexander Seton, Earl of Dunfermline* (London, 1882)

Several Hands, *The Parliamentary or Constitutional History of England*, Vol XIV (London, 1763)

Society of Antiquaries, *Archaeologia Aeliana,* Vol XXI (SOA, 1899)

Stoyle, Mark, *Soldiers and Strangers* (Yale University Press, 2005)

Strickland, Agnes, *Lives of the Queens of England,* Vol VIII (Philadelphia, 1853)

Strickland, Agnes, *Lives of the Queens of England,* Vol IV (London, 1865)

The Confession of Richard Brandon the Hangman (upon his death bed) (London, 1649)

The Gentleman's Magazine, Vol XXVI (1756)

The Lord Digby's Cabinet and Dr. Goff's Negotiations (1646)

The New Monthly Magazine and Humorist (1839)

The Papers Which Passed at Newcastle Betwixt His Sacred Majestie and Mr Al: Henderson: Concerning the Change of Church Government (London, 1649)

The Sixteenth Century Journal, Vol 43, No 2 (2012)

The Volume of the Walpole Society, Vol 37, Abraham Van Der Doort's Catalogue (1958-60)

The Westminster Review, Vol LVI (1879)

Townshend, Dorothea, *Life and Letters of Endymion Porter* (London, 1897)

Transactions of Royal Historical Society, Vol I (1872)

Verney, Frances Parthenope, *Memoirs of the Verney Family During the Civil War,* (London, 1892)

Walcott, Mackenzie, *Memorials of Westminster* (London, 1851)

Warburton, Eliot, *Memoirs of Prince Rupert*, Three Volumes (London, 1849)

Warwick, Sir Philip, *Memoirs of the Reign of King Charles the First* (London, 1702)

Wedgewood, C.V., *The King's War 1641-1647* (Penguin, 2001)

Weldon, Anthony, *The Court and Character of King James* (1651)

Whitaker, Katie, *A Royal Passion* (Orion, 2010)

Wilson, Arthur, *History of the Life of James I* (London, 1653)

Wood, Anthony, *Athenae Oxonienses* (London, 1817)

Works of Francis Bacon (London, 1819)

Notes

Abbreviations used

CCP	Calendar of Cecil Papers
CSPD	Calendar State Papers, Domestic
CSPV	Calendar State Papers, Venice
HA	Hertfordshire Archives & Local Studies
HHC	Hull History Centre
IOW	Isle of Wight Record Office
LA	Longleat Archives
LANC	Lancashire Archives
LPL	Lambeth Palace Library
NA	Northamptonshire Archives
NAS	National Archives of Scotland
S&S	Staffordshire & Stoke Archives
SA	Sheffield Archives
TNA	The National Archives

Chapter 1: Precious Jewell

1. NAS: PA2/16/f.3r-7r
2. Arthur Wilson, *History of the Life of King James I* (1653), p.12
3. *Calendar of the Cecil Papers in Hatfield House, Volume 10, 1600*, ed. R.A. Roberts (1904), pp.353–371
4. NAS: PA2/16/f.12r-v
5. Richard Perrinchief, *The Life and Death of King Charles I* (1676), p.2
6. Leanda de Lisle, *White King: Charles I, Traitor, Murderer, Martyr* (2017), p.5
7. Jack Alden Clarke, *Huguenot Warrior: The Life and Times of Henri De Rohan* (1966), p.14
8. NAS: GD40/2/13/20
9. Richard Perrinchief, *Life*, p.4
10. CSPD, November 1602
11. Weldon Anthony, *The Court and Character of King James* (1651), p.2
12. *Memoirs of the Life of Robert Carey* (1759), p.150

13. CCP, *Volume 15, 1603*, ed. M.S. Giuseppi (1930), pp.1–24
14. *Memoirs of Henry Guthry* (1702), p.95
15. Thomas Birch, *The Life of Henry, Prince of Wales* (1760), p.25
16. Arthur Wilson, *History*, p.3
17. CSPD, March–May 1603
18. *Letters to King James the Sixth*, The Maitland Club (1835), p.33
19. George Seton, *Memoirs of Alexander Seton* (1882), p.55
20. CSPV, October 1603
21. Robert Carey, *Memoirs*, pp.162–63

Chapter 2: Sweet Duke

1. Phineas Pett, *Autobiography*, ed. W.G. Perrin (1918), pp.21–23
2. CSPV, April 1604
3. Frederick Devon, *Payments Made Out of his Majesty's Revenue – James I* (1836), p.10
4. HA: DE/B761/65447
5. 'The Illness of Charles, Duke of Albany', *Journal of the History of Medicine*, Volume IX, Issue 4, October 1954
6. HA: DE/B761/65447
7. *Journal of the History of Medicine*, Volume IX, Issue 4, October 1954
8. CCP, *Volume 16, 1604*, ed. M.S. Giuseppi (1933), pp.135–58
9. HA: DE/B761/65452
10. CCP, *Volume 16, 1604*, ed. M.S. Giuseppi (1933), pp.158–174
11. Ibid.
12. LANC: DDTO/E/16/1
13. CCP, *Volume 16, 1604*, ed. M.S. Giuseppi (1933), pp.174–195
14. Robert Carey, *Memoirs*, p.163
15. HA: DE/B761/65448
16. HA: DE/B761/65452
17. HA: DE/B761/65435a
18. CCP, *Volume 16, 1604*, ed. M.S. Giuseppi (1933), pp.221–268
19. Ibid.
20. CSPV, August 1604
21. CSPV, October 1604
22. LPL: MS/3192-3206/f.233

Chapter 3: Charles of Scotland

1. LPL: MS3192-3206/f.231
2. CCP, *Volume 16, November 1604*, ed. M.S. Giuseppi (1933), pp.357–373

3. Rev. Mackenzie Walcott, *Memorials of Westminster* (1851), p.58
4. *Memorials of Affairs of State in the Reigns of Q. Elizabeth and K. James I,* Vol II (1725), p.43
5. *The New Monthly Magazine and Humorist* (1839), p.253
6. CSPD, February 1605
7. Robert Carey, *Memoirs*, p164–68
8. CCP, *Volume 23, February 1605*, ed. G. Dyfnallt Owen (1973), pp.197–203
9. CSPV, March 1605
10. CCP, *Volume 17, 1605*, ed. M.S. Giuseppi (1938), pp.141–206
11. CCP, *Volume 17, 1605*, ed. M.S. Giuseppi (1938), pp.262–295
12. James Halliwell-Phillipps, *Letters of the Kings of England,* Vol II (1846), p.117
13. John Evelyn, *The Diary of John Evelyn,* ed. William Bray (1879), p.2
14. LPL: MS3201/f.115
15. Maitland Club *Letters*, p.38
16. CCP, *Volume 17, 1605*, ed. M.S. Giuseppi (1938), pp.423–474
17. Ibid.
18. Ibid.

Chapter 4: This Poor Boy's Innocence

1. TNA: SP78/52/338-340
2. HOLJ, Vol II, pp.356–359
3. CSPD, October–November 1603
4. CSPV, November 1605
5. LPL: MS708/f.83
6. CSPV, February 1634
7. CSPV, April 1606
8. *The Court and Character of King James* (1651), pp.215–216
9. Nadine Akkerman, *The Correspondence of Elizabeth Stuart*, Vol II (2011), p.77
10. CCP, Volume 18, 1606, ed. M.S. Giuseppi (1940), pp.220–235
11. Henry Ellis, *Original Letters*, Vol III, (1824), p.94
12. Christopher Hibbert, *Charles I* (2007), p.26
13. CSPV, February 1607
14. CSPV, May 1607
15. Halliwell-Phillipps, *Letters*, p.114
16. Ibid.
17. William Sanderson, *Life of King Charles* (1658), p.1
18. Charles Cornwallis, *A Discourse of the Life of the most Illustrious Prince Henry* (1626), p.27

19. CSPV, November 1607
20. CCP, Volume 19, 1607, ed. M.S. Giuseppi & D McN Lockie (1965), pp.397–521
21. Philip Warwick, *Memoirs of the Reign of King Charles the First* (1702), p.64
22. CSPV, January 1608
23. CSPV, February 1608
24. CSPV, January 1610
25. CSPV, November 1608
26. Ellis, *Original Letters*, Vol III, p.94
27. Halliwell-Phillipps, *Letters*, p.114
28. CCP, Volume 21, 1609–12, ed. G. Dyfnallt Owen (1970), pp.113–124

Chapter 5: Little Servant

1. Mary Hervey, *Life Correspondence and Collections of Thomas Howard* (1921), p.61
2. Josephine Ross, *The Winter Queen* (1979), p.20
3. CSPV, February 1610
4. Ross, *Winter Queen*, p.18
5. CSPV, September 1611
6. Richard Cust, *Journal of British Studies*, Vol 52, No 2 (2013)
7. CSPD, November 1611
8. CSPV, July 1611
9. Halliwell-Phillipps, *Letters*, p.118
10. CSPV, May 1611
11. CSPV, August 1611
12. CSPD, August 1611
13. CSPV, October 1611
14. Robert Carey, *Memoirs*, p.169
15. CSPV, June 1612
16. Arthur Wilson, *History*, p.61
17. Halliwell-Phillipps, *Letters*, p.119
18. Westminster Abbey (www.westminster-abbey.org)

Chapter 6: Weep Forth Your Teares

1. CSPV, November 1612
2. Ibid.
3. CSPD, November 1612
4. Thomas Birch, *Life of Henry, Prince of Wales* (1760), p.272

5. CSPV, November 1612
6. BL: C/194/a/1114 *Lachrimae Lachrimarum* (1612)
7. Cambridge University Library (https://specialcollections-blog.lib.cam.ac.uk)
8. *Works of Francis Bacon* (1819), p.61
9. Thomas Birch, *Court and Times of James the First* (1849), p.210
10. CSPV, November 1612
11. BL: C/194/a/1114 *Lachrimae Lachrimarum* (1612)
12. *Autobiography of Sir Simonds D'Ewes*, ed. James Orchard Halliwell (1845), p.46
13. The plaster face had been made by Abraham van der Doort, who later inventoried Charles's art collection.
14. CSPV, December 1612
15. Ibid.
16. *The Sixteenth Century Journal*, Vol 43, No 2 (2012)
17. George Hakewill, *Sermons* (1621)
18. TNA: SP/14/72/f.39
19. TNA: E/407/57/2
20. LA: PO/VOLII/f.8r
21. CSPV, September 1622
22. Bodleian Library (https://ota.bodleian.ox.ac.uk)
23. CSPD, September 1613
24. Thomas Birch, *Court and Times of James the First* (1849), p.307
25. HOCJ, Vol 1, 3 June 1614, pp.505–06
26. Arthur Wilson, *History*, p.77
27. Samuel R. Gardiner, *History of England*, Vol II (1895), p.240

Chapter 7: Steenie

1. CSPV, August 1614
2. Earl of Clarendon, *State Papers,* Vol II (1773), p.347
3. CSPD, February 1615
4. Maitland Club, *Letters*, p.109
5. LPL: MS/663/f.164r-v
6. LPL: MS/663/ff.155r-156v
7. NAS: GD124/10/113
8. LPL: MS/663/ff.99r-100v
9. LPL: MS/663/ff.192r-193v
10. CSPD, August 1616
11. LPL: MS/663/ff.191r-192v
12. LPL: MS/663/ff.192r-193v
13. CSPV, January 1620

14. Ibid.
15. CSPV, January 1615
16. CSPV, September 1618
17. CSPV, November 1616
18. CSPD, November 1616
19. Birch, *Court and Times*, p.437
20. Halliwell-Phillipps, *D'Ewes*, p.92
21. Birch, *James the First*, p.426
22. Arthur Wilson, *History*, p.147

Chapter 8: The Scotch Journey

1. CSPD, December 1616
2. Maitland Club, *Letters*, p.113
3. CSPV, April 1617
4. CSPD, June 1617
5. CSPV, May 1617
6. LPL: MS/664/ff.71r–72v.
7. LPL: MS/665/ff.166r–167v.
8. David Calderwood, *The True History of the Church of Scotland* (1678), p.675
9. John Rushworth, *Historical Collections of Private Passages of State*, Vol I (1721), pp.175–244
10. CSPD, February 1618
11. Arthur Wilson, *History*, p.105
12. CSPV, December 1617
13. NAS: GD124/15/27/56
14. Halliwell-Phillipps, *Letters*, pp.122–23
15. CSPV, December 1617
16. Mary Hervey, *Life*, p.143
17. IOW: OG/BB/32
18. CSPV, August 1618
19. CSPV, April 1620
20. CSPV, September 1618
21. CSPD, January 1619
22. NAS: GD40/2/13/20
23. RCT, Van Der Doort's Inventory (www.royal.gov.uk)
24. CCP, Volume 22, ed. G Dyfnallt Owen (1971), pp.83–87
25. CSPD, June 1622
26. CSPV, November 1618
27. Edwin Beresford Chancellor, *Life of Charles I* (1886), p.50
28. Mary Hervey, *Life*, p.152

Chapter 9: Crown of Thorns

1. Mary Hervey, *Life*, p.153
2. CSPD, March 1619
3. James Howell: *Familiar Letters* (1892), p.105
4. CSPD, March 1619
5. Mary Hervey, *Life*, p.154
6. CSPD, March 1619
7. CSPV, December 1617
8. CSPD, June 1619
9. CSPV, January 1620
10. LPL: MS/930/122
11. LPL: MS/930/161/ff.2
12. CSPV, January 1620
13. W. Noel Sainsbury, *Papers of Rubens* (1859), p.118
14. King James VI & I, *Meditation upon the Lord's Prayer* (1619)
15. William Harris, *Life and Writings James the First* (1753), p.37
16. LPL: MS/666/f.205v
17. CSPV, January 1620
18. Nadine Akkerman, *The Correspondence of Elizabeth Stuart*, Vol I (2011), p.216
19. Ibid.
20. CSPV, January 1620
21. NAS: GD40/2/19/1/8
22. CSPD, March 1620
23. CSPV, March 1620
24. CSPD, March 1620
25. Nadine Akkerman, *Correspondence,* Vol I p.254
26. CSPV, April 1620
27. CSPD, April 1622
28. NAS: GD124/15/27/79
29. *The Gentleman's Magazine*, Vol XXVI (1756), p.234
30. IOW: OG/BB/38
31. Pauline Gregg, *Charles I* (1981), p.417
32. Reginald Heber, *Life of Jeremy Taylor* (1824), p.202
33. LPL: MS/666/ff.120r-121v
34. CSPV, October 1620
35. Ibid.
36. CSPV, October 1619
37. CSPD, January 1621
38. Halliwell-Phillipps, *D'Ewes*, pp.166–67
39. CSPV, February 1621

40. CSPD, March 1621
41. Halliwell-Phillipps, *Letters*, p.162
42. CCP, Volume 22, ed. G Dyfnallt Owen (1971), pp.140–151
43. Rushworth, *Historical Collections*, Vol I, pp.24–62
44. CSPV, July 1621
45. CPSV, May 1621
46. CSPD, January 1622
47. CSPV, September 1622
48. CSPV, December 1621

Chapter 10: Jack and Tom Smith

1. CSPV, April 1622
2. CSPD, February 1623
3. Ibid.
4. Arthur Wilson, *History*, pp.225–26
5. CSPD, March 1623
6. CSPD, February 1623
7. Robert Carey, *Memoirs*, p.186
8. Halliwell-Phillipps, *D'Ewes*, p.224
9. Ibid.
10. CSPV, May 1623
11. CSPD, March 1623
12. Ibid.
13. CSPV, July 1623
14. CSPV, May 1623
15. CSPV, April 1623
16. Dorothy Townshend, *Life and Letters of Endymion Porter* (London, 1897), p.48
17. CSPV, May 1623
18. *Transactions of Royal Historical Society*, Vol I (1872), pp.104–219
19. CSPV, June 1623
20. Robert Carey, *Memoirs*, p.188
21. CSPV, June 1623
22. Ibid.
23. CSPV, July 1623
24. William Laud, *Autobiography* (1839), p.14
25. HOCJ, Vol 1, 3 March 1624
26. CSPV, July 1623
27. Dorothea Townshend, *Endymion Porter*, p.69
28. LA: PO/VOLII/f.41r
29. Phineas Pett, *Memoirs*, pp.130–131

Chapter 11: Ecstasy of Joy

1. Robert Carey, *Memoirs*, p.189
2. TNA SP97/9/71
3. CSPD, October 1623
4. Katie Whitaker, *A Royal Passion* (2010), p.33
5. Nadine Akkerman, *Correspondence*, Vol I, p.425
6. CSPV, December 1623
7. CSPD, February 1624
8. CSPD, March 1624
9. CSPD, March 1624
10. Ibid.
11. NAS: GD124/15/27/195
12. CSPV, September 1624
13. NAS: GD124/15/27/195
14. CSPV, June 1624

Chapter 12: Impatience and Love

1. Arthur Wilson, *History*, p.285
2. Robert Carey, *Memoirs*, p.190
3. Laud, *Autobiography*, p.33
4. Rushworth, *Historical Collections*, Vol I, pp.165–219
5. IOW: OG/BB70
6. CSPD, March 1625
7. TNA: SP81/32/149
8. Earl of Ancram, *Correspondence*, ed. David Laing (1875), pp.33–42
9. Ibid.
10. CSPD, April 1625
11. CSPV, May 1625
12. CSPV, September 1613
13. NAS: GD40/2/19/1/7
14. Julius Hutchinson, *Life of Mrs Hutchinson* (1806), p.65
15. Leanda De Lisle, *White King*, p.40
16. CSPV, April 1625
17. Katie Whitaker, *Royal Passion*, p.44
18. Ibid
19. CSPV, April 1625
20. CSPD, June 1625
21. Katie Whitaker, *Royal Passion*, p.51
22. Leanda de Lisle, *White King*, p.38
23. Laud, *Autobiography*, p.38

24. CSPV, July 1625
25. Halliwell-Phillipps, *D'Ewes*, p.100
26. Leanda De Lisle, *White King*, p.126
27. CSPV, July 1625
28. Laud, *Autobiography*, p.42
29. CSPD, August 1625
30. Katie Whitaker, *Royal Passion*, p.68
31. CSPV, October 1625
32. Laud, *Autobiography*, p.19

Chapter 13: Rights and Wrongs

1. M. Oppenheim, *Administration of the Royal Navy* (1896), p.220
2. CSPD, November 1625
3. CSPV, January 1626
4. CSPV, February 1627
5. CSPD, January 1626
6. *The Annals of England* (1877), p.58
7. CSPV, January 1626
8. CSPV, February 1626
9. Laud, *Autobiography*, p.58
10. Ibid.
11. Halliwell-Phillipps, *D'Ewes*, p.293
12. Sir George Radcliffe, *Earl of Strafford's Letters*, Vol I (1739), p.31
13. CSPV, February 1626
14. HOLJ, Vol 3, 6 February 1626
15. CSPV, February 1626
16. HOLJ, Vol 3, 6 February 1626
17. CSPV, March 1626
18. *Carew Manuscripts*, ed. J.S. Brewer (1867), p.62
19. CSPV, March 1626
20. Rushworth, *Historical Collections*, Vol I, pp.219–248
21. CSPV, March 1626
22. CSPV, May 1626
23. CSPV, April 1626
24. Rushworth, *Historical Collections*, Vol I, pp.219–248
25. CSPV, April 1626
26. HOLJ, Vol 3 21 April 1626
27. CSPD, April 1626
28. CSPV, May 1626
29. Laud, *Autobiography*, p.69

30. HOLJ, Vol 3, 1 May 1626
31. CSPD, May 1626
32. *The Westminster Review*, Vol LVI (1879)
33. BL: MS/22591/ff.31r-39v
34. CSPV, May 1626
35. CSPV, May 1626
36. Halliwell-Phillipps, *D'Ewes*, p.301
37. CSPD, June 1627
38. CSPV, August 1626
39. CSPV, November 1626
40. Leanda De Lisle, *White King*, p.55
41. CSPV, September 1626
42. Ibid.

Chapter 14: Man of Seyaton

1. Laud, *Autobiography*, p.87
2. CSPV, May 1627
3. CSPV, March 1627
4. CSPV, August 1627
5. Nick Page, *Lord Minimus* (2001), p.80
6. CSPD, August 1627
7. CSPD, July 1627
8. John Forster, *Sir John Eliot Biography* (1872), p.397
9. CSPD, October 1627
10. Halliwell-Phillipps, *D'Ewes*, p.364
11. CSPD, August 1628
12. Leanda De Lisle, *Phoenix Queen*, p.103
13. CSPV, September 1628
14. Ancram, *Correspondence*, p.46
15. CSPD, August 1628
16. CSPD, October 1628
17. NAS: GD406/1/11134
18. CSPD, November 1628
19. CSPV, September 1628
20. CSPD, August 1628

Chapter 15: Rejoice

1. NA: TH/2285
2. HOLJ, Vol 4 26 January 1629

3. Rushworth, *Historical Collections*, Vol II, pp.650–662
4. CSPV, May 1629
5. Halliwell-Phillipps, *D'Ewes*, p.403
6. CSPV, May 1629
7. Katie Whitaker, *Royal Passion*, p.103
8. CSPV, May 1629
9. CSPD, May 1629
10. TNA: SP92/17/17
11. Dr Doran, *The Princes of Wales* (1860), p.410
12. Rushworth, *Historical Collections*, Vol I, pp.650–662
13. Radcliffe, *Strafford Letters*, Vol I, p.51
14. CSPV, April 1630
15. Linda Porter, *Royal Renegades* (2016), p.21
16. TNA: SP92/18/235
17. CSPV, June 1630
18. Andrew Kippis, *Biographia Britannica* (1789), p.272
19. CSPV, May 1629
20. Nadine Akkerman, *Correspondence*, Vol II, p.147

Chapter 16: Some Few Vipers

1. Rushworth, *Historical Collections*, Vol I, pp.515–538
2. CSPD, April 1628
3. Radcliffe, *Strafford Letters*, Vol I, p.36
4. Rushworth, *Historical Collections*, Vol I, pp.662–691
5. Gregg, *Charles I*, p.263
6. TNA: PROB/11/162/692
7. Radcliffe, *Strafford Letters*, Vol I, p.111
8. CSPD, May 1633
9. Siobhan Keenan, *Progresses, Processions & Royal Entries of Charles I* (2020), p.54
10. Laud, *Autobiography*, p.133
11. CSPD, June 1633
12. *The Volume of the Walpole Society, Vol 37, Abraham van der Doort's Catalogue* (1958–60)
13. Ancram, *Correspondence*, p.86
14. CSPD, July 1633
15. CSPD, June 1633
16. CSPV, April 1635
17. Radcliffe, *Strafford Letters*, Vol I, p.187
18. IOW: OG/BB/247

19. CSPD, April 1634
20. SA: WWM/StrP/24/25/133a-d
21. Keenan, *Progresses*, p.45
22. Radcliffe, *Strafford Letters*, Vol I, p.141
23. P. Peckard, *Memoirs of the Life of Mr. Nicholas Ferrar* (1790), pp.220–223
24. Laud, *Autobiography*, p.74
25. CSPD, February 1634
26. CSPD, January 1634
27. Radcliffe, *Strafford Letters*, Vol I, p.141
28. L.J. Reeve, *Charles I and the Road to Personal Rule* (2003), p.195
29. Radcliffe, *Strafford Letters*, Vol I, p.387
30. CSPV, March 1636
31. Radcliffe, *Strafford Letters*, Vol I, p.214
32. Radcliffe, *Strafford Letters*, Vol I, p.125
33. Radcliffe, *Strafford Letters*, Vol I, p.124
34. CSPV March 1635
35. Radcliffe, *Strafford Letters*, Vol I, p.79
36. SA: WWM/StrP/40/6a
37. SA: WWM/StrP/40/9a
38. SA: WWM/StrP/40/10a
39. SA: WWM/StrP/40/23a
40. SA: WWM/StrP/40/24a
41. Radcliffe, *Strafford Letters*, Vol I, p.365
42. SA: WWM/StrP/34/2a-2p
43. Radcliffe, *Strafford Letters*, Vol I, pp.302–332
44. Radcliffe, *Strafford Letters*, Vol II, pp.16–27
45. SA: WWM/StrP/34/2a-2p

Chapter 17: Monk, Rogue and Traitor

1. CSPD, July 1637
2. Mary Hervey, *Life*, p.342
3. Christchurch Library, Oxford: MS540.
4. CSPV, August 1637
5. CSPD, August 1637
6. Radcliffe, *Strafford Letters*, Vol II, p.129
7. Phineas Pett, *Memoirs* pp.156–157
8. Ancram, *Correspondence*, Vol II, p.190
9. CSPV, October 1637
10. Radcliffe, *Strafford Letters*, Vol II, p.154
11. CSPV, April 1638

12. CSPV, October 1637
13. SA: WWM/StrP/40/23a
14. *Theatre and Government Under the Early Stuarts*, ed. J.R. Mulryne and Margaret Shewring (1993), p.75
15. TNA: SP/89/4/3
16. Norfolk Record Office: HMN7/307/772X8/ff.177r-179r
17. Radcliffe, *Strafford Letters*, Vol II, pp.173–186
18. Radcliffe, *Strafford Letters*, Vol II, pp.181–192
19. CSPV, July 1638
20. CSPD February 1639
21. CSPV, December 1638
22. Radcliffe, *Strafford Letters*, Vol II, p.276
23. CSPD, August 1640
24. CSPD, February 1639
25. Ibid.
26. CSPD, March 1639
27. Ann Hughes, *Politics, Society and Civil War in Warwickshire* (1987), p.121
28. Ancram, *Correspondence*, p.15
29. Rushworth, *Historical Collections*, Vol III, pp.885–946
30. CSPD, April 1639
31. CSPD, May 1639
32. Rushworth, *Historical Collections*, Vol III, p.313
33. Ibid.
34. Isaac d'Israeli, *Commentaries on the Life and Reign of Charles I* (1851), p.303
35. Radcliffe, *Strafford Letters*, Vol II, pp.371–372

Chapter 18: Beggarly Nation

1. CSPV, August 1639
2. CSPV, January 1640
3. Radcliffe, *Strafford Letters*, Vol II, pp.408–411
4. Ibid.
5. Halliwell-Phillipps, *Letters*, Vol II, p.327
6. Rushworth, *Historical Collections*, Vol III, pp.1085–1149
7. Ibid.
8. Ibid.
9. Rushworth, *Historical Collections*, Vol IV, pp.734–761
10. Rushworth, *Historical Collections*, Vol III, pp.1149–1189
11. NAS: GD112/39/79/14
12. NAS: GD112/39/79/14

13. CSPV, June 1640
14. CSPD, June 1640
15. David Hume, *The History of England,* Vol VII (1818), p.527
16. CSPV, November 1640
17. HHC: U/DDEV/79/G156
18. CSPV, August 1640
19. CSPD, September 1640
20. Ibid.
21. CSPD, August 1640
22. HHC: U/DDEV/79/G159-160
23. CSPD, August 1640
24. CSPV, September 1640
25. CSPD, September 1640
26. Ibid.
27. CSPD, October 1640
28. CSPD, September 1640
29. Nadine Akkerman, *Correspondence*, Vol II, p.940
30. Rushworth, *Historical Collections*, Vol IV, pp.1–45
31. Ibid.
32. CSPV, December 1640
33. Forster, *Sir John Eliot*, p.722

Chapter 19: Intestine Divisions

1. C.H. Firth, *Transactions of the Royal Historical Society,* Vol VI (1912)
2. CSPD, December 1640
3. Radcliffe, *Strafford Letters*, Vol II, p.414
4. CSPV, February 1641
5. CSPV, January 1641
6. Katie Whitaker, *Royal Passion*, p.191
7. SA: WWM/STRP/36/1-42
8. CV Wedgewood, *Strafford* (1949), p.304
9. CSPV, May 1641
10. Halliwell-Phillips, *Letters*, p.327
11. Rushworth, *Historical Collections*, Vol IV, pp.239–279
12. CSPV, May 1641
13. Radcliffe, *Strafford Letters*, Vol II, p.432
14. Wedgewood, *Strafford*, p.333
15. Radcliffe, *Strafford Letters*, Vol II, p.418
16. Wedgewood, *Strafford*, p.341
17. CSPD, May 1641

18. SA: WWM/StrP/40-61a
19. SA: WWM/StrP/40-60a
20. Laud, *Autobiography*, p.271

Chapter 20: Popish Hellhounds

1. Samuel Rawson Gardiner, *The Constitutional Documents of the Puritan Revolution, 1625–1660* (1906), p.181
2. Rushworth, *Historical Collections*, Vol IV, pp.304–333
3. CSPV, April 1641
4. CSPV, May 1641
5. CSPV, June 1641
6. Nadine Akkerman, *Correspondence*, Vol II, p.972
7. CSPV, July 1641
8. CSPD, August 1641
9. Society of Antiquaries, *Archaeologia Aeliana* (1899), p.104
10. Rushworth, *Historical Collections*, Vol IV, pp.358–385
11. CSPD, August 1641
12. Dorothea Townshend, *Endymion Porter*, p.192
13. CSPD, October 1641
14. CSPD, November 1641
15. Keenan: *Progresses*, p.183
16. CSPV, December 1641
17. Keenan: *Progresses*, p.188
18. Rushworth, *Historical Collections*, Vol IV, pp.421–436
19. *Huntington Library Quarterly*, Vol. 68, No. 1–2 (March 2005)
20. Nadine Akkerman, *Correspondence*, Vol II, p.1020
21. Keenan: *Progresses*, p.179
22. CSPV, January 1642
23. Rushworth, *Historical Collections*, Vol IV, pp.421–436
24. CSPD, December 1641
25. Leanda de Lisle, *Phoenix Queen* (2022), p.213
26. S.R. Gardiner, *Fall of Monarchy of Charles I*, Vol II (1882), p.378
27. HOLJ, Vol 4, 3 January 1642
28. Rees, *Leveller Revolution*, p.16
29. Rushworth, *Historical Collections*, Vol IV, pp.473–494
30. CSPD, December 1641
31. Rushworth, *Historical Collections*, Vol IV, pp.473–494
32. Ibid.
33. CSPD, January 1642
34. CSPV, January 1642

35. Glamorgan Archives: DTD/8-11
36. Dorothea Townshend, *Endymion Porter*, p.200
37. Nadine Akkerman, *Correspondence*, Vol II, p.1029
38. CSPD, January 1642
39. CSPV, February 1642
40. CSPV, March 1642
41. CSPV, February 1642
42. Margaret Cavendish, *Life of William Cavendish*, ed. Charles Harding Forth (1886), p.330

Chapter 21: Discord and Ruin

1. CSPV, March 1642
2. Michael J. Brown, *Itinerant Ambassador* (2021), pp.236–259
3. Earl of Clarendon, *History of the Rebellion,* Vol I (1731), p.451
4. CSPV, March 1642
5. Ancram, *Correspondence*, pp.133–134
6. Henry Ellis: *Original Letters*, Vol IV (1827), p.2
7. Warwickshire County Record Office: CR 2017/C1/108
8. Ancram, *Correspondence*, p.133
9. CSPV, May 1642
10. Ibid.
11. Rev. J.S. Clarke, *Life of James II*, Vol I (1816), p.4
12. Nadine Akkerman, *Correspondence*, Vol II, p.1036
13. NAS: GD40/2/19/2/5
14. CSPD, May 1642
15. CSPD, April 1642
16. HOLJ, Vol IV, 11 April 1642
17. Rushworth, *Historical Collections*, Vol IV, pp.559–564
18. Ibid.
19. CSPV, May 1642
20. Worcester Cathedral: D17-41 Letters to Prideaux
21. HOLJ, Vol V, 2 August 1642
22. CSPV, August 1642

Chapter 22: This Poore Kingdom

1. Worcester Cathedral: D17-41 Letters to Prideaux
2. Frances Parthenope Verney, *Memoirs of the Verney Family* (1892), p.98
3. Mary Anne Everett Green, *Letters of Henrietta Maria* (1857), p.147

4. Worcester Cathedral: D17-41 Letters to Prideaux
5. Worcester Cathedral: D17-41 Letters to Prideaux
6. Worcester Cathedral: D17-41 Letters to Prideaux

Chapter 23: Rabble Multitude

1. Gregg, *Charles I*, p.367
2. Clarke, *James II*, p.10
3. *The Vindication and Clearing of Sir James Ramsey.* Thomason Tracts, BM: 669/f.6/184.
4. HHC: U/DDEV/79/H150
5. Sir Richard Bulstrode, *Memoirs and Reflections upon the Reign and Government of King Charles the Ist and K. Charles the II'd* (1721), p.78
6. HHC: U/DDEV/79/H150
7. Clarke, *James II*, p.12
8. Philip Warwick, *Memoirs*, p.252
9. Ibid.
10. Ibid.
11. Clarke, *James II*, p.15
12. Christopher Hibbert, *Cavaliers and Roundheads* (1993), p.81
13. Clarke, *James II*, p.15
14. Ibid.
15. *The Edinburgh Review*, Vol 176, p.419
16. CSPV, November 1642
17. Ibid.
18. CSPV, December 1642
19. CSPD, January 1642
20. Worcester Cathedral: D17-41 Letters to Prideaux
21. Rushworth, *Historical Collections*, Vol V, pp.387–504

Chapter 24: Angel of Peace

1. Eva Scott, *Rupert, Prince Palatine* (1899), p.101
2. CSPD, February 1643
3. CSPD, October 1642
4. CSPV, February 1643
5. Sir Charles Petrie, *King Charles, Prince Rupert and the Civil War* (1974), p.40
6. Agnes Strickland, *Lives of the Queens of England,* Vol VIII & IX (1847), p.80

7. Dorothea Townshend, *Endymion Porter*, p.206
8. Halliwell-Phillipps, *Letters*, pp.340–341
9. CSPV, April 1643
10. Petrie, *King Charles, Prince Rupert*, p.39
11. CSPV, May 1643
12. *Memoires of the Life and Death of Henrietta Maria* (1685), p.27
13. Earl of Clarendon, *The History of the Rebellion,* Vol II (1732), p.286
14. CSPV, August 1643
15. CSPV, September 1643
16. CSPV, August 1643
17. Hibbert, *Cavaliers and Roundheads*, p.134
18. Frank Kitson, *Prince Rupert: Portrait of a Soldier* (1996), p.145

Chapter 25: Gallant Gospellers

1. CSPV, January 1644
2. CSPV, March 1643
3. CSPV, July 1643
4. Keenan, *Progresses*, p.140
5. Ancram, *Correspondence*, pp.105–110
6. NAS: GD40/2/19/2/5
7. NAS: GD40/2/19/2/7
8. CV Wedgewood, *The King's War* (2001), p.289
9. Mark Stoyle, *Soldiers and Strangers* (2005), p.74
10. CSPD, March 1644
11. Philip Warwick, *Memoirs*, p.299
12. CSPV, March 1644
13. Margaret Cavendish, *Life of William Cavendish*, p.355
14. Charles Petrie, *Letters, Speeches & Proclamations of Charles I* (1935), pp.143–144
15. Pauline Gregg, *Charles I*, p.383
16. CSPD, May 1644
17. Ibid.
18. CSPV, July 1644
19. Morrah, *Rupert*
20. John Barratt, *The Civil War in the South-West* (2005), p.70
21. Barry Denton, *Only in Heaven* (1997), p.100
22. CSPV, May 1644
23. CSPV, June 1644
24. CSPV, August 1644
25. CSPD, March 1644

26. Rushworth, *Historical Collections*, Vol V, pp.677–748
27. CSPD, October 1644
28. Rushworth, *Historical Collections*, Vol V, pp.677–748
29. CSPD, July 1644
30. Petrie, *King Charles, Prince Rupert*, p.44
31. Hannah Cowley, *Poetry of Anna Matilda* (1788), p.122
32. CSPD, July 1644
33. Green, *Letters of Henrietta Maria*, p.248
34. CSPV, August 1644
35. Petrie, *Letters, Speeches*, p.129
36. Samuel R. Gardiner, *History of the Great Civil War*, Vol II (1895), p.37
37. CSPV, November 1644
38. HOLJ, Vol VII 29 October 1644

Chapter 26: Crying Blood

1. Halliwell-Phillipps, *Letters*, p.358
2. Ibid.
3. Radcliffe, *Strafford Letters*, Vol I, p.365
4. Halliwell-Phillipps, *Letters*, p.361
5. Agnes Strickland, *Lives of the Queens of England*, Vol IV (1865), pp.242–243
6. CSPD, April 1645
7. *The Parliamentary or Constitutional History of England*, Vol XIV (1763), p.326
8. Samuel R. Gardiner, *History of the Great Civil War*, Vol II (1889), p.70
9. CSPD, April 1645
10. CSPD, August 1645
11. Rushworth, *Historical Collections*, Vol V, pp.843–895
12. Strickland, *Lives*, p.223
13. Halliwell-Phillipps, *Letters*, p.369
14. Glenn Foard, *Naseby* (1995), p.108
15. CSPD, May 1645
16. Eliot Warburton, *Memoirs of Prince Rupert* (1849), p.396
17. Samuel R. Gardiner, *History of the Great Civil War*, Vol II, p.193
18. CSPD, May 1645
19. Nick Lipscombe, *The English Civil War* (2020), p.214
20. CSPV, August 1641
21. Earl of Clarendon, *The History of the Rebellion*, Vol V (1826), p.185
22. Halliwell-Phillipps, *Letters*, p.357
23. CSPD, July 1645

24. TNA: SP/89/4/26
25. Worcestershire Archives: 8579
26. Petrie, *King Charles, Prince Rupert*, p.9
27. Ibid.

Chapter 27: Hunted Partridge

1. CSPD, July 1645
2. *The Lord Digby's Cabinet and Dr Goff's Negotiations* (1646)
3. CSPD, August 1645
4. *Certamen Religiosum* (1649)
5. *Certamen Religiosum* (1649)
6. Earl of Clarendon, *The History of the Rebellion*, Vol IV (1849), p.83
7. Halliwell-Phillipps, *Letters*, p.389
8. Halliwell-Phillipps, *Letters*, p.384
9. CSPV, August 1645
10. CSPD, August 1645
11. Philip Warwick, *Memoirs*, p.317
12. Ibid

Chapter 28: Farewell Harry

1. CSPD, September 1645
2. Lipscombe, *The English Civil War*, p.240
3. Petrie, *King Charles, Prince Rupert*, p.10
4. Clarke, *James II*, p.24
5. Philip Warwick, *Memoirs*, p.308
6. Warburton, *Memoirs of Prince Rupert*, p.129
7. *Making the News,* ed. Joad Raymond (1993), p.349
8. CSPD, March 1645
9. Eva Scott, *Rupert,* p.191
10. Foard, *Naseby*, p.339
11. CSPD, August 1645
12. Rushworth, *Historical Collections,* Vol VI, pp.26–89
13. CSPD, September 1645
14. Ellis, *Original Letters,* Vol III p.312
15. Halliwell-Phillipps, *Letters*, p.393
16. CSPD, September 1645
17. Ibid.
18. CSPV, October 1645

19. *English Historical Review*, Vol VIII (1893)
20. Morrah, *Rupert*, p.204
21. Morrah, *Rupert*, p.205
22. CSPD, October 1645
23. Eva Scott, *Rupert*, p.213
24. CSPD, November 1645
25. *Letters of King Charles I*, ed. John Bruce (1856), p.20

Chapter 29: Conscience

1. Leanda De Lisle, *White King*, p.211
2. *Letters of King Charles I*, ed. John Bruce (1856), p.37
3. Anthony Wood, *Athenae Oxonienses* (1817), p.233
4. CSPV, January 1646
5. *Letters of King Charles I*, p.37
6. Richard Cust, *Charles I* (2014), p.413
7. *Letters of King Charles I*, p.50
8. *The Papers Which Passed at Newcastle Betwixt His Sacred Majestie and Mr Al: Henderson: Concerning the Change of Church Government* (1649) & viewed via: https://ota.bodleian.ox.ac.uk
9. CSPV, June 1646
10. Halliwell-Phillipps, *Letters*, pp.410–411
11. Ibid.
12. S&S: D(W)1778/I/I/66
13. Halliwell-Phillipps, *Letters*, p.413
14. Halliwell-Phillipps, *Letters*, pp.414–415
15. *Letters of King Charles I*, p.80
16. Halliwell-Phillipps, *Letters*, p.419
17. *Letters of King Charles I*, pp.80–82
18. *Letters of King Charles I*, p.19
19. Leanda De Lisle, *White King*, p.47
20. *Letters of King Charles I*, p.77
21. Clarendon, *State Papers*, p.265

Chapter 30: Golden Ball

1. Clarendon, *State Papers*, p.326
2. Clarendon, *State Papers*, p.342
3. CSPD, March 1647
4. CSPV, February 1647

5. Ancram, *Correspondence*, p.213
6. Clarendon, *State Papers*, p.348
7. Ibid
8. HOLJ, Vol IX, 21 May 1647
9. CSPV, June 1647
10. Leanda De Lisle, *White King*, p.221
11. Richard Perrinchief, *The Works of King Charles the Martyr* (1687), p.156
12. Ibid.
13. Leanda De Lisle, *White King*, p.224
14. CSPV, August 1647
15. Clarendon, *State Papers*, p.373
16. Leanda De Lisle, *White King*, p.226
17. CSPD, September 1647
18. S&S: D(W)1778-I-i-66
19. Halliwell-Phillipps, *Letters*, p.444
20. Clarendon, *State Papers*, p.372
21. Clarendon, *State Papers*, p.383
22. HOLJ, Vol IX, 12 November 1647

Chapter 31: Hellen

1. Andrew Hopper, *Black Tom* (2007), p.213
2. HOLJ, Vol IX, 31 December 1647
3. Clarendon, *State Papers*, p.346
4. Charles Carlton, *Charles I, the Personal Monarch* (1995), p.327
5. John Matusiak, *Prisoner King* (2017), pp.242-243
6. Ibid
7. Nadine Akkerman, *Invisible Agents* (2018), p.52
8. Matusiak, *Prisoner King*, p.234
9. Akkerman, *Invisible Agents*, p.56
10. Matusiak, *Prisoner King*, p.235
11. Cordell Firebrace, *Honest Harry* (1932), p.346
12. *Letters of King Charles I*, p.13
13. Clarendon, *State Papers*, p.283
14. Matusiak, *Prisoner King*, pp.242–243
15. Akkerman, *Invisible Agents*, p.58
16. *Eikon Basilike* (1649), p.107
17. IOW: OG/CC/65
18. Philip Warwick, *Memoirs*, pp.363–364
19. CSPD, October 1648
20. Earl of Clarendon, *The History of the Rebellion,* Vol II (1732), p.560

21. Cromwell: Letter dated 25 November 1648, Cromwell Association www. olivercromwell.org
22. Halliwell-Phillipps, *Letters*, p.454
23. Ancram, *Correspondence*, p.232
24. HOCJ, Vol VI, 4 January 1649

Chapter 32: Deadly Blow

1. Leanda De Lisle, *White King*, p.261
2. Rushworth, *Historical Collections*, Vol VII, pp.1379-1431
3. Leanda De Lisle, *White King*, p.261
4. Philip Warwick, *Memoirs*, p.379
5. Rushworth, *Historical Collections*, Vol VII, pp.1379–1431
6. Ibid.
7. Samuel R. Gardiner, *History of the Great Civil War*, Vol III (1891), p.573
8. Rushworth, *Historical Collections*, Vol VII, pp.1379–1431
9. Ibid
10. Leanda De Lisle, *White King*, p.265
11. CSPD, July 1624
12. Katie Whitaker, *Royal Passion*, pp.14–15
13. Mary Anne Everett Green, *Lives of the Princesses of England*, Vol VI (1857), pp.369–370
14. Ibid
15. François Guizot, *History of the English Revolution* (1846), p.461
16. In 1676, Richard Perrinchief stated in his *History of the Life and Death of King Charles I* that General Fairfax intended to 'hinder the Execution'. Suspecting this, 'Cromwell, Ireton and Harrison coming to him, after their usual way of deceiving, endeavoured to perswade him, that the LORD had rejected the King'. The men supposedly prevailed upon Fairfax to seek God through prayer, and Perrinchief asserts that Fairfax was unaware that the king's death warrant had even been signed.

This ignorance fits with Thomas Herbert's *Memoirs of the Two Last Years of the Reign of King Charles I*. In attendance on the king that day, Herbert recalled that after the execution, he came across Fairfax. The general 'ask'd how the King did' which was a strange question. Herbert put it down to the fact that Fairfax was unaware of proceedings and specifically states that the general had been at prayers 'in Colonel Harrison's Apartment', which ties in with Perrinchief's account. Continuing on through the palace, Herbert then met Lieutenant General Cromwell, who 'knew what had so lately passed' and discussion centred on the king's burial.

In April 1649, a pamphlet appeared called *A most Learned, Conscientious and Devout Exercise, or Sermon of Self-Denyal*. It is preserved within the British Library's Thomason Tracts. The sheet recounts that two days before the execution, Cromwell went with two troops of his cavalry 'to remove the scruples' of Fairfax regarding the king. Though satirical in parts, that doesn't automatically invalidate it. Couple these three sources with the accounts of the Dutch ambassadors, who said Fairfax intended to intercede for the king's life on the day of execution, and found soldiers stationed outside his door and in the streets. As second in command of the army, this was one occasion where Cromwell could not disguise his key role, nor remain in the shadows for one of his associates to take the lead.

17. Hibbert, *Cavaliers and Roundheads*, p.286
18. Rushworth, *Historical Collections*, Vol VII, pp.1379–1431
19. Ibid
20. Ibid
21. Ibid
22. Hibbert, *Charles I*, p.279
23. Gloucester Archives: D979A/F3/8

Chapter 33: Who Killed the King?

1. *The Confession of Richard Brandon the hangman (upon his death bed)* (1649)
2. LPL: MS930/21
3. CSPD, May 1644
4. Denzil Holles, *Memoirs* (1699), p.198
5. Mark Noble, *Regicides* (1798), pp.267–268 & Geoffrey Robertson, *The Tyrannicide Brief* (2005) which says Grey was 'at Pride's elbow'.
6. *Lord Grey, Old English blood boyling afresh in Leicestershire men* (1648)
7. *Mercurius Pragmaticus (Dec 26 – Jan 9 1649)*
8. *Cobbetts Complete Collection of State Trials*, Vol V (1810), pp.1185–1186
9. *Relation veritable de la mort barbare et cruelle du roi d'Angleterre* (1649)
10. William Dugdale, *Life, Diary and Correspondence*, ed. William Hamper (1827), p.96 – states the action 'bruis'd ye face' of the king.
11. William Lilly, *History of his Life and Times* (1822), p.148
12. William Lilly, *Monarchy or No Monarchy in England* (1651), p.51
13. HOCJ, Vol VI, 31 January 1649 & Heneage Finch, *An Exact and Most Impartial Accompt of the Indictment, Arraignment, Trial, and Judgment (according to Law) of Twenty and Nine Regicides* (1679) – states '100l. for the Service of the Common-wealth'.

Index

Vane, Sir Henry, 92, 99, 103–4,
111, 138
Venice, 18–19, 21
Vere, Sir Horace, 49
Verney, Sir Edmund, 29, 54, 121, 126
Victor Amadeus of Savoy, 39, 80
Villiers, George, Duke of
Buckingham, 33–40, 43–6,
49–50, 64, 66–7
and the 'Spanish match', 51–8
criticised by Parliament, 69–70
accused of killing King James,
70–1
assassination threats, 73
commands fleet against French,
74–5
assassinated by John Felton, 76–7

Wake, Isaac, 35
Wales, Prince of, *see* Charles I, King;
Charles II, King
Waller, William, 130, 137–9, 142
Warwick, Sir Philip, 20, 125, 135,
154, 176–7
*Weep forth your Teares and doe
Lament* (John Ward), 28

Wentworth, Sir Thomas, Earl of
Strafford, 31, 64, 67–8, 82–3,
87–8, 95–6, 101–6, 143
Wentworth, Sir William, 9
Whalley, Colonel Edmund, 167
Whatman, Immortal, 40–1
Wheeler, Elizabeth, 170
Whitehall Palace, 12, 42, 91, 95
White Mountain, Battle of, 48
Whorwood, Jane ('Hellen'), 171–2
William II, Prince of Orange, 107–8
Williams, John, Archbishop of
York, 112
Willis, Richard, 156
Willoughby, Lord, 126
Windebank, Sir Francis, 101
Winter Queen, *see* Elizabeth, Queen
of Bohemia (Charles' sister)
Winwood, Sir Ralph, 32
Worcester, Marquis of, 10–11, 150–1
Worksop Manor, 9
Wray, Lady, 47
Württemberg, Duke of, 48

Yelverton, Sir Henry, 49
York, 118, 122, 129, 135–41